TV DRAMA IN TRANSITION

Also by Robin Nelson

BOYS FROM THE BLACKSTUFF: The Making of TV Drama (*with Bob Millington*)

TV Drama in Transition

Forms, Values and Cultural Change

Robin Nelson

First published in Great Britain 1997 by
MACMILLAN PRESS LTD
Houndmills, Basingstoke, Hampshire RG21 6XS and London
Companies and representatives throughout the world

A catalogue record for this book is available from the British Library.

ISBN 0–333–67753–6 hardcover
ISBN 0–333–67754–4 paperback

First published in the United States of America 1997 by
ST. MARTIN'S PRESS, INC.,
Scholarly and Reference Division,
175 Fifth Avenue, New York, N.Y. 10010

ISBN 0–312–17276–1

Library of Congress Cataloging-in-Publication Data
Nelson, Robin.
TV drama in transition : forms, values, and cultural change /
Robin Nelson.
p. cm.
Includes bibliographical references and index.
ISBN 0–312–17276–1 (cloth)
1. Television broadcasting—Social aspects—Great Britain.
2. Television programs—Great Britain—Evaluation.   3. Television
programs—United States—Evaluation.   I. Title.
PN1992.6.N47   1997
302.23'45'0941—dc21   96–47005
                                                                          CIP

This book is printed on paper suitable for recycling and made from fully managed and
sustained forest sources.

10   9   8   7   6   5   4   3   2   1
06   05   04   03   02   01   00   99   98   97

Printed and bound in Great Britain by
Antony Rowe Ltd, Chippenham, Wiltshire

To Avril, without whom nothing

Contents

Acknowledgements

I am grateful to Sage Publications for permission to use in Chapter 4 material which appeared (in another version: 'From Twin Peaks, US, to Lesser Peaks, UK') in *Media, Culture and Society* 18(4) October 1996. I am grateful to colleagues and friends in the academy and media industries who have shared their insights and made helpful suggestions on reading drafts of the book. I should like particularly to thank Fred Inglis, Bob Millington, Jane Jackson, Stuart Doughty and Richard Pinner. In a book as wide-ranging as this, I have inevitably drawn heavily on a number of sources. I trust that, in summarizing sometimes complex arguments, I have represented views accurately. The good ideas are often other people's, the faults are all mine.

ROBIN NELSON

List of Abbreviations

BBC   British Broadcasting Corporation
BBFC   British Board of Film Censorship
BFI   British Film Institute
CCCS   Centre for Contemporary Cultural Studies
C4   Channel 4
CMT   Country Music Television
HMSO Her Majesty's Stationery Office
ITV   Independent Television
MTV   Music Television
NHS   National Health Service
OPEC   Organization of Petroleum Exporting Countries
PSB   Public Service Broadcasting
TV   Television
VT   Videotape
YTV   Yorkshire Television

Introduction

In the future 'quality programmes' will depend less on a nod and a nudge from a regulator and more on funds and organisational structures that grow up alongside and within a more conventional, internationalised, industry structure (Mulgan, 1990: 30).

A repeated question about TV drama in the 1990s is that of its ability in the future to equal the glories of its past. A pessimism resounds in some quarters that increasing commercial competition in a global market-place will dislocate and devalue established traditions of excellence in Britain in particular. As George Brandt reflects on the 1980s:

> if some of the omens at the end of the decade are anything to go by, [TV drama's] brightest moments of glory in the eighties may prove to have been the golden glow of a setting sun (1993: 17).

Such sentiments lead me to write this book. Not because I share them, but to explore my own sense that, whilst TV drama has changed markedly since its beginnings with some losses on the way, current TV drama output is by no means all bad.

Acknowledging, then, that change may be for the better as well as for the worse, a key idea, traced throughout this book, is that of 'transition' in its title. Many aspects of television production and reception, as well as our understanding of these processes, have changed. Series and serials, inclining to the format of soaps, have undoubtedly displaced the single television play as TV drama's dominant mode. But it is not only the forms of the dramas that alter. New technologies continue to influence television's qualities of sound and vision, and they also introduce into the home competing electronic means of 'infotainment' (video, computer games, CD-Rom). Accordingly, viewing habits change. Many homes have more than one TV set, reducing 'family viewing' by allowing individuals to watch the channel of their choice. Shifts in work and leisure patterns and other social relations similarly have an impact on viewing, and broader cultural change gives rise to new ways of seeing. Over the past decade, deregulation of industry generally – and of television

1

institutions in particular – has been an influence on TV production, product and reception alike.

Last, but not least, of the transitions to be considered is the shift in Television Studies of the site where the meanings and pleasures of television are seen to be located. Nowadays, any notion of good television is understood to refer not simply to the intrinsic merits of the text itself but also, if not instead, to the productivity of meanings and pleasures by viewers as they watch. Brandt pays too little attention to this aspect of television and marks the decline he perceives only in terms of textual quality judged by specific literary-dramatic criteria. These last, I shall argue, have less relevance as TV drama turns increasingly cinematic, though they remain an important factor in my estimation.

This book offers, then, an account of new, as well as established, forms in TV drama. Secondly, it locates developments in a reformulating ecology, embracing technological, economic, institutional, cultural and aesthetic factors in a force field. It also asks what kinds of TV drama are of value in these changing circumstances.

Against one strain of current critical orthodoxy, I discuss the qualities of a range of TV drama texts. These case studies are interspersed with the more descriptive and theoretical chapters. They represent a gentle, but firm, insistence on my part that the 'television text' remains a useful analytic category. Attitudes to programmes have changed several times in the past twenty years of Media Studies. A general drift away from the dominant 1970s film theory idea of the spectator being ideologically positioned by the text is evident in reception theorists' increasing stress on what people do with texts. A shift in approaches to textual analysis itself appeared in late 1970s/early 1980s production of 'redemptive readings' (Brunsdon, 1990a)[1] of popular texts. But, by the early 1990s, a tendency to celebrate the populist[2] resulted from the coincidence of a number of cultural forces.

The agency of the reader in constructing meanings and pleasures came to seem paramount. Indeed Schroder has gone so far as to assert that:

[t]he text itself has no existence, no life, and therefore no quality until it is deciphered by an individual and triggers

the meaning potential carried by this individual. Whatever criteria one wishes to set up for quality, therefore, must be applied not to the text itself, but to the readings actualized by the text in the audience members (1992: 207).

Whilst recognizing that viewers taken generally engage with the flow of television only semi-attentively and that such viewing habits impact on reading, I note that many people pay particular attention to specific programmes ('I never miss *Morse*') and talk about them in those terms ('Did you watch *EastEnders*, *The X Files*, *Pride and Prejudice* last night?'). At times viewers select texts (possibly on video hire) to watch with some concentration. There is even a discernible tendency, against the tide of a three-minute culture, for products of longer duration in recent television and film.[3] Thus, as in the other transitions under consideration, there are continuities as well as discontinuities.

Debate goes on, amongst commentators from different schools of thought, as to the nature of any cultural rupture in the late 1960s/early 1970s. Lacking both the scope and qualifications fully to treat the many facets of the 'postmodern debate' in this book, I wish nevertheless to locate my discussion of TV drama broadly in the contemporary. Callinicos (1989) has argued vigorously that continuities – both in the socio-economic sphere of 'postmodernity' and the cultural products of 'postmodernism' – suggest that no 'paradigm shift' has taken place at all. Whilst the empirical evidence (including some significant changes) which he brings to bear serves as a timely corrective against the more hyper-fibrillated pronouncements on a postmodern apocalypse, the significance of any cultural shift lies precisely (as his discussion of Baudrillard acknowledges) more at the level of mediated consciousness than in the economic base, a 'reality' which commentators such as Baudrillard deny.

Whatever the continuities, metaphors have shifted significantly from those of community, rigidity, mass, homogeneity, to figures of (individual) difference, flexibility, dispersal, diversity. These characterize at least a perceptual shift from modernity to postmodernity and I use the term 'postmodernity' in this book to indicate the sum of those transitions as perceived to be emergent in the socio-economic sphere of the past twenty-odd years. Besides delineating the principles of construction of postmodern texts, furthermore, I explore the idea of a new affective order, a distinctive postmodern experience – a consciousness even – increasingly disarticulated,[4] if not quite detached, from the empirical world.

Amidst accelerating commercial influences and a profusion of technological developments, a new, intensely privatized, way of experiencing the world in attenuated bursts of energy turning over at rapid pace tends towards dominance in marked contrast with the slower, more prolonged, reflective apprehension of the traditional aesthetic disposition. This notion extends the familiar idea of a soundbyte media culture in which attention spans have been drastically reduced and surface image is all. Whilst some see in this phenomenon signs of cultural decline (Postman, 1987; Booth, 1988), and I myself express reservations about the new affective order, there is potential in the energies released in contemporary culture and perhaps in the resistances afforded through play in the spaces created by the break-up of traditional grammars. Accordingly, I shall distinguish different kinds of postmodern text and experience as well as various realisms.

Tempering the individualist emphasis of recent media theory in which the agency of the viewer is exaggerated, this book is quite consciously concerned, in Giddens's phrase, with 'situated activities' (his emphasis, 1979: 54),[5] the setting of agency in structure. The anti-humanism of poststructuralist thought (in the wake of Nietzsche) over-stresses the potential for the self-creation of subjectivity by down-playing, or ignoring, the factors constraining all individuals, albeit not in equal measure. For example, as Callinicos summarizes, 'most people's lives are still ... shaped by their lack of access to productive resources and their consequent need to sell their labour-power in order to live' (1989: 90).

My reservations about the fashionable tendency to stress the agency of the reader at the expense of the authority of the text (let alone the author) is made, then, partly in political terms which recognize the extant power relations – operating at any given time within any given community – which constrain people's imaginative and political freedom. In the rush of 'new revisionism' in Television Studies, Fiske's former recognition of commercial discourse's interest, 'to circulate some meanings rather than others, and to serve some social interests better than others' (1987:20), appears to have been forgotten by many commentators, including Fiske himself (see 1992), or seen to be so pervasive that no resistance, other than a knowing irony of recognition, is possible. If nothing else, an over-emphasis upon the active reader plays into the hands of the more ruthless financial managers of television companies who are implicitly invited to abandon any concern for programme quality since they are roundly told that such quality as may be derived is made up by the reader. At worst, the endemic structural inequities of power and wealth in postmodernity's global village are masked by the immediacy of pleasurable intensities for individuals isolated from historical consequence.

Particularly in the light of accounts which overlook the market as a dynamic force in social transformations, it is timely to recall Raymond Williams's strictures about previous changes to broadcasting. Writing in the early 1970s, Williams observed that:

> [t]he 'commercial' character of television has to be seen at several levels: as the making of programmes for profit in a known market; as a channel for advertising; and as a cultural and political form directly shaped by and dependent on the norms of a capitalist society, selling both consumer goods and a 'way of life' based on them (1974: 42–3).

In the twenty years since Williams made these observations, attitudes to the market and its influences have changed variously. On the one hand it has been observed (extending Williams) that, 'in the society of the simulacrum, the market is 'behind' nothing, it is *in* everything' (Burgin, 1986: 174). But this implied inability of any aesthetic production or critical practice to stand apart from the market has led other commentators, in a shift to the political right, to abandon critique altogether seemingly on the grounds of 'if you can't beat 'em, join 'em'.

In this light, this book responds to McGuigan's recent call for 'a *critical populism* which can account for *both* people's everyday culture *and* its material construction by powerful forces beyond the immediate comprehension of ordinary people' (1992: 5). Accordingly I set the over-emphasis of some commentators on the agency of viewers against the consumerist drift, to be discussed in Chapter 3, which characterized both Britain and America in the 1980s. Amidst the consumer choice made available by multi-channel narrowcasting, it should not forgotten that, in Murdock's formulation, 'a positive response to diversity depends on a collective exploration of difference, not the perpetuation of separate spheres' (1992: 39).

It is in this context that I address questions of cultural as well as textual value. Some readers will no doubt take the view that in so doing I am merely asserting and privileging my own tastes, reverting even to, 'the full authority of the modernist intellectual' (Storey, 1993: 183). If discourse is never neutral, however, it is impossible to say anything value-free and, in this light, I readily acknowledge what Ang terms 'double partiality' (1996: 67). As a university teacher of contemporary arts prac- tices, I am perhaps more concerned than most with textual quality and cultural value. But when, in the television industry, a team sets out to make a TV drama, its aim customarily is to make the best programme in the given production circum- stances. Many, usually tacit, value-assumptions are made, liter- ally in the process.

This is precisely the point at issue. Values are made in the everyday practices of making and watching television drama series, and the estimability of those values depends to some extent on the qualities of the programmes we watch. Ang's view that media researchers must themselves '*construct* such [political] aims and purposes' (her emphasis, 1996: 79) accords with Rorty's (1989) sense that, if solidarity does not reside in the core self of human beings, it may have to be made rather than found. Distractions from ethical issues in a 'culture of contentment'[6] must be acknowledged equally with the pleasures generated.

It will be evident that the discussion of TV drama to follow will be wide-ranging. My interest – stirred by Brandt's sugges- tion that a decline has set in – in what is valuable about drama on television leads me from a narrow concern with literary- dramatic qualities of texts to the theory and sociology of tele- vision viewing, and on into questions of aesthetic and cultural value. Indeed, the more I have thought about what I value in TV drama, the more I believe that matters of aesthetics are inescapably bound up with matters not only of politics but of ethics.[7]

Since full discussion of values and evaluation is held back until Chapter 9, it is helpful broadly to indicate the criteria

which inform the debate throughout. I share the basic standpoint established by John Mepham:

High quality television is television which is excellent as
measured by its faithfulness to these principles – the rule of
diversity, the cultural purpose of providing usable stories,
and the ethic of truth-telling (1990: 59).

The rule of diversity involves pursuing a means to sustain a
diverse output such that varied social – as well as individual –
needs are served. Usable stories are those told according to
conventions the audience understands but which – in order to
pursue the ethic of truth-telling – avoid mere conventionalism.
The debate here about forms in transition centres on the usable
familiarity of realist forms as compared with the disorientating
tendencies of postmodern construction.

Shifting relations in the cultural sphere have led – both in
everyday life and in institutions such as universities and public broadcasting – to a dislocation of established cultural and
aesthetic standards. To inquire into the aesthetic quality of
TV drama, then, is shortly to be drawn, as noted, into broader
questions of ethics and politics. Mepham remarks, however,
that:

[i]t is precisely because there is no Truth, no guaranteed
foundation of true principles which could act as a criterion
of truth, no certainty derived from access to reality independent of our research and instruments, that an ethic of
truth-telling is essential (1990: 69).

Just because there is no single answer or one right way of
seeing, then, the principle of truth-telling does not have to be
abandoned.

A nervousness that any talk of truth in an age of relativism
implies absolute Truth, or a Eurocentric essentialist conception
of humanity as truth-foundation, has led commentators, as we
shall see, to be hesitant about making distinctions of worth. To
avoid, refuse even, to engage in value debate – as many contemporary observers do in the name of respecting difference
– is at worst, however, a self-deceiving evasion. We live our
values: they are made in all our discursive practices, not merely
in intellectual debate.

In general, the stance of this book is what some have termed post-culturalist.[8] It is taken as read, that is to say, that all culture – and all accounts of culture – are shot through with and filtered by human perceptions, themselves socio-historically constructed. Acknowledging that a key value of Derridean deconstruction lies in its challenge to the binary 'either/or' of dichotomous thought patterns, then, the aim is to think together opposing traditions on a number of fronts. Drawing upon Wittgenstein's 'family resemblances' (1994: 32e),[9] a conceptual framework which challenges set theory's categorization of things as belonging either to one set or another with no grey area inbetween, a 'both/and' approach is taken in this book to many issues where binary divides have previously driven sharp distinctions between culturalist and essentialist, authoritative approaches.

There is no doubt an element of academic fashion in this. The collapse or blurring of boundaries is a feature of postmodern philosophy in a number of its manifestations. Whilst it may well be too soon to assess any lasting significance in postmodernism, its apparent challenge to a tradition of categorial distinctions in Western thought (traceable back to Kant and beyond to Descartes' mind/body dualism) is potentially profound. It offers, I believe, a range of new conceptual tools appropriate to contemporary ways of seeing.

To ground these abstractions, the both/and approach may be related to a number of aspects of TV drama. With regard to writers and texts, for example, it is proposed that the distinctive signature of an author can be acknowledged without abandoning the socio-historical and collective sense of writing or textuality. In the case of dramas which blur any clear distinction between fact and fiction, furthermore, it will be argued that texts may be both conventional and referential to everyday life. Similarly, with regard to cultural value, distinctions of worth will not be made along a fault line between 'high' and 'low' culture. Indeed, no clear boundary will be drawn between the two: *Middlemarch* will be recognized both as a canonical nineteenth century novel in 'the great tradition'[10] and a popular television drama serial, commercially produced in 1994 for a transnational market.

The bridging of 'the great divide'[11] between 'art' and 'popular culture' is a key aspect of the postmodern erosion of categorial distinctions under consideration. There is no reason to jettison the notion of a critical art altogether, however, even in the popular medium of television. Where some popular culturalists merely invert established aesthetic hierarchies to assert that the popular (defined as what many people like) is good, but leaving the extant power relationships in place, I explore the possibility of retaining a critical aesthetic in a popular medium as an agent of social progress. The both/and task, as Huyssen puts it:

> is to redefine the possibilities of critique in postmodern terms rather than relegating it to oblivion. If the postmodern is discussed as historical condition rather than only as style it becomes possible and indeed important to unlock the critical moment in postmodernism itself (1986: 182).

Precisely because 'quality' is ultimately undecidable at a theoretical level, it can only be demonstrated by proffered example inviting intersubjective affirmation in given circumstances. That is why this book intersperses chapters analysing specific examples of British or American TV drama series and serials with more abstract theoretical discussion. Each case study illustrates a key theoretical perspective of the preceding chapter whilst together the examples suggest the range of provision of the past decade. Readers more interested in TV drama examples may prefer initially to read Chapters 2, 4, 6, 8, 10. I hope such an approach might lead them back to the more abstractly theoretical Chapters 1, 3, 5, 7, 9 which sketch the force-field of contemporary culture, because my case for worthwhile television embraces both text and context.

Finally, if the 'agents of commercialism are . . . hegemonic' (Ang, 1996: 33), it may be that I am perpetuating 'residual idealisms and obsolete concepts of what television watching should be about' (Ang, 1996: 33). But I like to think that self-reflexive, rational argument may still make a difference. For, as Hall notes, '[t]he politics of infinite dispersal is the politics of no action at all' (1987: 45). Indeed, this book will have fulfilled its key aim if it encourages resistance to wholesale capitulation to the desire-producing logic of consumer capitalism by provoking informed debate about the television industry and the worth of its drama output. To privilege rational argument for ideals in this way remains preferable to the mere retrospection on setting suns on the one hand or, on the other, the hyper-fibrillated talking up of contemporary ecstacies.

1 From Electronic Theatre to ... Cyberspace?

Technology and Televisual Form

> It is an underrated truism that all television aspires to the
> condition of soap opera. . . . The structures of television defer
> attention away from consequence (Maltby, 1983: 303–4).

I TV FUTURES

Much has changed technologically in little more than half a
century since the domestic television apparatus first became
widely affordable. The mid-1990s hail the domestic availability
of a global, two-way information and communications network. Cables are being laid apace across America, the UK and
elsewhere to facilitate digital fibre optics carrying 500 or more
channels and capable of interfacing computer technology with
more traditional television transmission. This adds to the developments in satellite TV already operating alongside the longer-
standing terrestrial modes. A key difference in fibre optics,
however – one to which I shall return – is the potential inter-
activity of the digital network replacing one-way transmission
with the possibility of two-way communication. Even one-way,
however, digital technology potentially affords cinema-style
definition and CD-quality sound in everyone's home.

New conceptions of TV space accompany the various technological developments in play. On the one hand, television
remains vision at a distance, that 'window on the world' through
which events beyond our parochial horizons can be seen by
way of news or current affairs documentary programmes. On
the other hand, the space behind the screen has become, in
the minds of some, not a direct recording or even a structured

reflection of the real world we inhabit, but a virtual world, cyberspace, a simulacrum constructed of non-referential codes and conventions in media ideolects divorced from any referents in historical reality.

The new technologies encourage new ways of thinking about television since it is possible like never before to construct and manipulate televisual imagery from a computer database. At the extreme, it is feasible to make from digital samples a virtual world without any trace of an 'original' recorded sound or image. Even moderately assessed, images of the historical world can be edited and treated with image-manipulating special effects on a scale such that technological mediation takes on new dimensions. A medium still to some extent trusted to document what happens is in fact increasingly less trustworthy, given its extended capacity to manipulate the images it mediates.

Furthermore, the very process of off-line, digital editing, along with the modes of access to – and reformulation of – information on the InterNet, calls linearity in question. A constellatory approach to relating one item pulled from an extensive and multifarious database to another gives rise to accidents of contiguity, displacing the logic of effect related to cause in linear time. The practice of 'zapping' between channels functions similarly. Some postmodernists accordingly suggest that digital technology either gives rise to a new episteme, a new way of mapping and knowing the world, or indeed heralds the end all together of a humanist theory of knowledge. Indeed the new technologies raise a range of quite fundamental philosophical questions, ethical and political as well as aesthetic.

There are clear implications for TV drama in technological developments and the new mind-sets associated with them. I propose to deal with matters technological and practical before turning to developments in narrative form related to new ways of seeing. This order does not imply technological determinism, however, since there are feedback loops – particularly through market research into audience preferences – which make TV drama processes and product concepts mutually influential. To illustrate their inter-dependency and to mark by stark contrast the transitions in progress, however, I begin with a sketch of two viewing experiences, *Boys from the Blackstuff* in Autumn 1982 and *Twin Peaks* almost a decade later.

II *BOYS FROM THE BLACKSTUFF* AND *TWIN PEAKS*:
A COMPARATIVE SKETCH OF VIEWING
EXPERIENCE

Joining the audience of almost 8 million watching *George's Last Ride*, the final episode in the repeat showing of *Blackstuff* on BBC1 on 8 February 1993, viewers were part of an event. So widely did the shockwaves of the series resound through British culture[1] that it approximated the impact of *The Wednesday Play* which – in mythology at least – had people in pubs up and down the country talking about it the next day (see Brandt, 1981). *Twin Peaks* (transmitted in the UK in 1990–91) caused a different kind of stir. In contrast with the social realism of *Blackstuff*, *Twin Peaks* was hailed in critical discourse as the ultimate postmodern text, a marker of a paradigm shift in TV drama.

To generalize broadly by way of opening up a comparative debate, the viewing experience of *Blackstuff* drew viewers in emotionally, through character identification, into a historical narrative. The final episode centres on the figure of the dying socialist, George Malone. For the first thirty minutes, there is virtually no action, just talk. It is only after a long conversation in which the doctor recounts to Mrs Malone his lasting memory of hearing, as a small boy, her husband speak at a political rally, that George is discharged from hospital to die at home. There are monologues, the first when George, having absconded from hospital, leans on the gravestone of his youngest son, Snowy (who died in an accident in Episode 1), and talks to camera in Close-Up for two minutes punctuated visually only by the occasional cutaway. There are conversations – all shot in tight Close-Up – between husband and wife, father and sons, and George and Yosser Hughes – one of the many visitors seeking Malone's advice. For George has long been a mentor to his community on practical and theoretical politics. In that rich admixture of Catholicism and Marxism typifying much of the Liverpool working class, George advises on marital problems and strike action alike.

The build-up to George's final passing in a wheelchair at the derelict Albert Dock in Liverpool, where Chrissie has taken him for the last ride of the episode's title, is an eight-minute-long monologue. Visually, Close-Ups of George are broken up by tracking shots of the wheelchair ride, cutaways to heaps of rusted metal and the general dereliction of the docks, and wider angles revealing the containerization which contributed to the redundancy of traditional dockers like Malone. But the emphasis is on George's verbal reflections on personal and labour history intermingled. He alludes to politics, football and cricket in the same sentence, and juxtaposes the 'revolution' with Blackpool illuminations. The effect is to convey a texture of mingled yarn in George's life in a form overtly realist in that, as Clifford summarizes, 'it does not refer to other art forms or other television or film genres, though, of course, it does utilise those genre's conventions' (1991: 18). Where George makes explicit reference to other films and series by way of making light of his emotional communion with Snowy ('I feel like James Stewart in *Shenandoah*') or explaining his impending death to his grand-daughter ('it's like the next episode of *Spiderman*: until it happens, nobody knows'), *Blackstuff* is not so much indulging in the intertextual play of *Twin Peaks* as articulating lived experience in the language of popular culture.

The moment of George's death is, however, heavily symbolic. As the camera angle widens from George slumped dead in his wheelchair to reveal the derelict docks, the series' equation of the personal and the political – the unemployment and the enforced disempowerment of trade unions in the early 1980s – is explicitly drawn. But to offset the danger of both a nostalgic sentimentalism and a heavy-handed political preachiness, Chrissie is shown in a Chaplinesque manner running, first one way and then the other, unsure of the shortest route by which to seek assistance.

In terms of technology and production practices, *Blackstuff* challenged what is 'essential' to television by pioneering hybrids mixing studio and cinematic forms and techniques.[2] Notwithstanding its production innovations, its humour and occasional non-naturalistic devices, *Blackstuff* sits in a televisual drama tradition:

> realist, character- and plot-based and with relatively unambitious themes and direction. . . . conforming to accepted technical and artistic limitations and possibilities and able to sit as happily in the studio or on video as on film or on location (Clifford, 1991: 20).

Such drama privileges words over visual images, being led by writers with tap-roots in naturalist theatre. It sets agency in structure, having believable characters and plausible, linear plot progression. It is socially engaged, evidencing documentary tendencies privileging story over performance. The viewing experience it offers is one of affective and cognitive engagement likely to lead to reorientation by, in the case of *Blackstuff* for example, interpreting the early 1980s to a displaced industrial working class.

Twin Peaks does not share these features. It is an intertextual weft, the tropes of which refer less to a recognizable historical world than to rhetorical figures in other television and film. Unlike George's explicit references, however, *Twin Peaks* relies for its ironic intertextual play on the audience's self-awareness of the discourses of popular culture. The serial has been variously described as, 'a cross between *Peyton Place* . . . and *Happy Days*' (Dana Ashbrook cited in Chion 1995: 103–4) and *Columbo* walking into *St Elsewhere* (Cambell in Lavery 1995: 177). There are quotations and allusions to specific films and film-styles (to Preminger's *Laura* and Hitchcock's *Vertigo*[3]), and to actors and their roles in previous movies (Beymer's role in *West Side Story* or Walter Neff, Fred McMurray's character in *Double Indemnity*[4]). Indeed the series combines a considerable range of film and television fiction modes: the soap opera, the detective series, the horror movie, the commercial, the sit-com, the western. Re-cycling the tropes, styles and forms to make a new series, *Twin Peaks* may be experienced as a free-play of signifiers or a pastiche of tropes, and, accordingly, as postmodern television.

But there are other ways in which the series might warrant these credentials. The blurring of time boundaries in its setting in an apparent 1990s 'present' but with strong resonances of the 1950s and 1960s in its *mise-en-scène*. *Twin Peaks'* echoing of *Happy Days*, a 1980s sitcom set in the 1950s, further confuses location in time. Familiar narrative structure is similarly affirmed and undermined. The detective series dimension of *Twin Peaks* lends it a plot-resolution narrative frame. There is a 'whodunnit' at its core: who killed Laura Palmer? Indeed, at the end of episode 16, there is closure of a kind: Laura Palmer's murderer is revealed to be her father, Leland.[5] But he committed the act when possessed by a diabolical and perhaps imaginary figure with the everyday name of Bob, and so a major enigma – beyond the closures of a regular detective series – remains.

The series then proceeds for another thirteen episodes until episode 29 in which agent Dale Cooper enters a parallel universe through the entrance to the Black Lodge which leads into the red room. As Chion puts it, '[h]e manages to leave it alive but he is transformed and perhaps possessed in turn by Bob, or by his evil double. The series ended, in theory definitively, on this enigma' (1995: 106).

It is not necessary here to follow Cooper and *Twin Peaks* into other time/space dimensions to acknowledge that, even at the level of the detective plot, there is a postmodern blurring of everyday reality, dreamworlds and the supernatural. Agent Cooper, unlike his mainly rational-deductive or intuitive predecessors in the detective fiction genre, follows aspects of Tibetan philosophy to establish a trail. His dreams play a significant part in his investigation which leads him, as noted, into non-natural territory. Insofar as the multivalency of the presentation of 'reality' in *Twin Peaks* amounts to a softening of a categorial boundary between the everyday and the supernatural, inviting an interrogation and redefinition of 'reality', the series may be claimed to be (philosophically) postmodern. In the world of *Twin Peaks*, for sure, the regular hierarchies of meaning and experience by which sense is customarily made in television series, if not in actuality, appear not to operate.

Turning to the characters, Chion's distinction of three over-lapping categories is helpful (1995: 107–10): typical soap opera characters who remain true to type; those identified explicitly as bizarre; characters with mythical qualities. Chion's particular insight into the sense of strangeness in the characters' interrelationships, however, is that it 'is not that everyone is mad, but that those who are not mad do not find the eccentric characters eccentric' (1995: 110). Paralleling the dislocations of time, space and hierarchy so far noted, then, is a decentring of society. The lack of recognition within the diegesis of an eccentricity, such as the log lady's – so evident to viewers accustomed to the plausibilities of the unexceptional – renders a curious sense of liberal tolerance taken beyond extreme, as if the community has no ethical bearings. There is just experience without distinction, an equivalence of randomly selected events.

The photography of *Twin Peaks*, as might be expected from

a production involving an established art-film maker, is exceptional. Although various directors made different episodes and there are stylistic variations, *Twin Peaks* has a distinctive experimental spirit. The cinematic qualities are evident in Chion's summary:

> Episode 24, for example, directed by James Foley, uses more chiaroscuro, that is to say, a more cinematic treatment of light and shade than the others, while the episodes directed by Diane Keaton and Caleb Deschanel respectively contain bolder framing (such as extreme close-ups on faces in episode 22) and more complex camera movements which create a truly cinematographic suspense (such as Lucy walking through the police station in episode 19). . . . [I]n some of the sequences he directed Lynch also managed to throw a spanner into customary television style. His long shots were vaster and deeper than the American cinema and, *a fortiori*, television usually dares to make them (1995: 102).

More visual than verbal in its impact like most film for television, *Twin Peaks* uses the forest locations of Twin Peaks in addition to augment its attraction as visual spectacle.

The experience of viewing an episode of *Twin Peaks* in 1991, then, is a distinctly different one from viewing *Blackstuff* a decade earlier. To overstate the case to make the point, where *Blackstuff* offers to interpret contemporary history to viewers by setting agency in structure in a familiar realist mode referential to the everyday reality of working people in Britain in the early 1980s, *Twin Peaks*, constructed from fragments of past film and television in a signifying system divorced from everyday reality, offers transnationally the pleasures of intertextual play. Where *Blackstuff* privileges story – told mainly in dialogue – over performance, *Twin Peaks* valorizes the visual in a collage of attractive images, and performance for its style, isolating character from normative 'reality' and lending it immunity from narrative consequence.

Structurally there is a shift away from linearity of cause and effect to parataxis,[6] that is a collage of discourses eschewing any attempt to smooth out their differences into a sense-making, harmonious whole. It is, in Barthes's terms, a shift 'from work to text' (1977: 155). Such a change parallels a mind-set related to computer networks where a vast amount of information is stored in bytes – without a linear order – to be retrieved at random. The very enormity of the mass of information circulating in an image-saturated communications world leads to a post-modern experience of assimilating juxtaposed bytes which bear no logical relation to each other. The experience of watching *Twin Peaks* is akin to what I shall explore in this book as a new affective order, a new way of dealing with a media-saturated, information overload in place of more explanatory sense-making in terms of the linearity of cause and effect in specific contexts.

The break-up of information into small bytes with a rapid rate of turnover extends the established gravitation of all tele-vision – and TV drama in particular – towards the condition of soap opera, as proposed in the epigraph to this chapter. In popular TV forms, the combination of new technologies and semi-attentive mindset of the television audience facilitates a transition towards the condition of entertainment rather than instruction, to scopophilia, the pleasure of looking, rather than 'epistephilia' (Nichols, 1991: 178), the love of knowing. As is evident in the comparison of *Blackstuff* with *Twin Peaks*, visual performance for its own sake increasingly takes precedence over the situated practices of historically located narratives. The TV space has begun to depart from a (humanist) depic-tion of characters and events grounded in a historical world in which actions have consequences to a (postmodern) collage of attractive but dislocated images and sounds.

It is worth noting at this juncture, however, that the ways in which the language of television operates in the lived experi-ence of many – possibly the majority of – viewers may well be at odds with discourse theorists' insistence that discursive prac-tices make rather than reflect 'the real'.[7] For all the theoretical work undertaken to demonstrate that the camera is not an innocent eye, a strong impulse to read photographs as copies of a visual reality remains. This inclination stems partly from the indexical mode (in Peirce's classification)[8] of many televisual signs but also, as Bourdieu's research suggests (1979, rep. 1992), from a popular disposition to ignore the visual construction and to read images only at the level of their basic code.[9]

To take a cross-sight on current transitions, then, I turn briefly to the differences between the media of film and tele-vision and their processes of production. I shall return to my two examples from the early-1980s and early-1990s at the end of the book, but it must be noted here that – each being exceptional of its kind – they do not represent typical drama of their respective periods other than in the broad tendencies I have sketched.

III   TECHNOLOGY AND PRODUCTION PROCESSES

The mediums of film and television are less distinct from each other today than in the past – another postmodern blurring of boundaries. The film for television is now commonplace, whilst successful TV series have originated or culminated in feature films (*Star Trek, Twin Peaks, Dr Who*). In addition, the growth of the home video publishing market for films might seem to blur any sharp distinction between film and television. Lynch, invited to comment on the difference, answered:

> Before distribution, none. After that, on television, unlike in the movies, you have a bad small image and bad small sound. But the construction processes are the same (in Chion, 1995: 102).

Indeed, partly due to improving technology, a closer relationship between film and TV production methods grew rapidly in Britain in the 1980s.[10] Television companies, anticipating the delegation of production to be inscribed in the Broadcasting Act of 1990, began diversifying their output. Many chose to invest heavily in feature films destined ultimately for the emergent specialist slots on television.

One aspect of earlier TV production should particularly be noted, since it marks an initial technological tendency to isolate character from environment. A significant constraint of the TV studio, as compared with filmic production, concerns the placing of character in space. In early studio production, shooting strategies were limited: the shot/reverse shot over the shoulder developed in cinema, for example, was not possible without inadvertently including one of the several cameras in the shot. Indeed, the telephoto lenses – developed for television and the multi-camera studio so that the three or more cameras operating could keep out of each other's field of vision

– contributed significantly to the emergence of a shooting grammar which is ultimately disposed against a drama of agency in structure and towards isolated celebrity performance. The poor resolution initially of the TV image militated in any case against the Long Shot – other than for briefly establishing the scene – and TV drama, making a virtue of necessity, developed the Close-Up as its characteristic trope.

Consequently, as Maltby has established 'the television image concentrates the viewer's attention on a single object, commonly shown in spatial isolation, to be regarded in itself rather than in its context' (1983: 332–3) since the background is compressed, defocused and therefore neutralized. This tendency is exacerbated by the aspect ratio of the television set which, unlike that of the film screen, leaves no side-space against which to set the image. Multi-camera studio practice is now rare in TV drama production since methods largely approximate those of film (that is, single-camera with post-production editing). It is thus possible to shoot wide-angle with the lens turret close to the object. Nevertheless the different aspect ratios remain, and Lynch still notes that '[t]elevision is all telephoto lens where cinema is wide-angle' (cited in Chion, 1995: 103).

Ironically, the shift from the studio-based, literary/theatrical to the visual/cinematic product is most marked in the historically cherished, authored, single-play slot. In a gradual process, one-off, authored TV drama has loosened its tap-root in theatre and gravitated towards the visuality of cinema. The old single play strands in Britain, 'Armchair Theatre' (ABC), 'Play for Today' (BBC1), 'The Wednesday Play' (BBC1), and 'Theatre 625' (BBC2), have become 'Screenplay' (BBC2), 'Screen on One' (BBC1) 'Screen Two' (BBC2) and 'Film on Four' (C4).

Whilst, in a strongly visual postmodern culture, TV drama with an emphasis on dialogue derived from its theatrical heritage might be considered outmoded, however, the domestic context of reception with all its distractions continues to constrain the extent to which television in its popular forms might yield to the cinematic/visual. Thus, even given a high resolution image produced by digital technology, surround sound, and flat screens with cinematic aspect ratios, the experience of film viewing on a domestic television screen is likely to remain different from that in the cinema, if not absolutely distinctive. For both contextual and technological reasons, then, films for television remain hybrids which often make neither for the best cinema nor the best TV drama (see Clifford, 1991: 17–18).[11]

In addition, there is an important residual difference in the disposition of viewers to television and cinema. A sense of immediacy in viewing, of observing parallel lives as they are being lived, continues to inform the modern TV drama viewing experience. The naturalist theatre's sense of looking in through the 'fourth wall' to apparently live action taking place in real time and located typically in domestic interiors[12] is sustained in TV studio production of soaps, the dominant genre of TV drama. As Raymond Williams points out, this is 'a drama of the box in the same fundamental sense as the naturalist drama had been the drama of the framed stage' (1974: 56). Indeed, early television plays retained a sense of the immediacy of theatrical presence since actors performed 'live' as the audience watched.[13]

In contrast with the mark of the absence of presence in the cinema image, furthermore, there is an apparent directness of relationship between TV drama characters and television viewers, since the audience is not obliged to negotiate two spaces – that of the living room and that of the screen world. The characteristic domesticity of the TV drama setting parallels that of the home viewing context and therefore, in its familiarity, does not need to be graphically represented in detail for it is taken as read. Character and viewer seem to inhabit the same space. Contrastingly, in cinema, the problem of negotiating two complex spaces is overcome differently by darkening the auditorium and occluding the viewing space, thus inviting the audience to inhabit the screen space as 'invisible guest', in Peter Wollen's coinage (1980: 59).

The significance of this difference cannot be overstressed since the immersion of the spectator in the dreamworld of the cinema screen space is fundamentally different from the quotidian of the domestic viewing context of TV. Emotional identification between viewer and character is encouraged in television viewing by the sense in which people on television seem to inhabit the same domestic space as noted, but this engagement is offset by a potential detachment occasioned by the inclusion of other objects and people besides the television screen in the field of vision, and by other domestic distractions. This context begins to account for television's tendency to the melodrama of the everyday – in the news as well as in soaps – since excessive sound as well as vision must attempt to distinguish specific items from the televisual flow, and hail viewers away from domestic distractions to watch. TV must compete for attention whilst the cinema can rely on a more or less captive audience.

It also points up the need for tools of analysis of text–reader relations different from those of the psychoanalytic approaches prevalent in Film Studies. As Metz observed, the cinematic signifier is 'closer to phantasy at the onset' (1985: 43). Cinematic fictions bring out libidinous relationships in an audience whose conative ties with the historical world are loosened by both viewing context and a strong emphasis on subjectivity in the dominant and spectacular screen image. TV drama, in contrast, notwithstanding its current inclination to scopophilia, retains – through its viewing context and screen image characteristics – a distance for cognitive reflection and a pleasure in knowing. To echo Nichols on documentary, with which TV drama (in Britain at least) has historical associations, TV drama 'calls for the elaboration of an epistemology and axiology more than of an erotics' (1991: 178). The postmodern drift towards cinematic and visual spectacularity on television is thus in tension with its established, but by no means inevitable, characteristics.

IV TV DRAMA FORMS

Having sketched some key aspects of film and television technologies, working and viewing practices, I turn now to sketching similarly the place of dramatic fictions in the flow[14] of (post)-modern television.

Once interludes punctuating television output were abandoned,[15] TV drama ran into the flow of programming which for primarily commercial motives, seeks to engage its audience with an endless fictive experience.[16] Television now provides an uninterrupted stream of programmes for up to twenty-four hours per day. In many households the apparatus is permanently switched on in waking hours irrespective of whether or not it is actively being watched. A sporadic attention is thus paid to programmes such that their forms and content have accordingly been developed. The stream of television's transmission is broken down into items in familiar genres: soaps, the news, single plays, games shows, current affairs, quizzes, drama series/ serials, chat-shows and so on, each announced by its own distinctive musical signature. In commercial television the programmes are in addition overtly segmented by advertisements, but the internal structure of most modern television is further broken down into short narrative sections with smooth (to the point of invisibility) transitions between them. The structure of the news is typical: each item lasts between thirty seconds and two minutes paralleling the advertising segment.

According to Skovmand and Schroder, '[t]he conceptualisation of television as flow rather than as strings of distinct texts further emphasises that such notions as *intertextuality* and *meta-fictionality* are central to any conceptualisation of what is happening between audiences and television screens' (1992: 11). This is to beg a number of questions. Whilst recognition of established conventions no doubt contributes to the pleasures of some viewers reading at a metafictional level, others continue to become engrossed in the diegesis, the fictive world of an individual text.

Intertextual play has undoubtedly been established as a feature of popular culture, but this may not, however, amount – as some poststructuralist theorists would have it – to all viewers at all times consciously taking the world to be text. The pleasure of watching a favourite actor in another film or TV series does not necessarily preclude engagement in the fictional world represented: indeed both detached awareness and involvement is possible for an audience experienced in film and television watching (see Morley, 1986). The extent to which the majority of the audience is media-aware in such a way as to challenge the predominantly 'realist' illusions of TV drama and to lead to demand for a self-conscious postmodern product remains an open question at the core of this book.

Whereas current emphasis is placed squarely on the diversity of channels and readings, the offering in the UK, limited until relatively recently, has sustained something of that sense of a national communal audience for TV drama,[17] established in the 1960s when, Maltby argues, television displaced cinema as the 'primary source of consensus' (1983: 363). But occasions commanding widespread attention (royal weddings, Wimbledon, the soccer Cup Final, international sporting events) are rapidly diminishing in the profusion of channels and the incessant flow of television. As a consequence, any specific TV drama – whatever its form or content – is diminished in impact. New conceptions of audience and reading, along with various other developments, have contributed to revised dramatic forms.

The interweaving of different narrative strands developed in soaps has become TV drama's model form. Indeed, John Ellis has famously remarked that the unresolved narrative structure of soaps, 'is the central contribution that broadcast TV has made to the long history of narrative forms and narrativised perception of the world' (1992: 154). Segmented, capable of minor innovation through the introduction of new characters in a rapidly changing range of stories, it can afford the satisfaction of the occasional closure of narrative strands, whilst perpetually deferring the final satisfaction of ultimate closure overall. Multiple stories are necessary since some kind of larger narrative structure is needed in television if only for the benefit of the scheduler filling larger time-slots. For, whilst a story can be told in dramatic form in ninety seconds – as advertisements demonstrate[18] – the tradition of TV drama is on average for a thirty or fifty-minute slot. In this time-frame, a more fluid, open text better matches the sporadic attention span of a three-minute culture. But the form is not ideal for the developed narratives of a drama wishing to develop an argument by taking a point of view aimed at engaging critical reflection and/or profounder feeling.

As the unresolved multiple narratives of soaps and series found favour with schedulers and were accepted by audiences, the plot/resolution narrative diminished in importance. Narrative drama in a liberal consensual tradition, with convincing characters whose actions had consequences, privileged story over performance – performance alternatively conceived, that is, in terms of a display of celebrity status or lifestyle. As the single play slot gave way to series, the outcome of plots – in terms of the consequences of actions – similarly diminished.[19] For in each episode of a series, '[t]he central characters are re-established in their normal milieu, and shown to be immune from the consequences of the narrative they have just participated in' (Maltby, 1983: 331). The development of series thus marks an early shift of significance from the telling of usable stories to the presentation of performance. The value to popular

TV drama of repetitious, formulaic narrative structures may partly be accounted for in terms of the suitability of these vehicles for showing of this kind.

A further development of a gradual accommodation of TV drama's illusionistic narrative realisms with looser narrative forms is evident in current multi-narrative serials or series. They have embraced the flexible sound-and-vision byte approach of the three-minute culture to yield a new form, to be coined 'flexi-narrative' in this book. Neologisms can be problematic but a new vocabulary is needed to describe a TV drama product which is not generic in that one mode of presentation is used for a number of genre forms. The cutting rate and the rapid turnover of narrative segments in all TV drama have increased exponentially. 'Flexi-narrative' denotes the fast-cut, segmented, multi-narrative structure which yields the ninety-second sound-and-vision byte form currently typical of popular TV drama. As noted, the narrative structure derives in part from soaps but cross-cutting to gain pace and to juxtapose incidents and images has long since been a cinematic device.[20] Besides telescoping time, the temporal and spatial ellipses serve to cut out what is deemed unimportant to leave 'the significant'. There is thus, as we shall see, a politics of salience in play in flexi-narrative forms. It suffices in the interim to note that flexi-narrative has extended into virtually all popular series and serials.

Television has always been inclined towards a rapid change of shots since, in comparison with cinematic images of greater visual depth and complexity, the limited information of each shot is readily accessible. The growing ability of viewers to read visual imagery in contemporary culture in addition has accelerated the rate at which information can be absorbed. Televisual literacy has educated viewers to accept bigger jumps in visual narration and even to accommodate – through their very awareness of established patterns – occasional breaches of normative perspective conventions without undermining the illusionistic world presented.

There is, however, an additional feature which increasingly distinguishes popular (post)modern TV drama output: the aestheticization of the image. To bring out this additional connotation in Chapter 4, where an example will be explored, I coin the term 'flexiad drama'. 'Flexiad' refers to the mode (in flexi-narrative form) which echoes advertisements and pop video in deploying signifiers for their intrinsic 'values and lifestyle' aesthetic appeal rather than in any referential sense to denote the 'real'. This second neologism arises from an obvious play in 'flexiad' on '*ad*vertisement' and on the '*flexi*bility', both of flexible accumulation in consumption and of multiple narrative strands organized to sustain intermittent appeal to different segments of the target audience. The new terms serve as useful shorthand in what follows to convey that, whilst perhaps remaining loosely within the frameworks of TV narrative realisms, a new form and style of presentation have emerged to dislocate sense-making realist conventions.

The tendency towards visual spectacle – against the tide of, at least British, TV drama traditions – is accompanied by a discernible shift in the soundscape. Popular music on radio has become a dominant feature of (post)modern life. Correspondingly music soundtrack features more in television drama than in the past when a stricter naturalism precluded non-diegetic sound. Traditionally music is used, as in film, to mask visual edits by sustaining a rhythmic structure of sound or to create atmosphere or underscore the mood of the action. As TV drama has drifted away from sense-making narrative structures to looser compilations reflecting new patterns of production and consumption, however, music is increasingly used for the sake of its own appeal and only loosely related to the dramatic action.

To sum up contemporary production, modern television drama single plays, series and serials are today mostly made 'cinematically' with a single camera and post-production editing on either digital video or film. Soaps remain the exception since, owing to the fast turn-around time in production to feed a voracious schedule, they retain some studio-style strategies in a hybrid multi-camera/single camera approach. Given the developments of television technology, it is possible to deploy compositional strategies from veristic documentary to abstract art video. Although there is a drift, as noted, towards the idea of screen space as virtual reality, broadcast television as yet operates within a relatively narrow range of its potential rhetorical field. Tradition and audience horizons of expectation in the reception context as well as commercial interests are key factors in its conservatism. Flexi-narrative, arising from a combination of forces in the field, is dominant.

V ISSUES

The role of the writer, the TV dramatist, has changed. The drift to series marks a move from an authored, literary tradition of the playwright. The consequence of this change is the production of more formulaic drama with a team of writers for the most part working within the prescribed framework of a series or serial in either a thirty or fifty-minute slot. Producers and script editors, moreover, frequently re-work commissioned scripts in current production processes. Both film and television production are, of course, inexorably collaborative processes but the hierarchical relations of production are historically different in the two mediums. Perhaps because of its literary theatrical heritage, TV drama started with the writer, and the production process has traditionally aimed to realize the writer's vision. Film, in contrast, is a director's medium with screenplay writers relatively subservient.

The change from a verbal to a visual culture diluting the literary/theatrical tradition has been seen by such commentators as Postman and Booth, as noted, as evidence of a cultural decline. Postman's case is that a verbal and print culture is rational and discursive and engenders that informed debate which is the cornerstone of democracy, whereas the visual culture of television is solely a medium of entertainment. Postman is careful to distinguish between a technology and a medium:

A technology is merely a machine. A medium is the social and intellectual environment a machine creates (1987: 86).

He contends, however, that technologies are not neutral and that modern television is disposed to be a visual medium. In America the television medium is:

a beautiful spectacle, a visual delight, pouring forth thousands of images on any given day. The average length of a shot on television is only 3.5 seconds, so that the eye never rests, always has something new to see. Moreover, television offers viewers a variety of subject matter, requires minimal skills to comprehend it, and is largely aimed at emotional gratification. . . . American television, in other words, is devoted entirely to supplying its audience with entertainment . . .

[and] has made entertainment itself the natural format for the representation of all experience (1987: 88–9).

Whilst Postman's case is overstated and smacks of a technological (or media) reductionism taking no account of the activity of the audience and the sense-making frames negotiated by viewers, there may be something in his distinction between a verbal and visual culture pertinent to the development of TV drama. There is a strain in contemporary television drama, led by ratings discourse to common denominator production, which seeks to maximise audience gratification in the way he suggests. It resonates with the account here of television's historical tendencies technologically to performance as spectacle. Culturally, in addition, the entertainment value of TV drama has come to be placed above other possible functions of usable stories such as, in Dennnis Potter's words, 'discovering something that you did not know'.[21] But as Potter saw, in 'the palace of varieties' which television offers, the hierarchies of print culture which excluded many people, might be overcome. It is a question of how television culture is developed and on the available cultural forms in a verbal/visual medium.

Guy Debord's formulation of the 'society of the spectacle' brings out the political downside of postmodernism's drift to the visual, seeing beyond surface decoration:

> The spectacle is not an aggregate of images but a social relation amongst people mediated by language. The spectacle, grasped in its totality, is both the result and project of the existing mode of production. It is not a supplement to the real world, its added decoration. It is the heart of the unrealism of the real society. In all its specific forms, as information or propaganda, advertisement or direct entertainment consumption, the spectacle is the present MODEL of socially dominant life (1992: 63–4).

To read the increased influence of the visual spectacle purely as a mark of wholesale cultural decline, however, is to take too totalizing a view. Whilst it can be acknowledged that in postmodern culture everything is presented, dramatized, turned into a show, it may be possible for a critical postmodernism to do more in visual culture than merely placate. A sophisticated, visually literate audience is able to read complex visual statements in a context of intertextual, even metafictional, awareness which in the demands of its engagement might approximate to the intellectual activity of verbal debate. Viewers situated in specific socio-historical sites, moreover, do not buy into all the market offers. Thus the tendency towards the mindless entertainment Postman alleges is not simply attributable to visual culture, but perhaps to some of its more overtly populist forms and functions.[22]

Indeed, it may be that programmes more loosely constructed on a paratactical frame afford greater space for readers actively to construct meanings and pleasures. Plural cognitions may thus replace the (contrived) liberal consensus of an earlier age. A new dimension in this regard of the established debate about the mindlessness of the mass media is currently provided by the context of developing communications technologies bringing the relative activity or passivity of the user again in question. I thus return in concluding this chapter to the implications of new technologies for TV drama.

Some argue that the greater accessibility of knowledge to individuals in their own homes through horizontal dissemination will significantly increase participatory democracy (Masuda, 1990). Others are less sanguine (the political and ethical dimensions of this broad debate are matters for Chapter 9). The circulation of images and sounds through the new technologies are yet profoundly to affect TV drama production and circulation,[23] though fast feed-back to the producers of *The X Files* via the InterNet is alleged to have had some influence on the development of the series (see Lowry, 1995) and interactive computer games, offering choices in the progression of narratives, mark possible developments. Indeed, the key feature of the new technologies is their interconnectedness leading to 'a single high capacity digital network of networks' (Neuman, 1991: x). Thus TV drama is by no means technologically isolated from the broader context of an electronic universe.

Extension of such developments into TV drama might lead to an active audience beyond the expectations of recent media theory. In non-professional production, furthermore, Enzenberger, placing emphasis on the increased agency and creativity afforded to users, envisages new art forms and popular, guerrilla video (see 1974: 95–128). This optimistic perspective must, however, be set in the context of an established production industry where economies of scale, 'generate strong counterpressures toward mass-produced, common-denominator, mass-audience media . . . rather than promoting narrowcasting and two-way communication' (Neuman, 1991: 13, 42). Similarly, according to Neuman, 'the psychology of the mass audience, the semi-attentive, entertainment-oriented mind-set of day-to-day media behaviour' (1991: 13) must be considered.

Should the development of digital wide-screen TV receivers not prove too expensive, it may be that improvements to the television image will extend the 'cinematic' possibilities of narrative fictions, with all their visual complexity and ability to situate agency in structure. Alternatively, the ability with digital technology to manipulate imagery and to edit with special effects may tend towards a shift from representing the real to 'jacking in to cyberspace'. With regard to the introduction of interactive video to date, however, the signs indicate conservatism rather than innovation on a wide scale, but time will tell.

Finally, it is evident that, in the force field of relations of production and consumption, there are numerous influences and no single factor is ultimately determinant of TV drama output. In the practice of its popular forms, illusionistic narrative fiction, inclined towards humanist ways of seeing and showing, has been dominant. It may not remain so as technologies develop, the boundaries of mediums are tested, and new aesthetics emerge along with shifts in the social formation. Cultural changes, under the influence of more radical technologies and new ways of seeing may have begun to redraw the cognitive maps of new generations. A key question in TV drama is whether further accommodation can be reached with narrative traditions or whether a point of crisis is imminent in which traditional forms and social functions are no longer sustainable under the pressures of a new affective order.

2 Flexi-Narrative from Hill Street to Holby City

Upping the Tempo; Raising the Temperature

> ... by the 1970s the attention span of the viewers had short-ened. They were spoiled. You had to come at them from all directions to keep their attention (Grant Tinker cited in Feuer *et al.*, 1984: 80).

I

Whilst multi-narrative, multi-character television drama was common in soaps by the 1970s, the origins of flexi-narrative in series might be traced to the MTM (Mary Tyler Moore) stable in Los Angeles and to *Hill Street Blues* (1980) in particular.[1] The context of the production of *Hill Street* was influenced by a range of factors bearing out the appropriateness of the eco-logical approach in this study to TV drama. One factor – as declared by Grant Tinker, financial head of MTM, in the epi-graph to this chapter – was a sense in 1970s America that the audience required a pacey television to sustain its attention. In addition, an early example of 'demographic thinking' about audience led NBC to take on the dominant CBS network not in terms of total numbers ratings but on the basis of maximising 'quality audience' – those sectors, that is, with highest disposable income (AB/C1's). Together with liberalizing cultural develop-ments arising from the 'beat generation' of the 1960s, the civil rights movement, and the feminist movement of the early 1970s, these influences led to a perceived need for sophisticated adult programming which could nevertheless hold the attention of an audience whose powers of concentration were diminished.

A change of format from the traditional narrative mode in TV drama of problem leading to resolution was called for. The protracted telling of a single story with perhaps a comic relief sub-plot demanded a level of sustained attention which could not be guaranteed. Narrative pace was not, however, the sole factor motivating change in MTM. The relatively unambiguous, established formulaic narrative did not facilitate new challenges leading to the examination of values, at a time of a sense of the greater complexity of issues. The 'quality' audience which MTM was striving to make its own was thought ready for multiple perspectives.

Hill St Blues is the successor to those programmes which established both the MTM stable and ultimately a flexible, yet 'quality', multi-narrative form. It was *Lou Grant* in 1977 – itself a spin-off from the *Mary Tyler Moore Show* (1970–77) – which shifted MTM output from 30-minute sit-com to 60-minute drama. As Feuer *et al.* notes:

> One can see in *Lou Grant* the beginnings of the multiple plot line construction often claimed as one of *Hill Street*'s great innovations in prime-time drama. . . . Already the TV convention of main plot and sub-plot is being deconstructed (1984: 45).

Hill Street, however, extended the functions of a richer texture achieved by juxtaposition of a number of narratives variable in tone, with a range of diverse characters. Going even further than soaps, many of the narrative strands were left open to be taken up in later episodes whilst others simply trailed off un-resolved. Thus *Hill Street* achieved its dense textures and sense of a lack of resolution to difficult problems for an audience who sensed the complexity of things in the historical world. As Feuer – picking up on a review by Tom Carson in *The Village Voice* – remarks:

> 'Character ensembles', 'motivation', 'a set of little epiphan-ies', have transformed the problem/solution format of the sitcom into a far more psychological and episodic formula in which . . . the situation itself becomes pretext for the revela-tion of character (Feuer *et al.*, 1984: 35).

The flexi-narrative approach in *Hill Street* was by no means an unqualified success at the outset: indeed the first series was poorly rated. To renew the series for a second season, MTM was required by the NBC network to return somewhat to a more traditional television narrative structure, tying up at least one plot line within a single episode. Ultimately, however, *Hill Street* was both a critical and ratings success. With its particular blend of soap melodrama with aspects of the cop show, shot with a visual style borrowing from cinema verite and influenced, it has been suggested, by Robert Altman's fluid use of the camera in the film *M*A*S*H* (see Kerr, 1984: 148), *Hill Street* is distinguished.

MTM's conscious sense of itself as a familial, creative production company aiming to make 'quality' product for a 'quality' audience contributed also to the simultaneous introduction and innovative use of the flexi-narrative form in prime-time drama series. The use of a cinematic visual style emulating the fluid tracks and long takes of feature films is part of MTM's declaration that it is liberated from the visual grammar of the studio and is free to compete with feature films. The question of quality will be taken up in Section II. Meanwhile the influence of *Hill Street*'s structural approach on subsequent television drama series can be seen in *Casualty* (BBCI).

Casualty is set in a fictional hospital, Holby City, which took Trust status at the end of the Spring 1993 run of the series. This modification to a publicly owned, National Health Service hospital shadowed the actual policy of the Conservative government in Britain at the time to encourage independently-funded Trust hospitals. A violent response from local people in *Casualty* to what were perceived as 'government cutbacks' resulted, in the final episode of the previous run, in an inner-city riot which destroyed the 'A&E' (Accident and Emergency) unit.[2]

Casualty thus represents an ambivalent combination of actuality and fiction to be discussed in Chapter 5. It is a typical example of a more everyday use of flexi-narrative in the series genre and some general observations may therefore be drawn from it and *Hill Street* about the flexi-narrative form's functioning and broad appeal. These insights will in turn serve to suggest why flexi-narrative has spread to become the TV drama format most popular (as defined in ratings discourse) with audiences, the most serviceable to producers and schedulers, and therefore increasingly the most common in series and serials.

Flexi-narrative in soaps functions as follows. A number of

stories involving familiar characters in familiar settings are broken down into narrative bytes and rapidly intercut. Any lack of interest of an audience segment[3] in one set of characters or story-line is thus not allowed to last long as another story with a different group of characters is swiftly taken up, only in turn to give way to another before taking up again the first narrative, and so on in a series of interwoven narrative strands. It is through presenting a wide range of characters and issues to reflect a broad social spectrum in story-lines rapidly intercut that one half-hour or fifty-minute programme can attract and sustain interest, domestic distractions notwithstanding.

In contrast with the single narrative action-adventure series, the plot of which is goal-oriented, soaps' stories do not reach narrative closure at the end of an episode. In the problem/resolution narrative model, the story follows a circuitous route to the inevitable solution of a problem posed to the central characters. The paradigm is the detective story and the audience needs to follow the story to gain the pleasure of the pay-off in discovering 'whodunit'.

The traditional narrative pattern, as discerned for example by Propp's narratology (Propp, 1968), sees the forces of stability engaged with those of disruption. In this view a problem or force threatens the equilibrium in the social formation at the outset of the narrative only for order to be restored by the end, typically in Western culture through the agency of a white male protagonist. Thus such goal-oriented narrative structures have been termed 'masculine' in contrast with the 'feminine' narrative fluidity of soaps (see Fiske, 1987: 144). This conception, however, implies essentialist gender categories in one of those binary divisions which the both/and approach in this book aims to call in question.

Feuer, however, offers an alternative, ideological model for the tensions in soaps: a notional equilibrium in the unachieved ideal of a stable, happy family against which all the disruptions are plotted. Feuer notes of continuing serials that:

[i]ntegration into a happy family remains the ultimate goal, but it cannot endure for any given couple. The various sets of couples achieve in fulcrum fashion a balance between harmony and disharmony but no one couple can remain in a state of integration (or of disintegration) (1986: 113).

Narrative strands in soaps are periodically brought to a conclusion in a number of ways: as a feud is resolved, for example,
a secret is revealed, or an actor or character leaves the series.
At the end of each episode, however, one of the narrative
strands is brought to a point of dilemma and left suspended
as it were in mid-air. Hence the colloquial term for this feature: 'cliff-hanger'.

The difference between soaps and popular series with regard
to the deployment of flexi-narrative is that new characters and
narrative strands are introduced in each episode of a series.
Their stories are usually brought to closure within the episode
whilst a number of regular characters (smaller than in soaps)
is involved in unresolved narratives which give continuity across
episodes. The blurring of distinction between the series and
serial affords schedulers the joint advantage of an unresolved
narrative strand – a cliff-hanger to draw the audience to watch
the next episode – and a new group of characters and self-
contained stories in each episode. A serial sustains through its
episodes a single, complete (though complex) story, based on
a group of key, regular characters, and seeks to draw an audience by the power of a sustained narrative. A flexi-narrative
series has something of this attraction but, in contrast, avoids
deterring those potential viewers who may not watch a serial
if they sense they might have lost out on something crucial to
understanding by missing the previous episode.

First in a new series, the episode of *Casualty* written by Scott
Cherry and entitled 'No Place to Hide', was transmitted in
prime time at 20.10 hours on Saturday, 9 October 1993 attract-
ing 13.96 million viewers.[4] The episode includes four stories
and a narrative fragment exclusive to the episode. These are
interwoven with a strand, Story 1, involving the central character, the male head-nurse, Charlie Fairhead, and the receptionist,
Norma Sullivan, which develops a trans-episodic thematic concern in the series with the plight of the contemporary NHS in
Britain. The fifty-minute episode breaks down roughly (including the beginning and end titles) into sixty-two narrative bytes
(see Appendix). A narrative byte is defined in terms of the time
and space given to a particular narrative strand before cutting
to a byte of another narrative strand. The byte is distinct from
a televisual sequence which is defined in terms of a linked group
of individual camera shots distinguishing different times and

spaces within a given narrative. Thus the rhythm of the episode is governed by the duration and juxtaposition of both narrative bytes and sequences.

A brief account of the self-contained stories in the episode is needed prior to analysis. Story 2: 'the Millers' story' concerns a young middle-class married couple whose relationship is fragile because the husband, unbeknown to the wife, is involved in hard drugs. Both Mr Miller and an acquaintance of his receive minor knife-wounds in an incident connected with drugs dealing. The hospital and police consequently get involved. Story 3: 'Phipps's story' involves an elderly man, a Burma campaign veteran, who refuses treatment having been admitted following a fall. Story 4, 'the Westons' story' tells of the owner of a small clothing factory – in his thirties, married with a pre-teenage daughter – who has employed to run a creche in his factory his one-time au-pair, Kate. The two are having an affair, but Mr Weston cannot bring himself to tell his wife as Kate insists he must. In terms of prominence defined by allotted time, this is the main story of the episode. It is not, however, introduced until byte 22, approximately one-third of the way through the fifty-minute episode. This narrative strategy is another aspect of the flexibility of flexi-narrative as it affords viewers who join the episode late to experience a story complete in itself. The 'Westons' narrative' serves also for a crescendo in 'No Place to Hide', rising to high tension when Kate is seriously injured climbing to reach help after she is trapped in a lift at the factory with the Westons' daughter and a young boy.

The single 'narrative fragment' in the episode, in contrast, is undeveloped having only one byte. It involves a young couple whose son has inadvertently swallowed a rare coin belonging to his father. The doctor's recommended means of retrieval of the coin – that the parents should sift the child's faeces – allows this story to afford a little comic relief to the relative seriousness of issues raised in the other narrative strands: hard drug-taking and its effects on married life; loneliness and a sense of being unwanted in old age; marital infidelity and the consequences of not facing up to one's actions. Indeed, the function of humour may be the key to the inclusion of this otherwise dispensable fragment. *Casualty* has the reputation of being bleak in its concern with life's accidents and injuries in a context of a declining public sector health provision. At just the

moment when viewers might be considering switching off for
this reason, a lighthearted interlude leavens the episode. The
fragment of narrative serves also to authenticate the illusion of
a historical reality of life at Holby City by suggesting a through-
flow of patients in the 'A&E' Department which purports to
select from the flux of hospital life just those stories which the
episode chooses to highlight. In this respect it shares a structural function with the 'Westons' narrative' which, as noted, is
a late admission to *Casualty* in more than one sense.

Pacey cutting of dynamic images and a strong soundtrack
typify the modern drama series. Given the increasing competition between channels for viewers' attention, it is perceived to
be necessary at the start of any drama to capture the audience.
This demand has resulted in a range of conventions whereby
an exceptionally fast-cut sequence precedes the unfolding of
the action proper of the episode. Some series and serials give
a foretaste of the action by editing together excerpts – usually
the most visually dynamic – from the episode to come; others
have a titles signature with standard fast-cut action of the kind
which typifies the strand accompanied by a distinctive soundtrack to hail to the television set those members of the household not yet actually watching. *Casualty* follows the latter model.
In a fifty-second sequence, the fastest-cut and most cinematic
of the entire programme, the series, its central concern and its
general dynamic are introduced.

Under a soundtrack of a synthesized siren approaching, an
ambulance weaves through heavy traffic towards the camera and
out of frame right in seven seconds. The first part of the titles
sequence is shot through a blue filter conveying a cold, wet,
nocturnal mood underscored by an insistent synthetic strain
of sound echoing the ambulance siren. The dynamic pace of
the cutting is however sustained by a strong percussive beat.
After the ambulance, a Close-Up of a 'paramedic' arm band is
followed by a series of shots of accidents: a woman falls down
stairs in Mid-Shot; the masked eyes of a man welding who lifts
his hand to his mouth as if it is paining him; a rugby tackle
with the bodies coming to camera, a Close-Up of the tackled
man's face expressing the pain of a fall; in Mid-Shot a person attacked by somebody in a leather jacket; similarly shot a
young boy in bed with hands of a doctor (out of frame) treating him; a TV Long-Shot of somebody falling from scaffolding

to the horror of his helpless mates; mouth-to-mouth resuscitation of an old woman seen in Close-Up; in Mid-Shot somebody is struck and tossed over the bonnet of a car; a couple with a baby anxiously get into a car; a woman is apparently attacked, her face in Medium Close-Up; ambulance doors close. This sequence lasts for twenty-six seconds.

The soundtrack (still synthesized) changes to a more melodious strain in the lower registers evocative of deeper feelings. Against shots of the ambulance – still through a blue filter – travelling to Holby City, where it finally arrives to be greeted by a team of waiting 'A&E' staff, are insert frames. These frames are fragmented by the mosaic Special Effect Generator,[5] as if masked to preserve anonymity in a televisual news convention,[6] and in the warmth of full colour. These inserts show in seventeen seconds a number of people receiving prompt, professional but caring medical attention: a phone is answered; a drip is prepared; the bed-head of a patient in a white robe against fresh white linen is raised; a doctor feels a man's temple; another doctor treats a black man's arm; a trolley, accompanied by a team of doctors and nurses, is wheeled speedily to camera; a young boy receives electric shock in an effort to restart his heart. From the awaiting team at the hospital when the ambulance arrives, the episode cuts to the first studio sequence of a trolley being wheeled into a bay for treatment.

The titles sequence has been described in detail because it is a microcosm of the series. Accidents happen, people are treated – despite the pressures on the 'privatized' NHS hospital – and they recover medically, as the human interest aspects of their stories, revealing problems often associated with the cause of their illness or injury, are explored and resolved. The titles are also vital, as 'hook', to the programme's success. The metaphor is telling since it reveals the scheduler's need to pull in an audience as well as drawing attention to the means by which this is typically attempted. Fast action, fast-cut, appeals to sensationalism as the moments of highest dramatic temperature are collaged into a hotspot. At the same time, the distinctive musical signature and the reassurance offered by the images of professional medical care in the titles reinforce the formula. An economy of tensions and resolutions – more intense and dynamic than that in the single-drama problem/resolution model – is thus in play. Together the titles sequence marries high excitement with reassurance, the twin characteristics of formulaic, popular TV drama.

The titles sequence in *Casualty*, moreover, is a sophisticated cinematic montage quite different in style from the televisual construction of the body of the episode which evidences a studio heritage.[7] As used, it is a distinctive feature of the series or serial. Whereas in a single play basic narrative information must be imparted at the outset sometimes resulting in a slow start, the dynamic sense of pace introducing *Casualty* is generated initially by the titles. Thereafter, although the pace is much slower relatively, an energy is sustained by the inter-cutting of bytes of the multiple narratives. Bytes 2, 6, and 8 introduce the 'Millers'' narrative, bytes 3 and 5 introduce the 'Norma' narrative, and segments 4 and 7 develop Charlie's political engagement with the Hospital's Chief Executive. In the latter half of the episode, sections 33 to 43, tension mounts, as noted, in the accelerated pace of the build-up to Kate's fall in the lift-shaft through fast inter-cutting of sequences within the 'Westons'' narrative.

Handling a number of stories in this flexi-narrative form generates a high level of intensity since, once the strands of the narratives are established, it is possible to cut to the high points in the action of each, thus keeping up – if not always at fever pitch – the dramatic temperature. Extending viewers' increasing ability to fill in the narrative gaps as noted in Chapter 1, all but the most dynamic or dramatically intense moments of a story can be omitted.

A combination of human interest stories with at least the appearance of fast-action in the flexi-narrative form seems currently to maximize audience appeal. For in an apparent paradox, flexi-narrative, whilst it gives the appearance of fast action, does not rely on it entirely to sustain the pace which captures and retains viewers' interest. Indeed the form affords the treatment of personal human encounter in Close-Up in the humanist mode noted as traditionally distinctive of television. Precisely because there are a number of intercut stories, any given narrative does not in itself need to be action-packed. 'Phipps's narrative' is, for example, one in which the only action is the Major's enfeebled resistance to medical attention. It is sensitive, moreover, in treating the problem of loneliness in old age through the male nurse Ken's gentle insistence in talking to Phipps.

Flexi-narrative series would appear to have achieved an accommodation between traditional viewer interest in stories presented in the familiar naturalist mode and a market-driven need to maximize an audience with a short span of attention. It has achieved a narrative structure which combines the allegedly 'masculine' preference for action and narrative resolution with the supposedly 'feminine' fluidity and open-endedness in story-telling with an emphasis on human interest. By combining a number of stories in one episode, it is indeed possible to appeal to a range of audience segments. 'No Place to Hide' includes significant characters from the young boy who swallowed the coin, to a pre-teenager (the Westons' daughter and the boy trapped in the lift with her), to a young woman, Kate, on to the twenty-something couple, the Millers, the slightly older Westons, through to the elderly Mr Phipps. The regular characters cover a range of ages and, in the run of *Casualty* under discussion, include a black male (Martin Ashford) and black female nurse (Adele Bedford), a young woman receptionist of Asian descent (Mie Nishi-Kawa) and a homosexual male nurse, Ken Hodges (Christopher Guard). If the interest of individual viewers with regard to representational drama is at least in part a matter of empathy with at least one of the characters, then flexi-narrative offers a wide range of points of identification.

Similarly the flexi-narrative structure offers a range of stories with different content such that, particularly in the case of *Casualty* which deals with topics of contemporary social interest, there should be something in any given episode to attract all audience segments. An insight in the approach to construction is provided by Nick McCarty who has written episodes of *Casualty* though not the one under discussion. Invited by the producer to contribute to the series, the writer took to a preliminary discussion meeting 86 one-liner stories involving accidents.[8] A quick sift revealed that all but 24 of them had been covered in *Casualty* in one way or another. From this remainder the writer was then able to select four stories that might work together and include a range of characters and points of interest and identification in the manner described above. At best this choice might result in a thematic link between the stories which could potentially extend the resonance of any one of the narratives in just the way that a multiple plot play builds up an intricate cross-referencing of comparative worlds.[9]

Taking up the idea above of the flexi-narrative series as multiple-plot drama, the 'Charlie', 'Nora' and 'Phipps' narratives in 'No Place to Hide' might be seen to link thematically. In variant ways, each narrative strand demonstrates the pressures on staff and services in an NHS under threat of cost-accountancy and privatization. Charlie is engaged in a standing battle to resist some of the initiatives by Holby City's cost-accountant Chief Executive, Jane Scott, and Administrator, Mark Calder, both of whom are constructed through their appearance and attitudes as 1980s 'yuppies'.[10] Charlie is particularly disturbed in this episode by an instrumental productivity study – focusing on Ken, the homosexual male nurse – which threatens his job should his output be deemed unsatisfactory. In treating the resistant Phipps, Ken requests of Charlie permission to take time to talk to the old soldier in an effort to discover what is at the root of his self-denial. Charlie grants the request but viewers are in a position to share the irony that this apparent kindness is double-edged. Meanwhile Nora has a breakdown in the face of the insensitivity of her work context in turn occasioned by the cuts in staffing and funding. Charlie, who is normally sympathetic to his colleagues' troubles, rebuts Nora when she asks to talk to him early in the episode but the audience knows that he himself is under pressure and is preoccupied with an impending visit from the financiers.

As the episode unfolds, the 'Norma' narrative might be seen to be thematically linked as noted with the 'Charlie' story. It might be read as evidence and authentication of Charlie's perception that the NHS and its staff are suffering from the effects of cost-accountancy. 'Phipps's story' is also thematically linked to the concern in other narrative strands with the monetarist threat to time for treatment of the whole person in the NHS, the salutary need for which is demonstrated in Ken's resolution to Phipps's dilemma. Having talked to Phipps to establish that his main problem is loneliness, Ken locates and contacts members of the Major's old regiment who were not aware that he was still alive and yet who are delighted to come to take him home from hospital and befriend him again. The happy outcome of the story serves potentially as authenticating evidence that human interests are served by nurses having and taking the time to get to know their patients as people rather than merely as medical problems. The 'Norma' narrative and the

'Phipps' narrative thus support what emerges as the preferred view of the episode, and perhaps of the series. This is in part constructed through an organic relationship of plots available to an attentive and sophisticated reading, but it is also reinforced in *Casualty*'s central character Charlie, whose point of view the audience is invited to share.

Point of view is established televisually by the simple means in the first instance of allotting more narrative time, and thus more screen time, to a particular character. In a series this is likely to be a recurrent character structurally central to the institutional context of the fictional world, though not usually a person in a dominant position of power. The character may command sympathy by displaying qualities to which the society attaches positive values but since – as has often been noted – the diabolical is more interesting than the saintly – this is by no means a necessary condition. In the case of *Casualty*, however, Charlie Fairhead – the name connotes ordinariness but reasonable justice – is constructed as a decent human being trying to do a caring job under difficult circumstances. He is narratively central to Holby City's politics and human interest stories as the episode under discussion demonstrates. He is romantically unattached affording parts of the audience the pleasure of his notional availability. Love-interest – both hetero- and homo-sexual – has featured in his continuing personal story.[11] Extending his narrative centrality, Charlie's point of view is mediated through shots of his reactions to the key moments in each episode.

Although Charlie holds the preferred position for viewer identification offered by the text, he is no Hollywood hero. His ambivalent character is in itself an illustration of the strain, rather than the fix, theory of ideology (see Geertz, 1993: 201–7). Furthermore, flexi-narratives do not seek to channel a singular ideology but are plural in their very structures in recognition that audiences comprise a range of people with differing perspectives. Indeed, ethnographic research has demonstrated unlikely points of identification between audience sub-groups and points of view in television programmes. Similarly coincidences have emerged between groups with apparently disparate interests (see Morley, 1980 and 1986). Whilst, then, TV drama texts are by no means innocent in their discursive positions, flexi-narratives particularly evidence a model of negotiation of a range of meanings rather than an inoculation theory of ideology.

II

A facility of multiple-plot drama is its ability in its different narrative strands to explore and connect different viewpoints on a topic. Although part of the attraction of flexi-narrative form to producers and schedulers of TV drama series is to offer fragments of different narrative strands to different sub-groups in the plural audience, the form is by no means precluded from greater structural complexity. If, as Feuer suggests, 'quality' means 'more literate, more stylistically complex, and more psychologically 'deep' than ordinary TV fare' (Feuer *et al.*, 1984: 56), then flexi-narrative is a contender. The inter-relationship of narrative strands can result in a complex dramatic construct with a range of multiple-plot relationships between them. Such a structure in turn invites a more complex response from audiences since one plot strand may be related to and negotiated with others.

Such a feature of plotting is not, however, a significant production factor in building the large audiences articulated in ratings discourse, because level of reading difficulty is associated with an AB/C1's 'quality' audience. Where a niche market is targeted as with *Hill Street Blues*, stylistic complexity may then be on the agenda, but little attention is paid to sophisticated compositional strategies in more regular flexi-narrative production. Writers are usually under pressure to produce scripts to tight deadlines and therefore lack the time to work on the thematic, multiple-plot construction of scripts. On occasion they find by design or accident that such an organic complex emerges, but it is not a high priority. It is a possibility of the flexi-narrative form, not its defining characteristic.

In mainstream series, quality scripts in terms of multiple-plotting are thus relatively rare but, when they appear, they have the potential to ask more of all sections of the audience. It is not, then, the flexi-narrative form in itself that gravitates towards the repetitious and the formulaic, but the institutional constraints which privilege prolific TV drama output and large audiences over dramatic quality more traditionally viewed.

With regard to a disposition to truth-telling, for example, the ways in which interpersonal and family relationships are handled in TV drama series is a central concern. Most television drama deals in the familiar. The setting of Naturalist 'chamber' plays – from which TV drama is in part derived – is intimate and literally based in the family. Raymond Williams sees this feature of television drama as a further social extension of the Naturalist trajectory. His perception of a continuity between that literary-theatrical tradition and both the family rooms people watch in and those observed on television is worth quoting at length as it synthesizes a number of points of the discussion thus far in this book:

> The great naturalist dramatists, from Ibsen, left the palaces, the forums and the streets of earlier actions. They created, above all, rooms; enclosed rooms on enclosed stages; rooms in which life was centred but in which people waited for the knock on the door, the letter or the message, the shout from the street to know what would happen to them; what would come to intersect and decide their own still intense and immediate lives. There is a direct cultural continuity, it seems to me, from those enclosed rooms, enclosed and lighted framed rooms, to the rooms in which we watch what is happening, as we say, 'out there': not out there in a particular street or specific community but in a complex and otherwise unfocused and unfocusable national and international life, where our area of concern and apparent concern is unprecedentedly wide, and where what happens on another continent can work through to our own lives in a matter of days and weeks – in the worst image, in hours and minutes. Yet our own lives are still here, still substantially here, with the people we know, in our own rooms, in the similar rooms of our friends and neighbours, and they too are watching: not only for public events, or for distraction but from a need for images, for representations of what living is now like, for this kind of person and that, in this situation and place and that ... to simulate if not to affirm a human identity (1975: 14–15).

It is to fulfil this need for representations which offer a space for negotiation between familiar, private lives and the public sphere that TV drama retains what Williams has elsewhere called the 'naturalist habit' (1973: 386), a habit which may well not ultimately be broken by current postmodern tendencies.

Casualty and other popular TV drama series might be seen, then, as the latest examples in a century-old line, though presented in flexi-narrative form. The central concern is with the private handling of events with public resonances. In the case of Casualty it is how people deal with accident, illness, injury even death, and how they negotiate the social problems of the day: drug abuse, a declining health service, the pressures of work, loneliness in old age. People would appear still to be interested in narratives about other people, particularly those who are similar to themselves but whose experience is perhaps slightly out of the ordinary, or of a kind which they anticipate encountering and perhaps are pleased to rehearse vicariously in engagement with representational fictions.[12] This is part of what is meant by usable stories.

When series employ the narrative strategies of realism and naturalism outside the structure of feeling which generated those conventions, however, the habit remains but without conviction of lived experience.[13] Actions are motivated in a simple and direct manner; predictable consequences result in a trite moral framework; narratives are contrived to reach foreseeable moments of suspense in high tension. Information is conveyed, but the usable story does not fully unfold.

In the episode of Casualty discussed, for example, the Millers' marriage is predictably brought under strain by Mr Miller's involvement in hard drugs, though it is indicated that his wife will stand by him. The Westons' family life – and ultimately Mr Weston himself – are left in ruins in a final moment of narrative suspension for viewers to contemplate the ill consequences of marital infidelity. In comparison with the problem/resolution plot model, there is incomplete closure but, to an audience familiar with flexi-narrative conventions, outcomes are equivalently predictable. The noted norm of the ideal family in tension with deviations from it is evident here. Consequently the more everyday versions of flexi-narrative do not invoke amongst viewers the imaginative resources that the best story-telling commands. They offer usable stories but, on the scale to be developed in this study, they are less usable because they do not challenge the moulds of TV drama's or society's habitual ways of seeing.

If, as Benjamin long ago observed, direct, interpersonal communication has 'fallen in value' (1992: 83), TV drama serves as an important substitute site for the negotiation of the contemporary personal and public spheres in the manner Williams proposes. At best, the stories of TV drama engage people's imaginations assisting them in making sense of their own lives in relation to a frame of reference which is at once vastly expanded and yet, through television and other modern communications, more immediately accessible on local levels.

Indeed, within the dramas themselves connections are made between the personal and the public. Soaps inter-cut public spaces in which the various characters can meet and intermingle with private domestic spaces. *Casualty* follows the pattern using the interiors of Holby City as the regular settings and the reception area particularly as a communal public space, whilst Charlie's office serves frequently as a staff meeting-point. With the decline of the nuclear family, *Hill Street* and other North American soaps and series developed the 'work family' and the workplace or the bar in *Cheers* or *NYPD Blue* (C4) to replace the kinship family and the domestic residence.

For varied reasons relating to target audience, production conditions and chance factors, however, some series interrelate the public and private spheres more successfully than others in terms of the referential specificities of viewers' personal and social lives. A technological tendency to over-emphasize the personal, dislocated from history – and therefore unlikely to be useful even in terms of 'the personal is political' – is evident as documented in Chapter 1.

To achieve a rapid turnaround it is not practicable in terms of time, let alone expense, to keep changing locations. Thus the sets for series are built as durable constructions. In visual terms, then, there is little new each week in the environment of *Casualty* other than the film-style inserts covering one or more of the accidents included in each episode. For reasons of time and cost these too have to be kept to a minimum. In 'No Place to Hide', the lift shaft sequence at Mr Weston's warehouse serves the function of extending the environment beyond the rooms of Holby City. The restricted space on the permanent sets draws the camera script towards the Close-Up and the emotional intensity of the personal human drama. This approach to shooting, echoing earlier studio production, remains the televisual norm.

To offset a limitation in the visual vocabulary of television at a cultural moment where the aestheticization of the image predominates, however, some series now include more cinematic sequences. Coupled with a current fashion for rural locations, the contemporary preference for the visual over the verbal has led series such as *Heartbeat* and *Peak Practice* to reveal the environment. Indeed, much of the popularity of such series would appear to lie in their rural settings.[14] Visually, however, they remain restricted, establishing a rural location but quickly turning to work in familiar conventions. A wide-angle shot or two is perhaps reinforced with a tracking shot following a car crossing the moors, but cutting quickly to interiors and the familiar narrow range of shots from Mid-Two-Shot to Close-Up mostly at eye level.

It has appropriately been suggested that the scale of television demands a readjustment of the camera angle terminology developed in film grammar. Ellis points out that 'the TV image shows things smaller than they are' (1992: 127), though a face in Close-Up is approximately life-size. The general point is that the scale of television is not only smaller than that of cinema but its singular advantage visually over the big screen leads to the Close-Up on personal relationships, largely to the exclusion of broader environments and subjects.

Besides isolating the individual from the context of the broader public sphere, the privileging of the face has additional cultural implications. It locates the measure of experience in the individual and equates proximity with sincerity. Seeing the face closely, the Close-Up implies, is to know the person: truth is identifiable in the felt human experience. Because the personal is so frequently decontextualized in television, however, the Close-up effectively becomes an instrument of propaganda. Its use in advertisements to authenticate claims about products serves to illustrate the point.

The Close-Up of the human face in drama, demanding subtle gradations of acting on the part of the performers, attempts to imply a depth to the human experience portrayed when all too often it is no more than a dislocated sign, a mere substitute for it in dramatic representation. This accounts, however, for the *ersatz* emotional power of even a fragment of TV drama caught in passing. The zoom in to Big-Close-Up on the reaction of a character at a moment of high dramatic temperature has indeed become the cliché for the cliff-hanger. Even though viewers may be aware of the convention, it nevertheless has an emotive power in which the fragmented flexi-narrative can trade. But high-temperature emotion, if neither anchored in credible representations of human experience nor heightened to the extent of sublime intensity, is curiously self-generating and unsatisfying. Through television and other media forms it has become, however, the way in which we learn culture and is key to the new affective order.[15]

In conclusion, a difference might provisionally be drawn between the conscious structuring of multiple-plot narratives in *Hill Street* and the almost random chance that other series will amount to more than the sum of their fragmented parts. The beginnings of a critical spectrum emerges in the difference between the series or episode which brings out organically a thematic concern and offers a highly usable sense of the complexity of issues, and the less usable formulaic drama.

Hill Street, and its descendant *NYPD Blue*, are exceptional in giving the impression of psychologically rounded character (the discussion of *NYPD* in Chapter 8 suggests how this is achieved). For the most part in popular flexi-narratives, however, even the permanent characters tend to reaffirm each week the limited range of qualities which distinguish them. In Charlie's case, for example, a marked disposition to privilege human concerns over instrumental medicine accompanies a long-suffering, but unshakeable, commitment to patient care in the NHS. His character is filled out slightly when, for example, his lack of involvement in personal relations with women is explained not by his commitment to his work but by either the hurt of a lost love or the possibility that he may have homosexual preferences (see episodes of 16 October and 23 October 1993). In such instances, however, it is less the agency of the character that drives the narrative than the opportunity offered to explore a topical issue. Whilst powerful emotional sympathy with psychologically rounded characters may lead to cognitive insights, the fast-cut structure of the flexi-narrative form would seem to militate against deep engagement.

Casualty does offer usable stories. As Michael Ferguson, an experienced producer appointed for its 1993 run, notes:

What I've been realizing over the past five or six years is the importance of popular drama. It is a way of society facing up to its fears and worries, and discussing them in safe surroundings.[16]

Casualty, however, tends towards that liberal balance by episode which MTM producer, Steve Bochco, sees as a neutralizing mechanism. It has received attention for being hard-hitting both in terms of its treatment of medical matters and social and political issues: Libby Purves observes that 'its realism is so impressive that it has always been a focus for controversy'.[17] Indeed the series draws on the British realist, almost documentary drama tradition of Loach and Garnett. But, because of its high dramatic temperature and tempo, the flexi-narrative form affords less narrative space for the camera to interrelate the public and private spheres.

With regard to truth-telling, a balance is struck: ideologically, between resistant politics and reassurance with regard to the NHS, and dramatically, between referential realism and melodrama. In spite of the pressures on the NHS verbally articulated in the dialogue, the action in the main shows all the patients receiving prompt and appropriate medical attention from a professional, if hard-pressed, staff. 'Phipps's narrative' particularly embodies – against the articulated feeling of the nurses – the apparent fact that staff do have time for human considerations beyond the purely medical.

The conclusion of this exploration of flexi-narrative form, then, is that its function with regard to drawing a large and plural audience may incline it towards the formulaic and away from truth-telling and the most usable stories. At worst TV drama's formulaic output contributes to a deadening, positivist sense that things can be no other than they are. Nevertheless, the form is precluded neither from 'quality' status nor critical potential. Given particular conditions of production, and personnel disposed to achieve something different from the regular television fare, the form may even lend itself to a critical practice. To offset any implications of a formal, textual determinism in the discussion of this chapter, furthermore, it should be noted that the polysemy of *Casualty*, as reflected in the range of views in letters from viewers about the series, affords various readings.[18] The disposition of the text to prefer some readings to others remains a concern in this book, though this never amounts to a formal reductionism: it is just one factor in the force field.

Extending the account above, discussion of an episode of *Between the Lines* (Chapter 8) will illustrate how it is possible within the popular series format to retain broad audience appeal and yet elicit a reflexive, critical response. The flexi-narrative structure allows it, but it may be that other forces in the field, in the relations of production, militate strongly against it.

3 Dislocations of Postmodernity
Transition in the Political Economy of Culture

CHRISSIE.   George is dead.
LOGGO.   So y've said.
CHRISSIE.   Yeah. But George is dead.
LOGGO.   I know, Chrissie, *I know*.
CHRISSIE.   But . . . you know what he stood for, don't y'?
LOGGO.   What do you mean?
Chrissie shakes his head.
CHRISSIE.   Yeah. Well that's dead an' all isn't it?

(Bleasdale (1982) 'George's Last Ride',
Boys from the Blackstuff, Sc.32.)[1]

I THE ECONOMY

George Malone stood for something, now past, which Chrissie strongly senses but is unable to articulate. Scene 32, the final scene of Alan Bleasdale's *Boys from the Blackstuff*, is set in an industrial wasteland against '*a derelict, part-demolished warehouse, "Tate & Lyle's 1922" written across the front*' (emphasis indicates directions). In terms of the specific history of Liverpool docks which George invokes in his last wheelchair ride (see Scenes 18–21) there is a sense of loss of a labour tradition stretching back to the trade of Empire and Britain's maritime past. What Chrissie cannot quite formulate in 1982 – the year of the series' first transmission – more specifically concerns, however, the breakdown of an economic, political and social formation: the post-1945 accommodation between labour and capital in Britain. George 'stood for':

> politics and power and come the day when we'd have inside toilets and proper bathrooms. Of Attlee and Bevan . . . (Bleasdale, 1982: 213).

50

What Chrissie senses to be symbolized in George's death is the passing of a historical moment, of a relative high-point of spirit and power in the British socialist, labour tradition. Following the marking of that historical moment, Section I of this chapter sketches the subsequent changes in the political economy and their impact on TV drama culture. The economic outline draws particularly on David Harvey's *The Condition of Postmodernity* (1989) tempered by Callinicos's *Against Postmodernism* (1989).

As outlined in the Introduction, the political economy is but one factor in the constellation with which this study is concerned. The emphasis, following Harvey's marxist analysis, placed initially here on the economic 'base' is a means of affording a framework for my discussion of what Williams termed 'structure of feeling' (1973: 10–11) and does not signal economic reductionism. In the new circumstances described, for example, the consumer ultimately has a greater reciprocal influence than hitherto. Any 'reflectionist' inscription of meanings and values in textual encoding, moreover, is provisional rather than determinant in a reception context where diversity of response is, textually and contextually, actively encouraged. Indeed, in the shift to be traced in the balance of influence between a producer-led and a consumer-driven economic process, reception is seen to become an increasingly powerful force not merely by way of those 'skewed and structured "feedbacks" into the production process itself' – famously observed by Hall (Hall *et al.*, 1980: 130) in his encoding/decoding model – but quite directly through extended market research.

Significant shifts in the operations of capitalism are, however, discernible, even if this does not amount to a distinct 'postmodern condition'. In reviewing the period 1945–73, Harvey broadly accepts:

> the view that the long post-war boom . . . was built upon a certain set of labour control practices, technological mixes, consumption habits, and configurations of political and economic power (1989: 124).

After 1973, centralized, labour-intensive industries of mass production declined in Britain, resulting in a dispersed labour force and weakened union power. High unemployment – particularly amongst the white males who had benefited most from the post-war British context – followed, and led to the predicament in which Chrissie and the other 'boys' find themselves.[2]

In the critique of political economy, Marx famously argues that capitalism is technologically and organizationally dynamic and that periodic crises of over-accumulation are inevitable. Harvey demonstrates that the accommodation between labour and capital in the post-war years was temporarily successful in containing capitalism's contradictory impulses, but that the tendency to over-accumulation made itself felt again:

> The sharp recession of 1973, exacerbated by the oil shock, evidently shook the capitalist world out of the suffocating torpor of 'stagflation' (stagnant output of goods and high inflation prices), and set in motion a whole set of processes that undermined the Fordist compromise (Harvey, 1989: 145).

The cultural ramifications of these circumstances will be discussed in Section III but a homology might usefully be indicated here between the various legitimation crises that have informed poststructuralist thought and that of the gold standard. A strong sense of a loss of fixed bearings informs postmodern cultural theory: it is alleged that signs are divorced from their referents; the *grands récits* of historical progress are called in question; the flux of process is privileged over the fixity of product.[3] As with the loss of gold as a guarantor of paper money, so the intellectual traditions of the Enlightenment have lost, in the view of some theorists, the power to legitimate Western culture.

For the purposes of this study, the key figure in Harvey's analysis (1989: 121 ff) is a shift of metaphors from the 'rigidity' of Fordism to the 'flexibility' of post-Fordism (see 1989: 142). In the economy, this reflects a change from a mode of production which yielded standardized and durable goods on a large scale for a mass market to one in which a range of relatively small-scale and diversified organizations produce, in rapid turnover, consumables for segmented markets. Harvey's deliberations on whether these shifts amount to a new regime or merely a 'new combination of mainly old elements within the overall logic of capital accumulation' (1989: 196) need not detain us. A change in 'structure of feeling' has occurred, and an interrelation – though not in my view an economic reductionist one – can be discerned between economic production and the cultural sphere.

Four key features, all manifestations of the general notion of flexibility, are of particular interest here: an apparent compression of time and space achieved in part by new communications technology; changes in the social formation related to new modes of production which in turn have a bearing on residual and emergent cultural taste; changes in marketing which attempt to affirm a new political economy of culture and to exploit it; deregulation, in order to facilitate change, in a number of areas by curbing allegedly restrictive institutional practices.

One means of addressing the tendency in capitalism to over-accumulation is drastically to increase the rate of consumption. To simplify and draw on part of that complex process which Harvey terms 'time–space compression' (1989: 201–308), a more rapid consumption of goods and services accelerates the 'turnover time (the speed with which money outlays return profit to the investor) so that the speed-up this year absorbs excess capacity from last year' (1989: 182). To achieve such an acceleration in consumption involves changes in the mode of production, labour relations and sales strategies such as are evident in the practices emergent in the past two decades. From the Fordist mass-production plant with its mechanization of repetitive tasks cheaply producing numerous but standardized products, modern industry has undergone a significant change from a production to a consumption-driven mode, variously described as 'Japanization' or 'flexible specialization' (Hall and Jacques, 1990: 45 and 56). In the cultural sphere, consumer drives, encouraged and established through market research, replace supply-side aesthetics.

On a global scale, flexible specialization effects the noted change in labour practices. In Western economies, fewer people are permanently employed in manufacture.[4] The traditional male industrial working class in Britain has been substantially laid off – partly because of rapid rises in productivity and poor competitiveness – to be replaced by a part-time, notably lower-paid, female labour force to feed the needs of the flexible production economy as required (see Harvey, 1989: 150–5). More people generally are employed in the service industries though, as Callinicos points out, this change characterizes twentieth-century capitalism generally and is 'primarily at the expense of agriculture rather than manufacturing industry' (1989: 122). Indeed, there has been a tendency to what Lipietz has termed 'peripheral Fordism' (cited in Harvey, 1989: 155): the location of high volume industry in areas of the developing world where advantage might be gained from cheap labour. Indeed, globally, the industrial working class has expanded (see Callinicos, 1989: 125). The manipulation of finance has, however, become a service industry in itself. The need for accurate knowledge circulated instantly around the world through the InterNet and other telecommunications channels has created, furthermore, a vast electronics service sector. Indeed information has become a key commodity in the postmodern economy.

Employment insecurity on temporary contracts, unemployment and the proliferation and dispersal of labour practices militate, in the West, against a sense of community with the loss of group solidarity amongst workers. The resurgence of neo-conservatism itself in the past two decades has been attributed to:

> a general shift from the collective norms and values, that were hegemonic, at least in working class organizations and other social movements of the 1950s and 1960s, towards a much more competitive individualism as the central value in an entrepreneurial culture that has penetrated many walks of life (Harvey, 1989: 171).

In what Hall and Jacques have termed a new 'anthropology of consumption' (1990: 43), flexible specialization is supposed to be demand-led according to individual choice. Fordist production was centralized to produce standardized goods for a mass market. In contrast, flexible specialization produces goods in small batches designed to meet the needs of various individual consumers, or microcultures. Market research – another rapidly expanded service industry – has consequently come to the fore. In comparison with the mass advertisements for the standardized products of Fordism, 'the new media' not only afford more advertising but more specific and targeted advertising. In the retail outlets, as Murray has observed:

> emphasis has shifted from the manufacturer's economies of scale to the retailer's economies of scope. The economies come from offering an integrated range from which customers choose their own basket of products (1990: 34).

The flexibility of the system is such that targeted markets need not be confined within any particular national economy. Indeed the accumulation of a substantial market by aggregating targeted consumer groups transnationally allows the advantages of some economies of scale to be retained.

The function of aesthetics in distinguishing commodities will be a matter for discussion below. In Harvey's summary meanwhile:

> The relatively stable aesthetic of Fordist modernism has given way to all the ferment, instability, and fleeting qualities of a postmodernist aesthetic that celebrates difference, ephemerality, spectacle, fashion and the commodification of cultural forms (1989: 156).

The impact of a 'short-termism' implicit in the mode of consumption integral to flexible specialization has far-reaching resonances within culture. The holism of this book, with its emphasis on historical context, stands against a cultural drift to fragmentation as a mode of experience impacting on the habits of television watching and specifically on TV drama products. For, there has been 'a much greater attention to quick-changing fashions and the mobilization of all the artifices of need-inducement and the cultural transformation that this implies' (Harvey, 1989: 156).

Under flexible specialization, consumption of experiences manufactured by service industries is privileged over consumption of goods, though built-in obsolescence sustains a demand for consumer durables for home entertainment, white goods and private transport (see Callinicos, 1989: 123). Rapid turnover in services may be more readily achieved, however, since, the more insubstantial though superficially attractive the experience, the more will be the demand for repeats. As in the ethos of fast food, the rate of consumption must be accelerated to afford more time for further consumption of the proliferation of goods and services generally on offer. Small, intensive bytes are required since 'the time horizons of both private and public decision-making have shrunk' (Harvey, 1989: 147).

The flexi-narrative explored in Chapter 2, and the flexiad narrative to be explored in relation to *Heartbeat*, are textual forms appropriate to a new affective order. TV drama constructed on the paratactical principle of juxtaposing only loosely related, but spectacular, fragments sustains attention, not by drawing viewers into the narrative to investigate the social condition as in *Boys from the Blackstuff,* but through the ideology of entertainment harnessed to a new form. There is a match, in short, between developing TV drama forms and new modes of experience, fragmented and free from the constraints of established sense-making structures.

II   THE TELEVISION INDUSTRY

Contemporary TV drama production is part of the international television industry, itself a significant aspect of the global economy sketched above. Satellite technology frees broadcasters from the constraints of the national boundaries of terrestrial transmission. The costs of production of a TV drama series, given accepted – though not unchallengeable[5] – production values, are such that institutions need increasingly to take advantage of transnational markets. Alternatively, the new technologies of video, cable and satellite can by-pass public broadcasting systems and target a specialist audience through narrowcasting. The economics here require a considerable audience for new, specialist production, though more characteristically they encourage recirculation from the stock of feature films or old broadcast programmes. Industrial structures, however, are currently adjusting to new technological and market conditions.

Owing to its omnipresence, the television medium can play an important role in promoting socio-economic change. In a shake-up of the Western economy's relations of production, the stream of information, and the channels of the discourses of popular taste and culture conducting it, are influential. On the one hand television serves as a cultural intermediary assisting the absorption of change. On the other, everyday life in postmodernity is saturated with images and sounds to the extent that communication and sense-making may be obliterated.

The entrepreneurial spirit tends towards deregulation on the grounds that an industry freed to respond to consumers' demands diversifies markets through product differentiation. But the structure of the British television industry has resisted the dynamics of commercial corporations. Indeed, because British television has been distinctive historically, a short case study of it illustrates clearly the impact of postmodernity on television culture. It highlights the tensions between commercial and PSB influences, between citizenship and consumerism, between regional, national or transnational media cultures in relation both to broadcasting and narrowcasting. Deregulation has emerged as a global feature facilitating socio-economic reformation, however, and the UK context is of necessity set in the broader context of transnational markets.

British television is distinguished by the BBC, which has held a central place in media culture quite unlike that of PSB institutions elsewhere. Financed primarily by a licence fee compulsory for the owners of television sets, its funding mechanism is taken as an important guarantor of the institution's relative independence of both government and markets. But, funding is not its only distinctive feature. As Krishan Kumar has long since observed, 'the striking thing is the singularity of the BBC's position, as a major component of national culture when compared with the broadcasting organizations in other countries' (1977: 234). In comparable countries such as America, Canada or Australia, a free-market approach to broadcasting has resulted in a small market share for PSB channels and little cultural influence.[6] Perhaps as a consequence these countries have a very different kind of programming generally from that in Britain.[7] The impetus of deregulation therefore impacts with particular force on traditional notions of British cultural identity.[8]

As Murdock has documented, from early on in the history of broadcasting, North America and Britain have followed different paths in attempting to safeguard 'public interest' from commercial self-interest whilst at the same time affording the space to freedom of choice offered by market mechanisms. By 1927 in America, he notes:

> [t]he result was a system based around packaging audiences for sale to advertisers. In contrast, the parallel British debate was resolved by constituting broadcasting as a monopoly, concentrated initially in the hands of a commercial consortium (1992: 26).

The consortium became a public corporation, the BBC, and conceived its PSB role as speaking for the nation (see Murdock, 1992: 28–9). It accordingly constructed a position of national consensus from which it presumed to speak, a position of apparent neutrality. If not exactly the voice of truth, the discursive position at least articulated what it took to be the two sides to any issue. This feature generated the notion of 'balance' in coverage for which the Corporation is renowned.

In fact, according to Murdock, that position built upon a late-nineteenth-century

> tradition designed to create new foci for national unity in a situation where the uneven development of industrial capitalism was creating deep divisions of class and religion (1992: 28–9).

The national unity was founded on notions of 'Englishness', however, and thus effectively excluded from the outset many in the UK. Furthermore, the BBC's allegedly positive function of contributing to a conception of society and citizenship by invoking consensus has its negative counterpart. Ethnic, gender, age and regional differences tended to be suppressed by a white, male, middle-class viewpoint in the BBC's London centre.

In more recent times, however, the British television industry has followed the American way. The increasing diversity of outlets following deregulation has eroded the centralist authority of the BBC as more waveband choice is on offer to consumers. The plethora of channels currently available in North America is shortly to be matched in Britain[9] and, under these conditions, the notion of a mass consensual audience has inevitably declined. If there ever were a British national audience, it fragments as the concept of narrowcasting to niche markets replaces that of appealing through broadcasting to mass markets. The future role of the BBC has been in question in these new circumstances and remains centrally at issue. The Corporation and the licence fee will be retained post 1996,[10] but the broader economic context, already market-led, has dislocated the BBC's historical role.

The justification offered for a commercial approach and multi-channeling is the extension of freedom through consumer choice. But as Ien Ang has remarked:

> the widely-held commercialist assertion that competition between channels is beneficial because it leads to more freedom for the audience implies . . . a way of speaking in the name of an invisible audience (1991: 6).

It is a moot point as to whether the installation of a fibre-optic grid is consumer-led or entrepreneur-driven. It is particularly significant that the cultivation of an accelerated consumerism is a motivating factor in deregulation to facilitate technological innovation. Robins and Webster note, for example, that the former advertising agency, Saatchi and Saatchi, 'is a leading opponent of the continuance of the BBC's public service traditions' (1988: 39). Indeed, target marketing of consumer segments has begun to have a more direct influence on the making of culture generally, and of TV drama in specific. Market research and pilot testing have increased significantly in importance in British television over the past decade and particularly during the past five years (see Chapter 4).[11]

Whilst the displacement of the BBC has positive, liberalising aspects, it is doubtful whether the expanded, deregulated industry will provide space in the short term for those local, regional voices excluded from the airwaves, notwithstanding the BBC's commitment to make 25 per cent of music and arts programmes outside London by 1997–8.[12] The capacity to meet through narrowcasting and the mechanism of the market the diverse needs of microcultures in a plural society, also remains in question. Indeed, a major difficulty in assessing the impact of the new circumstances is that what at first sight appears to be liberating and democratizing seems on further scrutiny almost the opposite.

Tony Dowmunt has observed – in apparent contradiction of the drift to flexible accumulation – that, '[t]he discipline of the world market is tending more and more to exclude the local, the culturally specific, the politically oppositional' (1993: 1). The logic of the Benetton economy should see, as noted, a shift from a mass television for a mass market embodied for TV drama in the alleged cultural imperialism of *Dallas*,[13] to a catering for – and a giving voice to – microcultures within the global audience. But television schedules are increasingly pre-committed and predictable. It thus remains to be seen whether flexible accumulation can make an unequivocally positive contribution to serving the needs of a segmented audience.

The tension between PSB and commercial institutions about how people in the audience are best served is appropriately formulated in terms of the debate over the construction of audience members as consumers or citizens in Chapter 9. With regard to the provision of TV drama, a wholly commercial approach may lead to proliferation of channels and programmes but to

diminished diversity. Rupert Murdoch, for example, acknowledges that under a fully commercial system, the work of Dennis
Potter would never have been produced.[14]

But it is too simplistic to assume that in an entirely commercial television industry there would never be counter-cultural
programmes. One of the contradictions in capitalism is that the
drive for profit might promote products which do not serve the
best interests of the system overall. The logic of flexible specialization might lead to the production of a range of products
for different market segments, some of which may value the
counter-cultural. Channel 4 in Britain, with its PSB-style remit
to cater for under-represented groups is a commercial channel,
albeit one protected until recently from direct market influence.[15] Nevertheless there is a strong tendency in television currently towards a drama of diversion privileging by way of style
the nostalgic or the up-beat.

Several key issues emerge. The first concerns the functioning of an economy on a national or transnational basis where
globalization of markets threatens to displace national political
regulation. Secondly, with regard to popular media, the question
is posed as to the need for national regulatory or institutional
mechanisms to constrain any threat of cultural imperialism, particularly from transnational corporate giants, usually based in
North America. Thirdly, an alleged tension – with particular resonances in Britain – between commerce and cultural/aesthetic
values is highlighted.

Early BBC policy and the cultural elitism of Lord Reith is well
documented and may be summed up in Reith's reply to critics:

> It is occasionally indicated to us that we are apparently set-
> ting out to give the public what they need – and not what
> they want, but few know what they want, and very few what
> they need (1924: 34).

Reith's words serve starkly to mark a difference from contemporary consumerism where what privatized individuals want has
become the key determinant of cultural value. The BBC has
changed very significantly, of course, since the days of Reith
and his idea of disseminating high culture to the masses, but the
charge of unresponsiveness to its audience nevertheless remains.
Even measured and sympathetic assessments, such as Murdock's,
recognize that the corporation has failed to develop sufficient
flexibility to meet the needs of a shifting social formation.

The forces currently instigating change, however, may have less to do with popular choice than commercial influence. The notion of 'what people want' in modern society cannot simply be divorced from the influences of advertising and the ideology of consumerism, even recognizing that advertisers frequently miss their targets.[16] Robins and Webster note, echoing Williams, that:

> [a]s transnational corporations have developed, they have used television for a number of purposes: as a means of stimulating sales, to advertise themselves as socially desirable or, at least, as socially innocuous, and to project consumption as a way of life (1988: 39).

A tension emerges, then, between two approaches to media leisure. The paternalist, philanthropic approach of a centralized PSB institution, such as the BBC, works as a social and moral educator seeking to promote consensus in the public sphere of a bourgeois culture. The force of corporate capitalism in postmodernity, in contrast, seeks to fragment the audience into individuals addressed through diverse and specialist channels of discourse as consumers in the private sphere. The BBC may have tended to be undemocratic through a certain cultural elitism, privileging the tastes and outlook of an educated middle class and paying too little attention to the variety of taste formations. But market forces' construction of the viewer as consumer speaks in the name of a libertarian individualism which is partial in effacing the self-interest of corporate capital.

In recent years, the BBC has, of necessity, increasingly involved itself in the global market. With regard to production, moreover, it has introduced what is effectively an internal market, Producer Choice, a mechanism dependent in practice upon cash flow and borrowing. But the BBC's charter was renewed on condition that the corporation was, in the words of then national heritage secretary Peter Brooke, 'steadily to reduce and largely eliminate its annual borrowing'.[17] The implementation – over-zealous in the view of some – of this last injunction by managing director, John Birt, led in 1995 to a temporary moratorium on new commissions and, in particular to a crisis in the drama departments. As reported in *The Guardian*:

> Drama department staff are also anticipating job cuts. . . . It is understood BBC2's Screen Two series of single dramas may bear the brunt of the economy.[18]

Thus a strategy in the name of extending choice appears effectively to be reducing choice and the authored, single piece is further squeezed out of the schedules.

The overtly commercial sector of British television has also been the subject of an intensified spirit of competition in the early 1990s. The Broadcasting Bill introduced a blind auction mechanism for awarding the franchises of the fifteen ITV regional companies and the national 'breakfast' franchise. Significantly the central issue for debate was the criteria for the awards, since there was some confusion as to whether the highest financial bid would automatically succeed or whether there might be 'exceptional circumstances' involving criteria concerning quality. As deregulation has taken hold, concern is expressed in a number of quarters about impact on 'quality', but undecidability about what that term might signify has precluded a rigorous defence of it. An aim of this book is to engage that debate.

To summarize, it is apparent from the above that the British television industry is currently subject to fragmentation, cost accountancy and the direct penetration of capital in the context of global deregulation. A consumerist political drift has enshrined in law market principles which have direct bearing on television production and which dislocate the traditional BBC and impinge as well on the overtly commercial sector. The structure of the industry begins to mirror that of the 'Benetton economy'.[19] Opportunities for innovation in the making of a greater range of products appears to arise from a newly competitive situation. But in practice since the deregulation of 1990, the commercial companies have been seeking merger into larger corporations with oligopolistic power and diversity of programming has diminished.

Culturally, through target marketing, the drift is to the middlebrow, to the tastes of AB/C1's attractive to advertisers. Whilst the residual element of cultural elitism in the BBC has met with healthy challenge, then, the shift is in the middle ground and access to the media of society's seriously disenfranchised is not facilitated. Concern with social problems and contradictions, moreover, is displaced in the preference for the up-beat as an over-emphasis on style displaces content. The Broadcasting Act itself did not clarify criteria for quality though it introduced an Independent Televison Commission to regulate the independent sector. Ironically, in its 1993 Performance Reviews, the ITC looked unfavourably on a 13 per cent reduction in programme investment generally and remarked that the

> ITV Network Centre's schedule had been cautious and unadventurous with too heavy reliance on predictable game shows and light entertainment formats. Drama concentrated on police and crime stories to the exclusion of almost everything else.[20]

Such ambivalence reflects, and is reflected in, differing values of differing class fractions at a transitional historical moment in which there is considerable axiological uncertainty.

III TASTE FORMATION

In the 1970s, Bourdieu established a strong correlation between social classes and class fractions in terms of the distribution of both economic and cultural capital. There is, he attests, 'a certain configuration of this distribution to which there corresponds a certain lifestyle, through the mediation of the habitus' (1992: 260). In the event of economic and social reformation as sketched in Section I above, it follows that a new configuration of tastes will emerge and that a shift in the balance of cultural power will be negotiated. Any emergent group seeks expression aesthetically and, in seeking recognition of its tastes, looks to secure its identity. As Bourdieu puts it:

> changes in posts (and their occupants) are inevitably accompanied by a whole effort at symbolic restructuring aimed at winning recognition in representations and therefore by a permanent struggle between those who seek to impose the new system of classification and those who defend the old system. Taste is at the heart of these symbolic struggles (1992: 310).

A number of commentators have observed the emergence of a new social formation.[21] With the relative decline, in the West at least, of the white male industrial working class and the expansion of the service and white-collar sectors, a new group is 'in the vanguard of the transformation of ethical dispositions and world views occurring within the bourgeoisie as a whole' (Bourdieu, 1992: 311). The relatively stable class formations which characterized the 1945–73 period have given way to less rooted social groups. In specific, a new managerial fraction, the new bourgeoisie, has emerged through particular kinds of higher education into positions of economic power in the modern scientific, technological and service industries. Operating in the mobile and fluid world of national and transnational markets, these new executives are 'much less dependent on local privilege and prestige' (Bourdieu, 1992: 314) than their geographically rooted industrial predecessors.

Economically wealthy, and relatively rich in cultural capital, the new bourgeoisie is nevertheless outside bourgeois tradition in that its sphere of professional competence is not yet fully recognized. Distanced from the industrial bourgeoisie on the one hand, the new bourgeoisie is distinct also from the intellectual fraction of the dominant class which in Britain has traditionally held sway in public institutions such as the universities and indeed the BBC. Thus, as Lee has noted, the lifestyle of the new bourgeoisie, 'sits somewhat uneasily between the lifestyles of the old bourgeoisie and those occupied by the intellectual classes' (1993: 165). The new bourgeoisie, in Bourdieu's account, is supported by a new petite bourgeoisie which, aspiring to the managerial fraction, emulates its tastes and serves as its cultural intermediary. Indeed part of the challenge to the BBC related in Section II is precisely a displacement of the tastes, values and practices of the formerly dominant intellectual fraction by deregulation invoking sensitivity to new taste configurations.

Bourdieu's research is specific to France of the 1970s but patterns of taste formation – and shifts within them – are evident elsewhere in the 1980s and 1990s. My interest is in Bourdieu's outline of process rather than his specific details, for particulars of taste will vary relative to distinctive national and microcultural characteristics. Raphael Samuel has characterized, for example, a new British middle class which:

> distinguishes itself more by its spending than its saving. The Sunday colour supplements give it both a fantasy life and a set of cultural cues. Much of its claim to culture rests on the conspicuous display of good taste, whether in the form of kitchenware, 'continental' food, or weekend sailing and cottages. . . .

Class hardly enters into the new middle class conception of themselves [*sic*]. Many of them work in an institutional world of fine gradations but no clear lines of antagonism. . . .

The new middle class have [*sic*] a different emotional economy than that of their pre-war predecessors. They go in for instant rather than deferred gratification. . . . Sensual pleasures, so far from being outlawed, are the very field on which social claims are established and sexual identities confirmed. . . .

The influence of consumerism can be seen . . . in the value attached to novelty, imagery and style (1982: 124–5).

The pathways into this new configuration, particularly in respect of educational background relative to newly required skills, serve as a map of emergent dispositions.

In 1980s/1990s Britain, the new petite bourgeoisie is in some sense hardly a group at all, let alone a traditional class in its self-perception. It includes that sector of industrial and blue-collar workers who, taking advantage of post-war educational provision and the economic changes noted, have made over a generation the transition to white-collar jobs. Educational options available to this sector focus, however, 'on training and the acquisition of discrete occupational skills and knowledges . . . [rather than] the cultivation of the sort of all round cultural competences normally needed to valorise cultural capital' (Lee, 1993: 167). In addition to this, predominantly male, ascendancy, the new configuration is expanded by those many women finding part-time, semi-skilled, employment in the newly flexible work-place. The grouping also embraces those bright young people who, seeing no (or having no) opportunities in formal education, took advantage of a changing world and moved quickly into the rapidly expanding service sector (the financial markets, computing), where quick-wittedness and an openness to new technologies is more important than specialist knowledge. They are joined by members of the declining old bourgeoisie who have not attained educationally as well as might have been expected of them given the advantage of their class background.

Economically ascendant, this amorphous, *déclassé* configuration, aspiring to the new bourgeoisie, seeks both to consolidate its socio-economic power and to find and express its identity in the cultural sphere. Whilst Callinicos cautions that the new bourgeoisie itself constitutes no more than, 'perhaps 12 per cent of the British working population' (1989: 162), he acknowledges its social power and cultural influence on the other members of the broader social configuration described. The political result is manifest in the culture of 'new managerialism', the cost-accountancy and deregulation evident in the BBC, as noted, and particularly in all areas of the eroding public sector in Britian (hospitals, schools, universities). Whilst voting habits may have changed only marginally, a shift to the political right arises when members of the new configuration, relatively more wealthy than their parents, perceive themselves to be more able to buy into private services and therefore to be less dependent upon public welfare. In addition, cynicism about politicians, together with the force of electronic mediation of cultural representations, suggests that the political battle-front has shifted away from the traditional territory of class allegiance and policy debate. The temper of the times is more evident in the cultural sphere at large.

Here, Lasch has observed the emergence of a new, narcissistic self:

> Acquisitive in the sense that his cravings have no limits, he [*sic*] does not accumulate goods and provisions against the future, in the manner of the acquisitive individualist of nineteenth-century political economy, but demands immediate gratification and lives in a state of perpetually unsatisfied desire (1978: xvii).

This last observation offers an insight into the culture of postmodernity generally and specifically into developing dramatic forms on television in terms of flexi-narrative and flexiad drama. A fast turnover of narrative hot-spots tends instantly to gratify but to have little durable effectivity. Similarly, a specific taste is manifest for high production values and special effects and in some products – *The X-Files*, for example (see Chapter 6) – a toying with sophisticated ideas, rather than a profound engagement.

Owing to the eclecticism in its background, and particularly because of its ambivalent attitude to education, the new habitus-type affects an air of superiority partly based on educated taste, but at the same time it is not competent in the 'aesthetic disposition' of the intellectual fraction of the dominant class (see Bourdieu, 1992: 28–9). This leads the new configuration to ascribe value to objects it prefers in defiance of more 'legitimate' values. Broadly, it privileges, 'all the forms of culture which are, provisionally at least, on the (lower) boundaries of legitimate culture – jazz, cinema, strip cartoons, science fiction'. Its members flaunt 'American fashions and models – jazz, jeans, rock or the avant-garde underground, which is their monopoly' (Bourdieu, 1992: 360).

Hybrid dispositions emerge. Aspects of popular (as distinct from 'legitimate') culture are treated with a detached, academic disposition. Specifically skilled, the group draws to some extent on its education and proximity to the intellectual fraction, but tends to gesture at detached, analytic modes rather than deploying intellectual rigour. Disposition, attitude to an object of interest, becomes more important than the object itself as traditionally valued. The symbolic forms espoused by members of the new configuration have the substantial advantage over fully legitimized forms, according to Lee, of being 'generally far less demanding of the audience's interpretive capacities' (Lee, 1993: 170).

The new configuration thus stands for broad accessibility and in opposition to the established tastes of both the traditional bourgeoisie with its ' "rules" and formal etiquette' (Lee, 1993: 166) and the 'disinterested' contemplation and appreciation of 'high culture' characteristic of the intellectual fraction. The element of insecurity arising both from the novelty of the new group's emergent, but not fully established, position and from its consequent intellectual hesitancy thus manifests itself in undecidability.[22] In pursuit of a liberated lifestyle, the group tends to chafe against established values rather than for specific new ones (see Bourdieu, 1992: 370). With regard to cultural forms, undecidability is manifest in an aesthetic pose with a preference for hybrid symbolic products.

A noted characteristic of the postmodern construction of cultural artefacts is the blurring of category boundaries and the defiance of classification. Postmodern 'bricolage'[23] does not so much transgress, 'the normally well policed boundaries between popular, middle and highbrow culture' (Lee, 1993: 174) as leave unresolved a number of competing discourses in juxtaposition. The emergence of the flexi-narrative format for most popular TV drama corresponds with the irresolution of the new affective order. The more open the text, the more viewers feel free to construct their own narratives, pleasures and meanings, providing, that is, the dislocations are not so great as fundamentally to disturb normative frames of reference.

The new configuration achieves an aesthetics of liberation through, in Fred Pfeil's words, 'the bliss of escaping from codification and definition altogether, by dispersing and scattering [themselves] through the codes and cliches' (cited in Lee, 1993: 172). In the broader cultural market where distinctive goods are beyond the economic reach of the new petite bourgeoisie, the sale of image becomes all-important. As Bourdieu puts it, 'the new "substitution" industry . . . sells fine words instead of things to those who cannot afford the things but are willing to settle for words' (1992: 365). In a world of information overload and a bombardment of signs, it is alleged, signifiers become dislocated from their referents. The substitution of the sign of the thing for the thing itself – the 'free-floating signifier' of postmodernism – informs flexiad TV drama. Rather than becoming engrossed in a problem/resolution narrative, viewers dip in and out of paratactical structures picking up on the 'feel-good' imagery of isolated fragments.

To bring together in summary Harvey's and Bourdieu's marxian accounts, the aim of the new bourgeoisie is to expand markets and to accelerate sales by means of 'time-space compression'. It is necessary to transform the habitus from the ascetic thrift and parsimony of Fordism to a post-Fordist high-spending, fast-consumption mode. Newly aestheticized products and cultural services lead the market acceleration. The means by which a significant change of inclination to purchase over and above 'real needs' (see Chapter 7) is to be wrought is largely through changes of attitude. The role of the new petite bourgeoisie as cultural intermediary is to facilitate such change.

In the cultural sphere the keywords are 'pleasure' and 'fun' (see Bourdieu, 1992: 365). The identity of emergent groups is to be confirmed in the mutually reflective conviction of their pleasures of lifestyle. Habitual identifications must be dislocated and traditionally dominant allegiances (the male bonding of the industrial working class 'boys' in trade unions, for example) are called into question to this end. Values may be ascribed to goods, cultural or otherwise, that have not been accredited traditionally. Since signifiers of lifestyle are more important than the objects themselves, style or disposition towards the object are key. It is in the manner of consumption rather than in the object to be consumed that value is seen implicitly to reside. Thus value is more ascribed than described, an issue to be taken up in Chapter 9.

As Bourdieu summarizes it:

> The new logic of the economy rejects an ascetic ethic of production and accumulation, based on abstinence, sobriety, saving and calculation, in favour of a hedonistic morality of consumption, based on credit, spending and enjoyment. This economy demands a social world which judges people by their 'standard of living', their life-style, as much as by their capacity for production (1992: 310).

The critical tradition of the modernist intellectual (Adorno, for example) is thus not so much contested as by-passed, or in part usurped. Indeed, amongst the new bourgeoisie, as Bourdieu sees it:

> new intellectuals are inventing an art of living which provides them with the gratifications and prestige of the intellectual at the least cost (1992: 370).

These matters and their cultural implications will be revisited in subsequent chapters; it remains in this chapter to draw together the arguments above and provisionally to bring out their significance for the institutions of television and TV drama.

IV

In Chapter 1, flexi-narrative and flexiad drama were introduced as the developed narrative forms in an already segmented television. The findings of the accounts discussed above extend an understanding of the context of production and reception of contemporary TV drama by bringing to bear another dynamic in the force field – the political economy of culture. The emergent products in contemporary TV drama and attendant viewing habits may be seen to correspond with a new affective order more generally. Perhaps the most significant aspect to emerge is the reconstruction of the citizen as consumer. This transition is undoubtedly welcomed by people whose material quality of

life has dramatically improved through the economic developments from Fordism to flexible specialization but it disturbs
rooted traditions. The new habitus, indeed, has far-reaching
implications.

Drama constructed to circulate 'values and lifestyles' with the
ultimate aim of promoting commercialism is unlikely, whatever
pleasures it offers, to engage the viewer as citizen in an examination of public issues. Nor is it likely to offer stories usable
at the local level. Transnational product cannot address the
diversity and difference of locality, region, even nation and,
restricted in terms of verbal language, it privileges the visual.
Film can be a sophisticated medium. But the preference of the
new configuration for short-term aesthetic pleasure over reflective intellectual challenge puts a particular inflection on the
tendency established towards the primacy of the visual in contemporary culture.

At one end of the moving picture spectrum, art film – through
a range of devices such as montage and, more recently, multiple
framing – creates complex visual structures which demand a
concentrated effort to read. It is this kind of cinematic influence
which informs such minority TV drama strands as *Screen Two*
and *Film on Four*. At the other end of the spectrum, the aestheticization of the image is closely allied to the circulation of short-
term gratifications in consumption, whose ideal form is the
advertisement. The facility for consumers to dip into – and take
'hot' as little or as much as they want from – a TV drama text
reinforces the dynamic of an economy revitalized by accelerated
turnover in the service sector. The inclination of postmodern
texts to abandon sustained linear narrative to follow a more
random, constellatory, principle of construction thus impacts
on drama as well as on the other arts in both production and
reception. In this context, the visual style of advertisements
may be equally as sophisticated as television programmes – or
even more so. Indeed, some (post)modern advertisements are
dependent for their effect on a relatively high level of cultural
capital in their open textuality, parody, or quotation of the
visual styles of avant-garde arts.[24]

Amidst the new textual forms, blurring of conceptual boundaries and new dispositions to kitsch, it becomes difficult to distinguish a difference between a popular stylized aesthetic whose
main function is to accelerate consumption in an economy of

flexible accumulation and a stylized popular aesthetic in a tradition of critical practice, for example pop art or art film. For all its limitations, the BBC historically attempted to defend a public space, in Stuart Hall's phrase, 'for activities in common, the holding of space in trust for a social good' (1984: 28). Insofar as this space has been invaded by commercialism, the difference between commodity circulation and social intercourse is effaced. To draw the distinction sharply with regard to TV drama, where a realist aesthetic confronted a consensual society in the early 1960s with representations of contemporary life promoting social dialogue, a postmodern aesthetic of the early 1990s addresses individual viewers privately as consumers through the circulation of de-historicized, dislocated signs.

It is ultimately important, however, to guard against an economic reductionist over-emphasis on cultural change. Commentators on postmodernity and flexible accumulation stress the provisionality of their analyses and the tenacity of traditions (see Harvey, 1989: 196), marxist or otherwise. As Lee puts it:

> Long-established and solid social structures cannot be dismantled overnight, and distinctive sensibilities and the well-worn patterns and routines of ordinary life can never be functionally dissolved, even in the face of the enormous edifice and powers of transformation of capital (1993: 178).

Whilst the economic basis of people's lives is important, other discourses are influential.

With regard to television drama – at least in Britain – there remain amidst all the changes noted, features which militate against apocalyptic visions. Precisely because change breeds uncertainty there is demand for reassurance which is provided by the recognized narrative frameworks with their reaffirmation of order over chaos in the television's familiar formulaic realisms. Indeed, the tradition of linear narrative is so strong in the Western popular cultural forms in which TV drama has its roots, that it cannot readily be abandoned.

But a potentially powerful challenge has been made to the realist episteme. A weakening, at least, of the bond between sign and referent is effected in the reception context of a fragmented society wherein the uni-accentuality of a sign established through consensus in the speech community gives way to the multi-accentuality of pluralism. The disposition amongst members of the new configuration to stand against the fractions from which they have separated, itself extends to an anti-realism. Where slippery signs can be circulated in the realist aesthetic but without any need to anchor them to the realities of the world they appear to depict, a 'feel-good' drama can emerge in which signs of pleasant people play out their lifestyles in attractive circumstances loosely signifying 'reality'. Chapter 4 discusses examples of the 'nostalgic' and the 'idyllic' in the popular British TV drama, *Heartbeat* (YTV) as well as plausible ideal transnational types in *Baywatch*.

4 Signs of the Times?

Heartbeat and Baywatch

> TV is at the border-line of a great paradigm-shift between the 'death of society' (modernism with its representational logic) and the 'triumph of an empty, signifying culture' (the 'structural paradigm' of postmodernism) (Kroker and Cook, 1988: 272).

I

In this chapter I set out on an exploration of alleged shifts in television culture such that TV dramas might be seen less as representations of real (though fictional) worlds and more as pure textual practices. Through analysis of two TV drama series, one British- and the other American-produced, I consider aspects of the idea that in postmodernity signifiers have become dislocated from their referents such that signs do not stand for the things they represent in an object world but rather float freely. In this view, such connection as is made between one sign and another is more a matter of 'intertextuality', of play within and between languages, than it is a matter of a referential relationship between the linguistic sign and the object it might be thought to represent. Building on the political economy of culture established in Chapter 3, I sustain in addition a production context for TV drama in the economy of postmodernity, linking it to the kinds of pleasures generated in a new affective order.

Heartbeat and *Baywatch* call in question the idea that the language of television can simply be taken as, in the old models, a transparent window on the world or a mirror accurately reflecting reality. This does not, of course, imply that signifiers do not carry symbolic force, but it does suggest that the constructed worlds of television drama cannot be measured directly against those material worlds inhabited by members of the audience.

Heartbeat (YTV) is an example of the flexiad drama introduced in Chapter 1. It reinforces and extends the conception of flexi-narrative form in which multiple narratives are inter-woven in a fast-cut mode. In addition it displays features of a further shift from the dissolution of the problem/resolution narrative model in series or serials towards a paratactical struc-ture, increasingly influential in the 1980s and 1990s. Flexiad thus implies both new textual strategies and a new affective order. Visual and aural imagery at once construct and reflect the 'values and lifestyles' of audience segments, whilst the drama remains but loosely shaped by a narrative frame.

Heartbeat serves furthermore to illustrate the influence on audience-building in postmodern television production of that intensive market research, established in Chapter 3 to be a general feature of the postmodern economy. Whereas flex-ible specialization's adaptable small-scale production units may potentially serve different market segments in television by nar-rowcasting, British TV drama as yet strives to maximize audience for popular drama. In recognition of the heterogeneity of audi-ence members, however, attempts are made to establish what is attractive to a number of audience segments and aggregate them by including in the drama elements that will appeal to each. The dramatic mode remains ostensibly 'realist' in that the mimetic conventions of construction of an illusionist world are retained (see Chapter 5). But the signifiers are deployed increasingly for their intrinsic appeal as evocators of 'values and lifestyles' rather than – as they may have been in the refer-ential drama of the past – tied to signifieds which denote a contemporary, historical (though fictional) 'reality'.

II

The original series of *Heartbeat* (YTV, Spring 1991) shown on Friday nights at 21.00 hours drew an audience in the region of 10–13 million, the biggest ever Friday night audience for a drama series in UK. The second series (Autumn 1993) was scheduled on Sunday night in the prime-time 19.30 slot against *Lovejoy* (BBC1). In spite of the opposition of such a well-estab-lished series which itself approached the 10 million viewers mark,[1] *Heartbeat* showed even higher in the ratings than the first series, drawing 15.25 milion in the week of 18–24 October 1993. Second in ITV's weekly listing only to *Coronation Street*,[2]

Heartbeat is thus in the terms of ratings discourse an outstand-ing drama.[3]

The emphasis placed upon viewing figures reflects the sharp end of commercial television production where, as noted, rat-ings is the currency in which advertisers buy audience.[4] Per-ceived as consumers of both television programmes and other products, members of the audience – segmented into life-styles rather than taken *en masse* – are customers. In turn ITV Network's clients, the advertisers who buy space, are keen to know in some detail which viewers are attracted to watch which particular programmes. Thus, with more intensive commercial competition over the last decade, the importance of audience research has markedly increased. *Heartbeat* serves as an example of the development of a drama series in part through the application of the methods of market research undertaken by Audience Planning at the ITV Network Centre. The approach clearly marks a shift from the writer- and producer-led, supply-side aesthetics in drama production of the past. Its results raise interesting questions about dramatic structure and traditional notions of organic coherence in works of more traditional drama.

Prior to giving an account of the influence of market re-search on the development of *Heartbeat* as a TV drama, a brief description of the series will be helpful, particularly to readers who may not have seen it. Centred in the fictional village of Aidensfield near Ashfordly in the North Riding of Yorkshire, *Heartbeat* draws on the locational attractions of British series such as *A Country Practice* (ITV), *All Creatures Great and Small* (ITV) and the soap opera, *Emmerdale* (ITV). These all evoke regions of a rural England apparently little changed by the incursions of modernity, let alone postmodernity. But aspects of their construction reveal the influence of contemporary market forces. The casting of Nick Berry as the central char-acter, PC Nick Rowan, in *Heartbeat,* for example, adds to the series' attractions of rural, pre-industrial location the power to draw an audience of a conventionally good-looking young man with the intertextual rough edges of East London carried from his former role as Wicksy in the soap opera, *EastEnders* (BBC1). Berry's cover version of Buddy Holly's 1950s song 'Heartbeat' is used as the title music for the series, a recording which reached the top of the national popular music charts just prior to the launch of the series, thus providing additional revenue as well as advertising for the production.[5]

An overtly comic aspect to the series' generally light tone is supplied by Claude Jeremiah Greengrass played by Bill Maynard who brings intertextual associations of the lovable rogue from series such as *Oh No! It's Selwyn Froggit* and *The Gaffer*. As a poacher who spends his life looking for exploits which will make him money usually at the expense of the unsuspecting locals, Greengrass brushes frequently with the Ashfordly constabulary who sometimes use their awareness of his questionable activities to strong-arm him into conveying to them information which assists in solving more serious crimes. Since Greengrass's scams more often than not rebound upon himself he is accepted within the community as a 'colourful character' causing no real harm.

An additional feature of the series is the use of 1960s popular music as soundtrack over some of the incidents. The music is contemporary with the setting of the series in the 1960s, though the evocation of a mode of policing that would be recognizable to Jack Warner of *Dixon of Dock Green* (BBC1, 1954–61) could suggest the 1950s to some older viewers who might recall that early police series. Similarly some of the vintage vehicles used such as local buses and lorries belong to an earlier period than the mini-car which also features. The clothes, particularly of the younger adult characters, suggest the 1960s though to young modern viewers they may connote the contemporaneity of postmodern 'retro'[6] fashion rather than period nostalgia.

The production of *Heartbeat* was significantly informed by the findings of market research. Four aspects were undertaken by ITV: *concept*; *pilot*; *promotions*; *evaluation*. The formulations and terminology in what follows are those of Audience Planning at ITV Network Centre. At the initial stage an attempt was made to establish features which might be popular by *concept-testing*. This method offers to participants a choice of options on cards from which they select preferences. The findings of the test revealed three elements to have a popular following, namely nostalgia for the 1960s, interest in a potential north/south or London/rural culture clash, and a preference for a 'soft' character-based drama. The notion in itself of another police drama series received a relatively negative response which led to the policing aspects of the plots of the episodes becoming incidental and the human interest aspects of character interrelationships coming to the fore.

Indeed with regard to narrative structure *Heartbeat* slides flexibly between the traditional pattern of a problem/resolution frame and the flexi-narrative where some plots at least remain open-ended. The story-lines centre on the detection of mainly minor crimes in the rural environment frequently solved by PC Rowan often (in the first three series) with the indirect assistance of his wife (played by Niamh Cusack).[7] In the two episodes referred to in this discussion, the earlier one (the 'badger episode' of 21 November 1993) follows the plot/resolution model with a team of badger-baiters ultimately being caught in the act and arrested. The other (that shown on 5 December 1993, the 'Whitby episode') deals not with an enigma but with complications in the lives of the characters and comes to no clear resolution of any of its narrative strands. Potential dramatic conflict in that episode grows, not from the solving of crimes, but from the impositions of a new, young police inspector from the city who threatens to interrupt the cosy world of Ashfordly police station. In addition, the Inland Revenue catch up with Greengrass, and Sergeant Blaketon attempts to retrieve a relationship with his teenage son from an estranged marriage. A further possible conflict arises between PC Rowan and his wife who needs either to find new premises for her doctor's surgery or to take up the offer of a job in a modern practice in relatively distant Whitby. None of the narrative strands is contained or 'closed' within that episode. Action is provided in a mock car-chase with Greengrass in his lorry pursuing the Hillman of the tax inspectorate into a haystack, and PC Rowan's attempt to save a drowning man on the village visit to Whitby.

The findings of the concept testing may thus be seen to have had an effect on the narrative structure of *Heartbeat* which in early episodes adhered more closely to the traditonal series plot /resolution form. In addition to developing a flexi-narrative approach, human interest is privileged over police detection narratives. Other more direct changes similarly resulted from the second aspect of product marketing, the *pilot* with a focus group.

The pilot helped to establish 'viewergraphics', a more differentiated form of audience demographics than that of *Hill Street*

Blues, based on the targeting of 'values and lifestyles' of audience segments. Three audience target groups emerged in this patently diagrammatic approach showing a particular preference for the series through differing points of identification. The 'East-End girls' were attracted to watch by the centrality of Nick Berry playing the role of PC Rowan and bringing, as noted, a following from his role in *EastEnders*. Notwithstanding the poor showing of police series as such in the concept-testing, 'lager-lads', a second identifiable audience group, proved to be attracted to the police story-lines and the 1960s soundtracks. Thirdly, 'green mums' were drawn by 1960s nostalgia, the rural context of the series and its 'soft' approach to social issues.

The results of the focus group pilot assisted Yorkshire Television in developing a *promotional strategy* aimed at likely viewer groups. Indeed it led to the re-making of the Episode 1 of the first series to strengthen those aspects found to have greatest appeal. The original title track commissioned from Ray Davies – a musician famous in the 1960s with his band, The Kinks – was in keeping with the 1960s nostalgia found to be popular with the 'lager lads'. But a cover-version of Buddy Holly's 'Heartbeat', with Berry himself as singer, had additional pull on the 'East-End girls'. It also had simultaneous appeal to both memories of the past for the 'green mums' and, fashion *à la mode retro*, for the 'lager-lads'. Hence the original title track was replaced. Similarly, the opening graphics were changed to give a stronger sense of the North Riding location found to be popular with the 'green mums'. A promotional video trailer was produced bringing out those aspects which the viewer-graphics had shown to be attractive to the target groups to build up interest in the series prior to its showing. The success of the marketing and product strategy in ratings terms has been demonstrated.

The final stage of *evaluation* followed the first series and led to the development of the second. The two main characters, PC and Dr Rowan, proved to be strongly favoured in audience response, as did the other police constables working with Rowan, and Greengrass. The vague sense of period time and rural place were affirmed as popular, and the 'soft' treatment of social issues as the mainspring of narrative were likewise confirmed as features of audience appeal. The second series was consequently inflected as sketched above to foreground character relationships in stories based on 'soft-hitting' treatments of social concerns. The role of Greengrass, conceived originally as peripheral, was extended and more space was similarly created for scenes between the police officers in Ashfordly police station. 1960s music was retained as over-dub to sustain the draw of period nostalgia for the 'green mums' and *retro* interest for the 'lager-lads'. The stories were increasingly set against the scenic North Riding and 'cinematic', wide-angle shots of vehicles crossing the moors were included to extend the visual and connotative pleasures of location. The qualities of the programme and its broad audience appeal made it an ideal vehicle for the Sunday night slot when, in the wake of *Songs of Praise* and *Last of the Summer Wine* (BBC1), *One Man and His Dog* (BBC2) and *Dr Quinn, Medicine Woman* (ITV, a drama series set in the 1860s) the market seems to demand something light, unchallenging and evocative of a pre-industrial past.

It may be academic in more than one sense to engage in traditional drama or ideology critique of a series such as *Heartbeat* since to the producing company, Yorkshire-Tyne Tees, which 'has to find 52.7 million pounds every year just to meet the fixed cost of its franchise',[8] the ratings carry their own value. Whilst a different kind of drama product tends to gain the industry plaudits at the awards ceremonies,[9] suggesting that other values remain in circulation in the television drama industry, the popular series is literally a banker in an increasingly competitive and commercial production context. Given that, from a traditional critical point of view, *Heartbeat* has something of the feel of a drama made by a committee, however, a range of questions about dramatic form and structure present themselves as at least worthy of exploration if only to clarify by comparison with more traditional TV drama the changes to television drama forms and processes of production that have evolved in recent years.

Whilst on occasion the dramatic structure of a series like *Heartbeat* may correspond to TV drama's version of a classic realist text, the series came characteristically to function in the flexi-narrative mode. The various strands of narrative in the flexi-narrative form do not, however, amount to different discourses unresolved in their conflictual play, but rather the narrative closure of one strand brings out the atmospheric 'closure' of the others conveying the satisfaction of overall completion even where on-going narrative strands remain open. Other features of traditional Realist/Naturalist drama however are not so closely emulated.

Given the interest in the main characters revealed in the market research cited, it might be expected that in the course of the series the characters would be psychologically rounded and explored in some depth. This is not the case. In the 'Whitby episode', apart from the main pairing of the Rowans – whose marriage seems to reflect more a 1990s partnership conception of the new man and woman than a 1960s marriage – the characters are essentially two-dimensional. Indeed the Rowans, whose very name has a traditional country ring, are not explored in any depth. They serve as an allegory of 'England': as signs of caring people committed to traditional virtues such as helping the needy and fair play. Likewise, other characters remain the same in each episode, more signifier than individualized person. Greengrass is eternally the likeable rogue irredeemably up to no good in a small rural way. Sergeant Blaketon is typically severe in his hierarchical role in the police station but always with a wry smile to reveal his affection for and trust in his colleagues. They are less attempts to construct convincing 'people' in the mode of traditional Realism than signifiers of a tradition of a mythical human self-identity and stability. Indeed, where there are deviations from character stereo-typicality, the feel of the drama changes.

In the 'Whitby episode', for example, where he meets up with his son, Sgt Blaketon's popularity, evident in the first series' evaluation, seems to be taking him into new dimensions. To see him, out of uniform and vulnerable, in a completely new context struck a discordant note. The shift from established two-dimensionality seemed at first almost shocking, though it would become acceptable over time if character generally in the series were to be more fully rounded. Such a change would seem unlikely, however, since to make it would be to invite a complexity of emotional response which would militate against the established tone of the series. It would inflect it towards a psychological realism inconsistent with *Heartbeat*'s unchallenging Sunday night appeal. Similarly, as in the third series, where a more hard-hitting topic such as rape is taken on, the tone of the episode is distinctly changed. Both developments extend a traditional Realist/Naturalist aesthetic at odds with the circulation of signifiers of nostalgia for their own sake.

Apart from its use of music, the series remains within the bounds of mimetic televisual realism in the sense that a recognizable geography and time-scale, a few anachronisms notwithstanding, is sustained. The events are loosely motivated in a sequence through linear time. The characters are recognizable not as constructs approximating actual human beings as in the best of television's referential realism, but as signifiers of archetypes from the history of drama. Nor are the agents situated in structure. The treatment of social issues is (with the occasional exception noted) far removed either from the contemporary world of the watching audience or the 1960s in which the series is set. The 'soft' treatment of the issues of such matters as income tax evasion, changes to the structure of the police force, social deprivation and cruelty to animals in the episodes cited scarcely amounts to an interventionist socio-political agenda.

The series makes no claim to such a social realist or critical naturalist practice but it is noteworthy that its concept testing and evaluation revealed social issues – above crime detection narratives – to be a feature of appeal. In marked contrast to one of its predecessors in the police series genre, *Z-Cars* (BBC1) from the 1960s in which an 'aggressively realistic drama' (Brandt, 1981: 25) was favoured, however, *Heartbeat* elects to treat but not to confront the social problems of its day.

It is difficult to resist drawing the conclusion from the comparison above that there has been a marked change in the function of popular drama series from the 1960s themselves and *Heartbeat*'s construction of that era in the 1990s. It is not a question, however, of judging popular drama by high art criteria. In the early 1960s when Sydney Newman developed first *Armchair Theatre* for ITV and subsequently *Wednesday Play* for BBC1, he was committed to 'capturing the largest number of viewers possible' (Brandt, 1981: 16). He was thus a forerunner of the modern audience planners in the commercial sector but his means to the end differed from theirs particularly in having a criterion other than ratings alone. Newman believed, and proved through his success, that 'truth and audience identification are the first necessities of holding an audience' (cited in Brandt, 1981: 16).

To Newman, working in a context where the realist aesthetic went largely unquestioned as the dominant 'structure of feeling' of the period, 'truth' meant correspondence to the contemporary experience of the working classes who formed the mass television audience. Partly in reaction to the middle-class drama product of early television rooted in a theatre tradition, Newman commissioned 'plays about real people in provincial towns, people who worked in factories and shops and got dirty and had the sort of problems the majority of viewers might experience' (Redmond, 1979: 212). Having no high art pretensions, he nevertheless liked popular 'art that has something to say' and he believed that 'great art has to stem from, and its essence must come out of, the period in which it was created' (cited in Brandt, 1981: 16).

Measured by Newman's standard, *Heartbeat* does treat social problems but, opting for a period rural setting, it evades the realities of life in industrial (or post-industrial) contemporary Britain. Following an aspect of Newman's logic, then, it cannot deal in 'truth' and has nothing to say. Taking up his point that drama grows out of its epoch, however, it is possible, in the light of the cultural transition discussed in Chapter 3, to see that *Heartbeat* is produced and mediated in a very different milieu from that of Newman's time and that its popularity, matching that of Newman's productions in the 1960s, rests on something other than an aesthetic of social realism.

The 'structure of feeling' of the 1960s period, confident that it might begin to address social inequities by taking a clear sight on contemporary life, saw a resurgence of naturalism in the 'kitchen-sink' drama both in the theatre and on television. In contrast, the post-Fordist social reformation has caused in the 1980s a sense of displacement amongst a large fraction of the 'mass' audience of the 1960s. Alternative ways of seeing and negotiating (post)modern life have resulted, perhaps to the extent of a new affective order seeking – for different reasons according to social position – distractions from economic and social realities.

Viewed in this way, *Heartbeat* does indeed come out of the period in which it is created. Far from confronting contemporary social problems, however, it glosses over them. On the one hand evoking nostalgia for the headier days of the 1960s (amongst those who remember them), and on the other hand constructing (for those who do not remember or who have forgotten) a myth of pre-industrial, rural Britain, the feel of the series is of a 'golden age', a time when human values were central to a relatively simple life in a stable and knowable community. It draws on British cultural icons: indeed Greengrass could sit happily in the long-standing radio soap *The Archers* (BBC Radio 4) and would scarcely look out of place with Tony Lumpkin in the Three Pigeons of Goldsmith's *She Stoops to Conquer* (1773). Rather than constructing a coherent, acutely observed picture of contemporary reality for an audience with a sense at least of shared purpose, *Heartbeat* is constructed of loosely interwoven fragments reflecting the mythological (in Barthes' (1973) sense) visions of different microcultures identified by viewergraphics in a fragmented society.

In so far as it revisits the 1960s, *Heartbeat* is very selective, omitting, for example, reference to racial unrest, drug (ab)use and *les événements*. Instead, it brings together PC Rowan, a modern male lead with distinctly urban connotations as noted, and Greengrass, a stock comic figure from a literary/theatrical tradition, along with Sergeant Blaketon and PC Ventress from the cosy 1950s fictional policing world of *Dixon of Dock Green* (BBC1). It sets them in the rural location of *All Creatures Great and Small* and, over the visuals, sounds of the 1960s are dubbed bearing very little relation to the action. In a further blurring of referents, the construction of the Rowans' relationship suggests, as noted, the new man and woman of the 1990s in clothes that are both of the 1960s and 1990s. Such drama is, in Jameson's term, a postmodern 'pastiche' in which:

> the producers of culture have nowhere to turn but to the past: the imitation of dead styles, speech through all the masks and voices stored up in the imaginary museum of a now global culture (1993: 17–18).

Such pastiche is evident in *Heartbeat*'s use of music. Film and television music typically serves a range of functions supportive to the narrative such as underlining emotion or creating pace or suspense. In TV drama there are few examples (other than in the work of Dennis Potter) where music is used to comment on the action. *Heartbeat*, however, uses music simply for of its retro and nostalgic functions. As a consequence it finds it difficult to relate the tracks to the action of the drama. In the 'badger episode' referred to above, there is apparently little relation between the Beatles' gently surreal track 'I am the Walrus' and the visual action of snarling terriers attacking a badger sett, other than that one line of the lyric refers to 'city policemen' and 'sitting pretty policemen'. Similarly 'My name is Jack' bears little relation to the action over which it is played in which the simple character, David, is shown grinning whilst driving a tractor.

There may well be a pleasure on offer to the more media-literate members of the audience in conscious awareness of the various features of attraction to the 'viewergraphically' defined audience segments. But, howsoever it is read, *Heartbeat* poses a challenge to traditional notions of drama as an organic whole to which all the contributory parts are integral. Indeed, post-modernism's challenge to organic and totalizing structures (of history, nationality and cultural forms) would appear to have extended to a shift in TV dramatic form consonant with its new affective order.

If, resulting from the constellation of factors indicated in this book, a Realism with contemporary referentiality is outmoded, the question arises as to whether *Heartbeat* represents a new age of postmodern TV drama. It is possible to consider *Heartbeat*'s principle of construction as a 'bricolage', appealing through its multiple codes to a range of segments of a fragmented audience. Viewers might then either take from the drama those aspects which pleased them in line with the principle of viewer-graphics expounded above, or, perhaps more creatively, viewers might construct their own text from a collage of fragments as proposed by some theorists of textual reading.

There is an important difference to be drawn, however, between a critical postmodernism, a work composed through radical juxtaposition of different discourses without any attempt to harmonize or resolve the conflicting voices, and *Heartbeat*.[10] The latter puts together a range of features from different times and places in a mix of styles packaged in a loose and flexible narrative frame. In critical postmodern practice, in contrast, Jim Collins advocates:

> a careful, purposeful consideration of representational alter-natives – rather than [text constructed] by simple pastiche or the 'plundering' of history of art as though it were an attic filled with the artefacts of one's ancestors (1989: 138).

The juxtaposition of discourses in play without resolution of their conflicting voices is indeed characteristic of a postmodern aesthetic (see Jencks, 1989: 14–25). But in work of worth, Collins argues, 'a precise combination of styles forms the basis of a productive engagement with antecedent and contemporary modes of organizing experience as a way of making sense of life in decentred cultures' (1989: 140).

In so far as bricolage and parataxis are the principles of construction of *Heartbeat*, the juxtaposition of discourses does not offer a plurality of disparate voices such that readers are necessarily required to be active in negotiating the collisions of free-floating signifiers. The closures – either narrative or atmospheric – provide a sense-making frame to leave instead the impression of a resolution of any tensions set in play. The popularity of *Heartbeat* suggests that it gives the viewers what they want, but in so doing it dislocates, and perhaps diminishes, some functions of drama both as they have traditionally been perceived and as they might be produced in more progressive contemporary forms, either realist or postmodern.

There may for sure be a place in a fragmented culture for a television drama of comfort (see Chapter 7). The popularity of series like *Heartbeat* no doubt arises from the not unreasonable desire of viewers to be entertained and distracted from the difficult business of living in a fast-changing contemporary world when they sit down to watch television on a Sunday night. Nevertheless, if the comparison between *Heartbeat* and the social realism of the 1960s sketched above reveals a general shift from a socially and self-aware audience of citizens to a society of consumers in which the pleasures of postmodern surface are paramount, the cultural implications of such a transition deserve fuller consideration and I shall return to these issues in Chapter 9.

Meanwhile, it might be noted that entertainment and a more intelligent, challenging drama than *Heartbeat* are not mutually exclusive, as the track record of much British and other television drama illustrates.[11] It may be, however, that market research might not be the most fruitful approach in this regard. Indeed such research may yield unreliable results concerning people's needs and desires since, as is well known, the 'truthfulness' of the answers depends to a great extent on the mode of reception of the questions.

In relation to the strand of this book concerned with quality, there are a number of matters of interest in the market-led approach to making drama. Firstly, this means of establishing viewer preference is not likely to lead to a challenging drama even though viewers might actually enjoy (perhaps more) something with 'more to it'. British people, if stopped in the street and asked whether they would prefer a drama series set in rural Yorkshire and featuring 1960s pop music or one about unemployment in Liverpool, are most likely to opt for *Heartbeat* rather than *Boys from the Blackstuff*, though the popularity of the latter in the early 1980s testifies to viewers' intelligence and range of sympathies, interests and pleasures. Currently in Britain, however, an audience approaching the fifteen million mark remains the aim of the more dominant channels for popular series. *Blackstuff* initially achieved on average an audience of only 4.5 million and thus in the terms of ratings discourse is not worth making. As this chapter illustrates, given the conception of a plural audience, to maximize audience means to aggregate its segments. In this context, a coincidence has emerged between flexiad drama form and image-making generally in the television of postmodernity.

Flexible specialization is concerned with the creation of markets through the construction of consumer identities. The whole strategy of marketing in a post-Fordist context is one of product differentiation through aestheticization and consumer differentiation by lifestyle grouping. The approach to drama production outlined above is consonant with this quick turnover marketing strategy. A key question, then, is whether TV drama is fast becoming like advertisements in Lee's view of them:

> a visually arresting but narrativeless series of texts which . . . randomly stitch together the signs of one period (black and white imagery, typeface, fashion, hairstyles, mode of address and, indeed, the connotations of the product itself) in a manner that confuses the temporal origin of these signs (1993: 155).

The circulation of signs which appear to construct a recognizable world – such as that of *Heartbeat* – when placed under scrutiny amounts to nothing more than a simulation in Baudrillard's sense of copies for which there are no originals. Perhaps prefiguring the marketeers' construction of 'values and lifestyles' of audience segments, furthermore, Baudrillard has argued that 'present-day simulators try to make the real, all the real, coincide with their simulation models' (1988: 166).

In Baudrillard's conception of the simulacrum, signifiers either mask the absence of an underlying reality or bear no relation to reality whatever. Lee observes that:

> [t]raditionally, nostalgia has been used in advertising to establish a logical continuity between the past, the present and the future (1993: 154–5).

But more recent advertisements obfuscate a sense of time just as *Heartbeat* blurs the distinction between the 1960s and the 1990s. As Lee puts it:

> any attempt by the reader to focus cognitively upon one temporal dimension immediately finds the reader's concentration flooded by symbols (and meanings) that signify the other period. The result of this is that neither period of time finds a firm symbolic anchorage within the text but becomes free-floating and displaced (1993: 155–6).

Abandonment of a sense of history and of situating agency in structure thus emerges as a feature of the new circumstances, though the extent to which contemporary culture has been subsumed into hyperspace and the hyperreal remains in debate. There is no doubt a residue at least of the realist paradigm, and it may be that the latter is dominant yet – particularly in popular television (see Chapter 5). Nevertheless, as simulation rapidly encroaches on many aspects of (post)modern life, the question of an epistemic shift is repeatedly posed by theorists of the postmodern.

Whereas in the past, Baudrillard suggests:

> [a]ll of Western faith and good faith was engaged in this wager on representation: that a sign could *exchange* for meaning. . . . [today there is only] a simulacrum, never again exchanging for what is real, but exchanging in itself, in an uninterrupted circuit without reference or circumference (1988: 170).

Without going the whole way with Baudrillard to deny any reference points in a more grounded semiosis or the 'reality' of lived experience, it is evident in the analysis above that *Heartbeat* recirculates dislocated signifiers. In particular it recirculates the 'values and lifestyles' signifiers of the language of advertising. In addition to its flexi-narrative form, it comprises a pastiche of signs and symbols. These signifiers are wrenched from the rootedness of their meaning uni-accentually inscribed in the past to circulate within a, now fragmented, speech community. Indeed with regard to *Heartbeat* and similar flexiad TV drama series, it may be, as Baudrillard observes, that, '[w]hen the real is not what it used to be, nostalgia assumes its full meaning' (1988: 171).

III

Baywatch is informally categorized in America as a 'T and A' (tits and ass) show and it is referred colloquially as 'babewatch', 'buttwatch' or even (so my students inform me) 'wrist-watch'. Audience awareness of the specificity of the central attractions of *Baywatch* as indicated in these euphemistic tags does not amount, however, to a repudiation of the drama's overtly sexist treatment of women by switching off. On the contrary, 'new' *Baywatch* (Baywatch Production Company) is claimed to be 'the world's most popular TV show' (Billen, 1994: 16). It is transmitted in 72 countries and has an estimated audience 'of a billion – higher than any other TV series in history' (Billen, 1994: 16). It is 'new' in that, following only moderate ratings for the first showing in 1989, the sponsoring network in America, NBC, cancelled the series. It was revived by a group of co-producers including David Hasselhoff, the series' main star, who reduced the budget per episode from $1.2 million to $800.000 and marketed the show to individual transmitting stations across America. The series also purports to be new in trading less on the attractions of exposed, particularly female, flesh than in the first series.

Of the many analytic approaches which *Baywatch* invites, I am drawn, following on from the questions raised by the production and circulation of 'feelgood' imagery in *Heartbeat*, to focus particularly on two related concerns: plausible ideal type televisual imagery grounded only insecurely in empirical reality, and the commercial considerations which inform that imagery and its intertextual relations in television's flow. The aestheticism of postmodern culture is tightly bound up with the idea that certain kinds of consumption lead to the formation of a particular type of person: the abstracted lifestyle of personality displaces the situated life of citizens. In particular, I shall focus on a narcissistic obsession with the body, not – as in psychoanalytic accounts of cinema – in terms of the body as object of desire, but as index of a preferred lifestyle privileging specific moulds for youth, energy and health. This is to extend consideration of the idea introduced at the end of the discussion of *Heartbeat,* that television drama is becoming almost indistinguishable in its forms from advertisements. Indeed the term 'flexiad', as I have coined it, indicates precisely a flexibility of dramatic form to correspond with the 90-second sound-and-vision byte and circulating the 'feel-good' imagery of advertisements.

Baywatch has not built its audience on viewergraphic research. Its appeal lies rather in a more general conflation of pleasures: of the beach (invoking for many the liberations associated with holidays or an easy lifestyle); in sexuality, constructed particularly from a heterosexual male point of view, though not precluding aspects of female pleasure which (defying feminist critique[12]) some women, having ingested the cultural ideal types, might find in 'being-looked-at-ness', or indeed in looking themselves at the images of male or female bodies; and in an ideal of individualist freedom typified by the Western seaboard of California, *el dorado* of the American Dream.

A dominant feature of *Baywatch*'s camera style is to explore in the beach context the bodies of scantily clad men and women, but more specifically the erogenous zones of women. It is most evident in the titles.[13] In a fast-cut sequence under Hasselhoff's rendering of the rock-style song 'I'm Always Here', the fifth shot is a Mid-Shot following six bikini-clad bottoms along the beach. In a characteristic deployment of the rhetorical figure of synecdoche (the part of the female anatomy standing for the whole woman) *Baywatch* titles proceed to a fast zoom along the beach which ends by diving down a young woman's cleavage. The camera then tilts down her figure as she removes her shorts, cutting to an almost subliminal image – so fast is it cut in – of two young women in thong bikinis shot from behind running into the surf such that in the flash of the image they appear to be naked.

Body fetishism as lifestyle aesthetic applies, however, to both male and female. The shots of women are indeed intercut with Close-Ups of men in swimming shorts, but the men are presented characteristically in 'heroic' beach action and the camera does not isolate their erogenous zones as it does with the female form and thus does not objectify them sexually in quite the same way. For example, Hasselhoff is featured running along the beach as if on his way to rescue somebody, and he is shot in Mid-Close-Up from the front and side to show head and shoulders and the chest, and in another shot his feet and lower legs in Close-Up sprinting along the water's edge.

Many of the other images inter-cut with these in the titles are phallic: speed boats, helicopters, surf-boards, kayaks. Whilst Freud, in a moment of apparently corrective self-criticism, observed that a cigar is sometimes only a cigar, the context of the repeated phallic imagery in *Baywatch* does not require an over-imaginative reading in this respect. To bring out, moreover, the ethnic selectivity in the construction of plausible ideal types, the women featured are, with few exceptions, sun-tanned, though caucasian, mainly with long blonde hair and the hourglass shape prevalent in the idealizations of advertiser's imagery but typical of actual women even on Californian beaches only insofar as they have been caught up in the fetishism of ideal body-types.

The paradigm might be the lifeguard, CJ (Pamela Anderson), who, in her uniform orange swimsuit, features frequently swimming underwater, emerging from the water, or leaning against railings at the watchtower, or standing hands on hips on the boardwalk such that her thrusting (siliconed) breasts dominate the shot. Since she is formally contracted to submit to a number of cleavage shots per episode, it is perhaps not surprising that she is even shown conducting interviews in her office in this garb and posture.

Since, as Corner has remarked, 'it is only by analysing television at a primary level than (*sic*) we can ground generalities about the medium and confidently address the larger questions about its public character' (1995: 29), I shall discuss a specific showing of *Baywatch* on British television including the advertisements which punctuate it.

'Western Exposure', transmitted in the UK on 21 May 1994 (LWT and ITV Network), is flexi-narrative in form. It interweaves three simple stories: Hobie Buchannon's attempt to advance his adolescence by making a date with a class-mate, the fourteen-year-old Bridget; Sadie Jennings's attempt to make a success as a country music performer; and professional star country singer Jesse Lee Harris's attempt to find – and be reunited with – his son and wife, quite specifically in that order of importance. Although the episode's title evokes intertextually the more alternative cult North American series *Northern Exposure*, it does not depart from *Baywatch*'s tried and tested conventions. The separate strands of the narrative are causally interconnected but they do not otherwise add up thematically to much more than the sum of their parts.

By the end of the episode the problems posed in all three strands are conventionally resolved: the Harris family is reunited; Sadie, with Jesse's assistance, will sing on his tour in Las Vegas; Hobie does not get the girl – who has a crush on his father, the star of the show Mitch Buchannon (David Hasselhoff) – but Hobie does not care as he has seen through her immaturity and proved his 'masculinity' by rescuing from the sea Jesse's son, Jackson, who has fallen from the pier. Thus, the episode reinforces that patriarchal ideology endemic in Western culture and typified by *Baywatch* in spite of the fact that the episode in question is written by a woman, Deborah Bonann Schwartz, presumably related to the co-producer/director, Douglas Schwartz, whose use of the camera visually endorses his colleague's gender-coded narration.

With regard to the episode of *Baywatch* in question, 'Western Exposure' by no means adequates reality, even that dream-world of Venice Beach, Los Angeles. Indeed, its images rather relate intertextually to those of advertisements and MTV as much as they do to Californian beach life. But *Baywatch*'s fictional construct intersects through its textual discourses of gender with those patriarchal discourses pervading the non-fictional actuality of contemporary Western culture.

To put it plainly, *Baywatch* is sexist in its narrative structures, in the sexual politics of its fictional world, and in the ways in which it is shot. At the very least, it reinforces deeply conservative notions of 'family values' and endorses essentialist notions of distinctive male and female roles clearly separated along a binary divide. The closure of the narratives noted above accords with Fiske's conception of the 'masculine' narrative cited in

Chapter 2. Patriarchal social hierarchies are explicit and dominant in all the narrative strands. Following the titles of 'Western
Exposure', a (boy?)man-to-man dialogue between Hobie and his
single-parent father, Mitch, concerning how a male knows when
he is in love sets the tone of male confederacy from the outset.
Harris's pursuit is primarily of his boy, Jackson, conciliation with
his wife seemingly being little more than a necessary means to
that end. Harris himself is mobbed by young women in bikinis
as he combs Venice Beach in search of his son and driven by
their frenzy into the sea. CJ Parker, the female lifeguard on
watch, reports 'multiple victims caught in a rip' and, assisted by
colleagues, she pulls Harris and the women to the shore.

This event leads indirectly to Sadie's breakthrough as a
country singer which is only achieved through the intervention
of Harris whose approval confers on her immediate status in flat
contradiction of her girlfriend, CJ's, explicit repudiation of
country music in favour of rock, specifically Madonna, at the
beginning of the episode. Hobie's dates with Bridget are not
a success, as noted, but having gained personal status through
his heroism at the end, Hobie dismisses Bridget by asking to
borrow a quarter and responding to her positive response with,
'Go call somebody who cares!' in front of her friends who
ostracize her further by sniggering.

All this male chauvinism – handed down literally from father
to son – furthermore is superficially deflected by constant references to family values. First Harris and his manager, then CJ
and Harris, then Mitch Buchannon and Harris indulge in heart-
to-hearts about what it means to have family. Mitch observes
that he 'would have given anything for his [Hobie's] mother
to be there to hold him' when Bridget called Hobie a 'dork',
further stressing stereotypically that a man can only do so much.
Harris in turn envies Mitch those 'father–son times' he has
witnessed Mitch sharing with Hobie. At the end of the episode
when rescued from the sea and asked if he is all right, Jackson
replies, (to his mother) 'Mom, I told you dad loves us more than
anything. I knew he'd come. . . . I'm good now.' In the coda
following this reunion, Mitch confers his (series) patriarchal
blessing observing, 'that is a beautiful family'.

Turning to the economic considerations of *Baywatch* as commercial TV product, the series is successful in ratings terms in
its own right, and as a part of a network of mutually reinforcing

aspects of a culture of consumption. *Baywatch* is transmitted in Britain at 17.50 hours on Saturdays in the twilight slot following the afternoon sport programmes which attract a predominantly male audience, but at pre-teatime when a teenage audience is typically attracted on weekdays to the world of sun, sand and surf in the Australian soap, *Neighbours* (BBC1). Given that, as noted above, a fit between products and potential consumers is sought in modern scheduling informed by audience research through a demographic breakdown of the audience by market segments, it is predictable that the advertisements punctuating *Baywatch*, like the programme itself, should be aimed at adult males and teenagers. This proves to be the case.

For example, adult 'male' tools feature strongly (Black and Decker power drills run a repeat showing in the intervals of the episode under discussion) whose phallic shapes – encoded in Western culture with male power – echo the speedboats and helicopters in *Baywatch* titles. Appealing generally to teenage consumption of candy, there are advertisements for 'Lion Bar' and 'Bounty Bar' and, in recognition that some teenage females might constitute an audience segment, there is an advertisement for 'Oxy 10', presented by Nicola Stapleton (like Nick Berry in *Heartbeat*, an ex-*EastEnders* performer), exhorting young women to 'oxycute' their spots, presumably so they can begin to approximate to the idealized standards of the culturally encoded signs for women in *Baywatch*. Some of the advertisements (Black and Decker, for example) follow a traditional presentation of the object for sale with a voice-ever extolling its qualities. More typical of (post)modern television advertising, however, are those for 'Bounty Bar' and 'Brut Aquatonic' after-shave.

The descriptions below go some way to illustrate a key point which I might make better (in a context other than a book) by editing together a sequence comprised of extracts from the episode of *Baywatch* under discussion with shots from the advertisements which punctuated the transmission. A verbal description of the similarities is less potent than a full graphic illustration in revealing the marked similarities between the two in visual style. I focus on the advertisements for Bounty Bars and Brut Aquatonic.

Like the titles of *Baywatch*, each of these advertisements punctuating the episode comprises a fast-cut sequence of stylishly-shot cinematic images loosely framed by a narrative. In the case of the 'Bounty' advertisement, the whole thirty seconds is shot through a blue filter and set on the coast of a tropical island. The narrative involves a conventionally 'exotic' and beautiful young woman – or the signifier of one – ultimately joined by a conventionally muscular and handsome young man – or the signifier of one – shot in Close-Ups echoing, indeed replicating, those of Hasselhoff running along the beach through the edge of the surf. At the beginning of the advertisement the woman is seen in Close-Up sucking a (phallic) bounty bar in an overt simulation of oral sex, a trope originated in advertisements for 'Cadbury's Flake', but now a cliché in the language of television advertisements. A cutaway shot features in slow motion a coconut split asunder as it falls from the palm tree to hit the ground and release a spray of its juices as the shot dissolves into another of the foaming surf. Following the denouement in which the couple have met and embraced, a shot along the wave of a roll of surf echoes a similar shot at the top of the titles of *Baywatch*. Following a Close-Up of the faces of the pair – she supine passive, he moving to kiss her – a cutaway reprises the coconut again falling and issuing forth its juices plus the shot along the wave of surf. After this powerful movement of fluids, she is shown recumbent on his chest as she bites a 'Bounty Bar' and munches it with a look of profound satisfaction. The musical soundtrack features a male voice incanting a modern ballad of 'the reason for living, the reason for giving . . . listen to the sound of nature's charms', whilst in counterpoint a breathy female voice reprises the man's lines and concludes 'softly, softly with ('Bounty') the taste of paradise'. Again the relation of soundtrack to visual image corresponds to similar constructions in the *Baywatch* titles.

The Brut Aquatonic advertisement is shorter (nine seconds) and technically less sophisticated than that for Bounty Bar. It too is set on a sunny coast and its narrative also features a couple coming together in embrace. The opening shot of the A-shaped sail of a yacht on a sunlit sea is virtually identical to such a shot used in *Baywatch* over an MTV style insert (see below) of Sadie singing by the sea. Shot 2 is of the sea-sprayed face in Close-Up of a conventionally handsome caucasian male – or the signifier of one. The third shot features a bottle of the product, Brut Aquatonic, the pale aquamarine colour of which dissolves into the sea. The final shot features the man pulling into an embrace a slim blonde woman in white bikini, shot almost full figure in Mid-Shot but with the faces just out of shot such that the eye is drawn to the woman's breasts pressing against the man's chest. The female voice-over relates the product to 'the essence of man'.

Before drawing together the key points relating flexiad narratives in the dramas of *Heartbeat* and *Baywatch* to their counterparts in advertisements another structural feature of *Baywatch* demonstrates intertextual resonance with yet another TV genre, MTV (Music TeleVision). Additionally transmitted in Britain along with MTV (Europe) is CMT, Country Music Television (Europe), each a separate channel of the subscription outlet, Sky Television. Popular with teenagers who predominate in the market for pop music and videos, MTV has an appeal to that market segment. The flexiad form allows the inclusion of music – for its intrinsic attraction rather than its relation to the action as in more traditional cinematic and televisual modes, as noted – either as in *Heartbeat* dubbed over largely unrelated pieces of action from the drama's narrative, or, as in *Baywatch*, as an MTV-style insert. The visual content of some MTV videos is also, of course, dramatic narrative.

The innovation of CMT may throw light upon the narrative of the *Baywatch* episode, 'Western Exposure' and offer yet another level of meaning to its polysemic title. Whilst country music has a cult following of devotees, the aggregate may not be sufficient to sustain a music channel. At the outset of 'Western Exposure', as noted, CJ repudiates Sadie's music in favour of rock, but she is converted at the concert at Denim 'n Diamonds club, which Jesse Lee Harris attends at CJ's request and where he confirms Sadie's worth. Prior to the song, 'Life 9', Sadie sings at the club, she is given an MTV-style slot in the episode where she sings a rock/country hybrid 'My Baby Loves Me' whilst dancing barefoot in a loose-fitting cotton dress silhouetted against the sea and that A-shaped sail of a yacht, paralleling the one in the Brut Aquatonic advertisement. Similarly Jesse Lee Harris, besides strumming his guitar in his travel bus and singing a number 'Where was I?' at Denim 'n Diamonds to end the episode, has an MTV-style insert where, shot (in flash-back) on a sun-drenched fishing and camping trip with Jackson, he expounds his relationship with nature as a form of alternative prayer in a song 'Talking to God'.

Together the songs of Sadie and Jesse amount to a good deal of Western exposure in this episode of *Baywatch*, supported with the repeated tag: 'rock music doesn't come from the heart; country music's about life, its about love, its about family'. A democratic dance form, Texas line dance, featuring pleated mini-skirted young women in cowboy boots, shot in Close-Up of midriffs and feet, promotes in addition a popular cultural form. If a television company wished to extend its audience for CMT to embrace a section of the MTV teenage audience it could scarcely have constructed a better targeted advertisement vehicle than the *Baywatch* episode under discussion.

To summarize the flexiad features, the deployment of lifestyle signifiers, the use of music, the actors, the shot construction, the lighting, the effects, the editing rhythms, the imagery, indeed the televisual discourse are common to both the flexiad TV drama series and advertisements such that the boundaries between them, and other popular cultural forms such as pop music, pop video, MTV and CMT, are inevitably blurred in the televisual flow. *Heartbeat* and *Baywatch,* whilst they both illustrate the direct commercial interest in, and influence on, TV drama production, however, offer very different images for different segments of the audience.

The commonality of their approach to pleasing audience segments resides in a play on differences between people in different microcultures in marked contrast to the allegedly outmoded notion of a drama conceived for a mass audience based on an assumed shared experience and understanding of aspects common to humanity. At this point, pending full discussion later in the book, I will simply observe that there is a significant difference between an approach to making and marketing TV drama premissed on the idea of a shared experience implicitly emphasizing common capacities and values and one in which difference is commercially exploited by constructing audience segments and targeting them, perhaps exacerbating social divisiveness in the process for the sake of sales promotion.

To take up, by way of illustration, a particular aspect of the approach in *Baywatch* which reflects – and is reflected in – the social formation, children are increasingly constructed as diminutive adults. Hobie Buchannon is treated in 'Western Exposure' as a fourteen-year-old facsimile of his father, Mitch, though lacking as yet his father's irresistible sexual magnetism. Mitch talks of a double dinner date when he invites Bridget to join Hobie and himself with Stephanie, his friend and colleague, at home for dinner and subsequently at Denim 'n Diamonds. In the club, the teenagers dress, dance and drink like the adults only in diminutive form: their love relationships are treated on a par with those of adults. Nor is this phenomenon exclusive to *Baywatch*: it is replicated particularly in the sun, sand and surf contexts of the Australian soaps, *Neighbours* (BBC1) and *Home and Away* (ITV). Indeed, children's fantasy spaces on television are now strongly related to consumerism and the idea of life as a permanent holiday.

From one point of view such fantasy worlds might be seen to be electronic versions of children's play in which, traditionally, adult behaviour has been rehearsed in a safe, because imaginary, environment. The popularity of such TV drama series with adolescents – though they may be well aware of the series' limitations in terms of truth-to-life – might enforce the idea that they have something to offer in this way. From another point of view, in the light of the analysis above of both commercial and gender issues, however, an awareness that youth markets are being extended through the blurring of boundaries between programmes and advertisements, and that – however aware the audience might be of the fantasy element – images of ideals to which viewers are repeatedly invited to aspire in both drama and advertisement leaves a sense of unease. There is a difference, moreover, between children's construction of imaginary worlds in creative play and the presentation to them of idealized images in a fantasy world.

With regard to the latter, Alexandra Paul, who plays Stephanie Holden – the fourth at table in the double dinner date referred above – has suffered from bulimia and 'concedes media images of "perfect" bodies may have played their part in her illness' (cited in Billen, 1994: 24). As Andrew Billen sums up the issue and the series:

Baywatch is a show predicated upon fantasy, with fantasy heroes and fantasy heroines and many, many fantasy bodies. To complain about it, perhaps, is as fatuous as protesting at the lack of naturalism in Grimms' fairytales. Yet, as Paul understands, even fantasy connects with 'something real' (1994, 24).

I shall return later to the perspectives of those popular cul-turalists who, dismissing the Frankfurt school critique of the commodification and appropriations of 'mass culture', valorize uncritically the pleasures people take from all kinds of popular cultural forms. For the politics of pleasures in postmodernity has opened up interesting debates. An over-emphasis in acknow-ledgement that modern persons – children, teenagers and adults alike – are more media literate than their forebears and thus less subject to the lure of commodification tends, however, to mask that connection, that intersection, with reality from which people can, and do, learn about actuality whether posit-ively or negatively.

This chapter has emphasized various connections between commerce and programming in TV drama production, circu-lation and reception in postmodernity. A homology has been drawn between the formal construction of imagery in contem-porary popular TV drama and advertisements, both deploying dislocated signifiers of 'feel-good' or plausible ideal type imagery, loosely connected within a flexible narrative frame. Pushed to Baudrillard's extreme, it may be that such constructions are simulations disconnected from any basic or underlying 'reality'. Ultimately, however, I pull back from this position suggesting instead that postmodern constructs intersect with, if they no longer in any sense replicate, aspects of people's lived or ima-ginative experience. Exploring the quarrel between philosoph-ical realists and postmodernists can be put off no longer: it is the topic of the next chapter.

5 TV Drama Forms
Tradition and Innovation: Gradual (Un)realizations

The idealist nature of Hollywood's adopted ideology meant that it represented the world not as it was but as it should be. To describe an aesthetic so committed to illusion, artifice, and idealism as 'realist' seems a perversity sanctioned only by tradition (Maltby, 1983: 192).

I

The concept of 'realism' is highly contentious and debate about its usage in Television Studies has been re-engaged in the 1990s. John Corner, for example, has observed that, given the increasing looseness with which 'realism' is used, its 'abandonment might turn out to be a better bet than attempted repair' (1992: 3). Christopher Williams agrees that the term and concept are problematic but is convinced they must be retained (see 1994: 288). Differences of view about 'realism' are by no means new. In the 1930s, Brecht wrote:

> Now we come to the concept of *realism*. This concept, too, must first be cleansed before use, for it is an old concept, much used by many people and for many ends (1992: 81).

The colloquial interchangeability in modern usage of the terms 'realism' and 'naturalism' noted by Corner masks indeed a number of confusions. But, in particular, a long-standing problem is exacerbated by the emergence in the 1970s and 1980s of the related perspectives of poststructuralism and postmodernism. As we have already seen in taking note of Baudrillard, fundamental questions about languages of representation and their relation to an object world have been posed, adding to the prior complexities of the usages of 'Naturalism' and 'Realism' at the height of the cultural production of these aesthetic forms in the latter half of the nineteenth century. These are compounded by the debates in the 1930s between Brecht and Lukács as to the best critical method of historical realism, and the Brecht-derived *Screen* scepticism about the conservative politics of the 'classic realist text' in the 1970s.

In poststructuralism, a sense that discourses are locked in their conventions accompanies the severing of relationship between sign and referent. Additionally, conceptions of history as a developmental process are challenged by postmodernist loss of faith in grand narratives. In consequence, notions of a singular truth pursued either by scientific rationalism or in determinist marxist history have relaxed amongst some post-structuralists into a pragmatic pluralism of relative views without a valid means of distinguishing between them. A time of potential shift from the century-old dominance of the realist/objectivist paradigm to (philosophical) postmodernism, is an apt moment once again to review realism. The etymology of the terms 'Realism' and 'Naturalism' is well documented,[1] but it is illuminating to glance back briefly at their emergence. A subsequent selective sketch of the genealogy of the terms in literature, theatre and cinema brings out the key issues of philosophical debate concerning realism and naturalism (the lower case indicating modern usages) and postmodernism in contemporary TV drama.

At the height of scientific rationalism and empiricism in the latter half of the nineteenth century, a homology emerged between the premisses underlying artistic innovation and those informing conceptions of history and science. Indeed, the camera and the sound-recorder – subsequently the artistic media of film and television – arise out of the quest by science for means of objective documentation. The emphasis on empirical evidence apprehended through the senses and belief in the objectivity of scientific method fostered a climate in which artists such as Courbet and Flaubert pursued the idea that truth might be revealed directly through painting or writing. Broadly adopting the ideology of contemporary science, such artists sought to apprehend the world as it is by observing in detail the tangible facts and documenting them in their arts practices.[2] Many of the leading exponents of Naturalism and Realism had backgrounds in the natural sciences. Flaubert and Chekhov, for example, were medical practitioners and Chekhov asserted in a letter of 1887 that 'a writer should be as objective as a chemist' (cited in Styan, 1983: 83).

Succinctly to characterize key features of the ideology of science in the Enlightenment tradition of empiricism and rationalism: it had the potential of total explanatory power; there was to be one answer to every question (inviting consensus); a cause for every effect and progressive causal chains through linear time; the relation between sign and referent was direct, transparent and unproblematic. These features inform the initial development of Realist fiction and, more obliquely, narrative cinema, and subsequently television.

Realism and Naturalism made the arts an object of knowledge through accurate observation and representation of the perceived world. Their distinctiveness lies in their historical association with a positivist conception of truth.[3] As their respective usages settled, however:

> Naturalism was seen as that which merely produced the flat external appearance of reality with a certain static quality, whereas realism – in the Marxist tradition for example – was that method and that intention which went below this surface to the essential historical movements, to the dynamic reality (Williams, 1977: 65).

Thus each form makes its truth-claim on a different basis. Naturalism, consciously abandoning supernaturalism and metaphysics, claims to account for material reality by documenting the natural world objectively, free from a conceptual, sensemaking framework. Realism, in contrast, made sense of the flow of events but, from a historicist view, in terms of the dynamics of historical development perceived to be inherent in social reality. Both reveal positivist tendencies in purporting to offer value-free knowledge of 'the facts'.

That the truths offered are indeed shaped by their ways of seeing relative to the developing history of ideas is evident in marxism's structuralist, rather than objectivist, sense of realism. The conventions of realism, then, are discontinuous in a force field of influences. Realisms in the 1970s and 1980s came in turn to be typically perceived as conventionalized constructions, mimetic but without referentiality (see below). Then with the poststructuralist emphasis on discursive practices dislocated

entirely from historical reality, realism effectively becomes (philosophical) idealism in a confusing inversion of its premisses at
the outset.

Amidst the discontinuities, however, there are ingrained veins.
Throughout the changing history of ideas, realist texts have been
generally perceived to be in a hurry to explain everything. As
Christopher Nash summarizes their functioning:

> If the raw data of human experience tend to scatter and fly
> apart, literary convention has a compelling mechanism ready
> to hand in tropism – in above all, metonymy and metaphor.
> The centre can be made to hold by the synthesis, the synthetic
> use of rhythmically recurrent imagistic motifs producing the
> effects of a global harmony of a unified meaningfulness –
> without the aid of overt statement (1987: 26).

A key distinction between mimesis and referentiality, however, marks the difference between those referential realist texts
which claim to be explaining the object world, and those where
mimetic conventions merely make a story readily accessible by
giving it a plausible sense-making frame.

A text, Nash suggests, is:

> referential when it claims to tell us something about the
> world outside . . . mimetic when it *makes appeal to the verbal con-*
> *ventions* by which we 'imitate' the world outside. In a subtle
> but absolutely crucial way these are not the same (1987: 56).

The distinction begins to bring out the element of conventionalism in verbal and visual representations, even where the aim
is to reflect the historical world as accurately as possible. It has
important implications for the ethic of truth-telling:

> A mimetic text is one that borrows the strategies of imita-
> tion [e.g. *Heartbeat*] and may intend to be referential or it
> may not [*Heartbeat* does not]. A referential text is a text that
> may be replete with such strategies but it need not be so and
> – in the history of narrative – often is not (Nash, 1987: 59).

A mimetic textual strategy – particularly in the immediacy of
television's flow – may induce credibility by seeming transpar-
ently to offer a truth-to-life. But as Nash remarks:

> it guarantees not the what-and-how of a story but the manner
> of its treatment. Probability, to put it very crudely, is about

rules of being and happening; mimesis is about rules of telling. . . . A novel [or drama] may be an 'accurate description of life as we know it', as Realism claims. But there are actually three claims here – that the novel [drama] is mimetic ('accurate description'), that it is referential ('of life'), that it is probable ('as we know it') . . . a novel [or drama] need not be any more than two or one or it may even seek to be none of these things. Positive materialist Realism . . . alone maintains them to be inextricable (1987: 60).

It is, for example, a set of non-referential, mimetic conventions which generally informs the 'classic narrative realism' of Hollywood cinema. In developing as unobtrusive a style of narration as possible, 'classic realism' reworked in visual terms the conventions of Realist fiction but for the sake of the ease of audience understanding of the story. Motivated structuring provides a 'circumstantial realism' (Maltby, 1983: 196). The conventions include: the depiction of space and time through continuity editing, psychological characterization, a conventionally transparent linear causal development leading to resolution in plotting. Hollywood cinema did not, however, sustain Realism's commitment to seriousness (see below) let alone its purpose of replicating the historical world; indeed it veered towards idealism, though its constructs had political implications in contemporary life. As Maltby summarizes:

'Perfect reproduction' channeled audience response towards an unquestioning acceptance of the star's emotional, moral and ultimately ideological authority by providing spectators with a matrix of references to behaviour and circumstance in the external world which they would validate through their own experience (1983: 191).

Referentiality and mimesis are separable, then, though there is a loose relationship between even mimesis and the explanatory paradigm of scientific rationalism. It is evident in that sense-making frames are constructed in terms of the logic of cause and effect in linear time and the illusion of three-dimensional space. It is a matter of shared assumptions that a mutually known set of conventions represent a stable external reality. What to traditional science are explanatory causes verified by concrete detail empirically observed, however, become conventions for motivating and locating a story. At worst – as seen from the point of view of 1970s ideology critique – false representations were grounded in the validating strategies of realism.

A key feature of nineteenth-century narrative Realism – again paralleling the pursuit of truth in the natural sciences – was seriousness, subsequently to be seen as ethical or 'moral seriousness' (Leavis, 1972: 25). Where previously the everyday had been represented only comically in literature, Auerbach marks 'the entrance of existential and tragic seriousness' into Realist fictions of bourgeois life in a mixture of 'seriousness and everyday reality' (1953: 481). Taking ordinary people seriously rather than treating them as figures of fun is a politically significant aspect of Realism's trajectory, documented by Williams, towards 'the secular, the contemporary and the socially extended' (1977: 65). It gave rise particularly to theatrical representations of bourgeois domestic life in the chamber play. This emphasis on secular action, brought low class human beings literally to centre stage in the theatre and, metaphorically, to the centre stage of history. '[H]uman action is played through in specifically human terms – exclusively human terms' (Williams, 1977: 64).

Thus bourgeois life, particularly in the relative stasis of high Naturalist theatrical representation, comes to seem all-important. In the late 1950s, when – as a further extension of the trajectory – representations of working-class life were introduced to television, there was a significant – at times explicit – challenge to the dominance of middle-class concerns. Textual content makes its impact contextually in specific historical moments, and there is still a function for new representations by this means. An anti-humanist strain in poststructuralist thought overlooks, however, the significance of the question of who figures in contemporary representations, though appropriate images of women, non-caucasians and other mis- or under-represented groups remains a key debate in Media Studies in the framework of referential realism.

Before proceeding to consider realism and naturalism and why – albeit in diluted forms – they remain dominant in TV drama, it is helpful to summarize the main characteristics of the drama of the late nineteenth century to serve as a benchmark against which modern developments might be measured. The common premises of the style of theatrical Realism and Naturalism consist in:

(1) uncensored imitation of human behaviour
(2) telescoping of events and other manipulations of plot
(3) the conveying of information by implicit as well as by explicit means, entailing slow development
(4) a style of acting and production which does not overtly acknowledge the presence of the audience
(5) inclusion of the trivial, the commonplace, the inessential, the irrelevant detail, employed to further the illusion that the audience is seeing life and not an artefact
(6) dialogue written in the way people really speak
(7) the reproduction on stage of real locations
(8) the employment of real properties and the wearing of authentic costumes
(9) representative characterisation which, by economic deployment of detail, implies individual life.[4]

A strength (or weakness as perceived by somebody like Brecht) of Naturalism as a theatrical style is its tendency emotionally to involve the spectator through sympathy with the characters in their plight.

II

It is the coherent, explanatory yet illusionistic, ideal vision shared, primarily through an emotional relationship, between text and reader which has drawn much critical comment on realism in the late twentieth century. As Nichols summarizes it:

> [t]he attempt to represent a world illusionistically had the quality of deceit about it. . . . Realism contributed the lynchpin to this operation, drawing our attention past the apparatus and machination, past the enunciation and its ideology of containment, past the seeing to the scene and its imaginary, lifelike autonomy (1991: 175).

Redirecting structuralist attack from cinema to television in the mid-1970s, the well-worn *Screen* debate about the political effectivity of realist TV drama centred on Jim Allen's play *Days of Hope* (see Bennett *et al.*, 1981: 302–53). Although the production and direction (by Tony Garnett and Ken Loach respectively) was critical naturalist in the classifications to be

used in the exploratory model below, naturalism was seen by
its detractors merely as a degraded form of realist narrative in
a collapse of distinctions.

To define his conception of the 'classic realist text', Colin
MacCabe, a key figure in the debate, placed a formalist emphasis upon the structural features of realist narratives, upon
the mimetic conventions rather than the referential content.
In so doing he vastly expanded the range of texts that might
be included under the heading of 'realism'. As he states:

> The category of the classic realist text lumps together in
> book and film *The Grapes of Wrath* and *The Sound of Music*,
> *L'Assommoir* and *Toad of Toad Hall* (1974: 12).

Thus some of the key characteristics of nineteenth-century
Realism – verisimilitude, plenitude in material detail, fidelity to
observation of the textures of day-to-day life, ethical seriousness
– are explicitly overlooked in critical theory as they had largely
been abandoned in Hollywood cinema.

For MacCabe's conception of 'classic realism' collapses the
distinction between mimesis and referentiality on the anti-
realist ground that the world cannot be neutrally articulated
in language. As Catherine Belsey somewhat sweepingly puts it,
'classic realism':

> makes it possible to unite categories which have been divided
> by the empiricist assumptions that the text reflects the world.
> By implying Saussurean quotation marks round 'realism',
> the phrase permits the inclusion of all those fictional forms
> which create the illusion while we read that what is narrated
> is 'really' and intelligibly happening (1980: 50).

It is in this formalist, profoundly anti-empiricist, account that
the referential aspect of Realism is abandoned in critical theory.
In what became the new orthodoxy of Film Studies, 'classic realism' is defined not by any claim about what constitutes the real
but by an internal consistency within a recognizable system.

To contextualize the '*Days of Hope* debate' a little in respect
of its considerable influence, it should be recognized as form-
ing part of the broader structuralist controversy of the 1970s
contesting the capacity of signs – differentiated by poststructuralists purely in terms of their internal relationships within
linguistic structures – to be referential.[5] The controversy was

political within the academy, and in a broader sphere also. If language did not reflect the world but instead constructed it, as Althusser and Barthes amongst others alleged, the bourgeoisie could be said to have constructed reality to suit itself and presented its version of the world as natural.[6]

As Jameson summarizes the semiotic trajectory from modernism onwards:

> a [modernist] disjunction does not completely abolish the referent, or the objective world, or reality, which still continue to entertain a feeble existence. . . . But its great distance from the sign now allows the latter to enter a moment of autonomy, of a relatively free-floating Utopian existence, as over against its former objects (1993: 96).

But the next, poststructuralist stage of development in Jameson's account divorces sign and referent completely, to leave 'that pure and random play of signifiers that we call postmodernism' (1993: 96).

Echoing Nichols, however, this book keeps in play 'another set of propositions, ones in which the separation between an image and what it refers to continues to be a difference that makes a difference' (1991: 7). Indeed part of its critique of the drift of contemporary culture and TV drama practices is that they increasingly deny

> the persistence of history as a reality with which we must contend. . . . The reality of pain and loss that is not part of any simulation, in fact, is what makes the difference between representation and historical reality of crucial importance (Nichols, 1991: 7).

Whilst a new affective order emerges with changes in social and taste formations as proposed, there remains as yet a considerable residue of the realist paradigm which identifies 'the primary qualities of the world as objective and realist' (Inglis, 1988: 51). From a conventionalist view, even, as long as realist texts and their popular audiences agree that a set of codes represent external reality, they remain potent.

The neo-marxist case of the 1970s/1980s, harnessed to psychoanalytic approaches, was that subjective viewing positions are fixed by ideological inscriptions in the cinematic text. The consequent inference is that liberation is only possible through avant-garde textual strategies to break down 'mainstream film and the pleasure it provides' (Mulvey, 1975: 17). If the realist text could not create contradiction in the reader, as MacCabe claimed in addition (1974: 7–12), counter-realist strategies were needed to draw attention to the constructedness and hence the partiality of the text's vision. But the avant-garde can function only in negation with regard to realism. In any case, in a society in which cultural production has become so intensely competitive and accordingly requires rapid change in conventions, the avant-garde is constantly being overtaken, as Adorno foresaw. Callinicos instances, 'the regular use of Brechtian alienation devices by the televison series *Moonlighting*' (1989: 156). A key question for this book, then, is whether postmodernism is just another mode of consumption and not critical, in the avant-garde tradition, at all.

In the interim, as Nichols proposes:

> if we wish to apply our theory and criticism to works that remain within the popular mainstream . . . without driving them all into the same ideological corner, a more open-ended conception of realism and its possible effects will have to be entertained (1991: 176).

The socially extended television audience typically resists experiment with form. As Griffiths puts it, from a writer's point of view:

> When you're trying to speak to large numbers of people who did not study literature at university, because they were getting on with productive work, and you're introducing fairly unfamiliar, dense and complex arguments into the fabric of the play, it's just an overwhelming imposition to present those arguments in unfamiliar forms (cited in Poole and Wyver, 1984: 3).

The findings of Bourdieu's study of taste confirm that a materialist-realist paradigm has typified Western popular culture. Although he recognizes the current shift in the social formation, Bourdieu remarks that:

> [t]he hostility of the working class and of the middle-class fractions least rich in cultural capital towards every kind of formal experimentation asserts itself both in the theatre and in painting, or still more clearly, because they have less legitimacy, in photography and the cinema. In the theatre as in

the cinema, the popular audience delights in plots that proceed logically and chronologically towards a happy end, and
'identifies' better with simply drawn situations and characters than with ambiguous and symbolic figures and actions
(1992: 32).

If, following Wittgenstein, everyday language usage is taken
seriously, 'realistic' denotes conviction, truth-to-experience,
plausibility of character, setting and action.

Although realism in narrative practices has developed into
a set of conventions of representation which makes the worlds
it constructs readily digestible for readers, many realist texts
nevertheless use empirical realism, if only to anchor the story.
Much attention is paid in the making of period drama, for
example, to historically accurate costumes, decor, vehicles and
so on. Besides offering a range of pleasures in itself, such
authenticating detail can also lend the drama a sense of conviction. As Nichols observes:

> Empirical verisimilitude provides no guarantee of historical
> accuracy at the higher level of significance or interpretation
> ... but it does secure an existential bond between image
> and referent (1991: 171).

Whilst the textual determinacy of subject positioning may
be less absolute than alleged by the conventionalists, there is
undoubtedly a politics in the camera's gaze and formulaic principles of construction. There is a noted tendency in psychological realism, for instance, to underplay historical and social
differences and instead, through the empathetic relationship
between character and viewer, to overplay the commonality of
human experience. The truth-to-life of character portrayal tends
to rest heavily on universal notions of humanity and to draw
viewers to a way of seeing which, far from being objective, is
heavily laden with particular values. That, typically in Western
humanist culture, the most comfortable viewing position in
terms of empathy has been from a white, heterosexual male,
middle-class position needs no further exegesis here.

Nichols has proposed that a feature distinguishing documentary from fictional representations of reality is that, '[f]iction
harbors echoes of dreams and daydreams, sharing structures
of fantasy with them, whereas documentary mimics the canons

of expository argument' (1991: 4). Many TV drama's fictions are closer to documentary than to the dreamworld of the cinema. *The Big Flame*, like other naturalist plays of the 1960s (and since) with documentary overtones, interprets the working-class audience to itself by offering a hypothesis about class relations.[7] In this sense an argument is put with which the audience is required to engage. Indeed this intellectual, as well as emotional, aspect of critical naturalism (see below) in a single play is a feature largely – though not entirely – precluded from the open-ended narratives of soaps, series and serials.

That modern realisms in TV drama typically make sense of experience for human beings on individualist terms is undeniable. This feature leads to an emphasis in realism on human nature seen in what Stern refers to as 'the middle distance to which realism is committed' (1973: 161). It is this perspective which places emphasis upon 'common language, common knowledge, common experience' (Stern, 1973: 89) and finds truth in typical, average human experience. But until it is replaced as a linguistic code, it may be the most usable means of communication open to popular television. As Eco has remarked, it may be that '[n]aturally, life resembles *Ulysses* more than *The Three Musketeers*, but we prefer to think of it as the other way round' (cited in Armes, 1994: 61).

If realism is illusionistic in more senses than one, its illusions remain potent nevertheless for the human beings who give them credit, and for whom realist narratives are the key means of making sense of their world. Its dramatic power lies in involving the audience through sympathy with characters. The quality of feeling evoked and its object can vary significantly, however, between different realist texts. Focused identification with a character outside the realm of any individual viewer's experience can itself lead to cognitive reorientation (see Chapter 6). Sympathetic feeling, as much as rational distance, functions as an important part of cognition and by these means, realism can at its best afford new understandings of human truths. Because it is ultimately a system of conventions of a language for describing the world, moreover, realism is neither monolithic nor static. The conventions within realism change and indeed other conventions for talking about the world emerge.

A body of criticism from a late-twentieth-century 'post-humanist' stance questions, however, the anthropocentricity of a realism, which locates its truth in character. In a sceptical age which doubts the capacity of human rationality to make sense of things, the ontological status of the worlds of realist fictions is in question. Indeed, the very foundation of a realist episteme which purports to secure knowledge of an object world has, as noted, come under attack. The integrity of personality distinctive of character in realist fiction is in doubt amongst anti-realists who stress instead the decentred nature of subjectivity.[8] Heavy emphasis is placed on the pluralism and 'otherness' of the world's cultures in place of the shared capacities of human beings universally.

At a theoretical level, these challenges to a dominant, liberal humanist, Western way of seeing are important and, in remaking the case for realism and humanism in this book, I do not intend that they should be lightly dismissed. But television is an everyday medium domestically consumed and its realisms still seem to serve a broad audience. Some commentators have sought to claim television, or aspects of it such as MTV, as archetypically postmodern (see Connor, 1989: 158–73). In discussing *Heartbeat* and *Twin Peaks* in this book, I address postmodernist texts insofar as new priniciples of construction have been developed in TV drama, but wholesale claims about television as postmodern medium seem overstated.

To many of its advocates, postmodernism is a disposition, a ready capacity to move in and out of diverse modes of response and interpretation. It is a new affective order, contra realism, which – freely or fearfully – refuses sense-making in the face of an indigestible information overload. It may be, as Jameson suggests, that new codes and conventions may ultimately become the new forms of realism (or at least of the mimesis of reality) (1984: 86), a new perceptual set, that is, by which future beings apprehend the world they inhabit. In the interim before we all get wired, however, it is worth reviewing the state of the frames used by the majority to mould their understanding.

III

This section looks again at a range of texts which – under the umbrella term 'realism/naturalism' – have not recently been distinguished. A spectrum is proposed in which family resemblances are not allowed to obscure significant differences. Provisionally the continuum runs from *photographic* to *critical naturalism* at the more 'objective', documentary end. It proceeds through a range of realisms: *fantasy realism, formulaic realism* and finally to *critical realism*. The purpose of distinguishing the faces in the family is to acknowledge the range of ideolects in TV drama realisms, provisionally only, since a full discussion of realist strategies is material enough for another book.

Different television programmes tacitly make differing truth-claims. The many news and current affairs programmes purport to be reflecting without bias what is happening in the historical world. That they do not simply do so – but tend rather to present, 'as the natural, self-explanatory and common-sensible way to see things. . . . the way things are seen from the offices of those in charge' (Inglis, 1990: 85) – has been explored in depth elsewhere and needs no repetition here.[9] With regard to drama, however, which is characteristically fictional though representational in British television, there are few overt truth-claims but there are certainly implications that the world of actuality is being reflected with greater or less fidelity.

In the range of documentary dramas, observational television approximating to the least interventionist *photographic naturalism* of the documentary methods are relatively rare and do not have a strong record of success. Documentary drama deploys some devices borrowed from 'factual' programmes to authenticate its truths, however, and these in turn have been borrowed by some veristic forms of dramatic naturalism and realism. The continuum between fact and fiction proposed here seems to suggest a duplicitous blurring of the distinction between truth and untruth and has indeed been the basis of ideology critique in media studies. In a more recent figuration, already noted and to be explored further below, both/and thinking offers the dissolution of the clear distinction between fact and fiction less as a conspiracy theory and more in terms of the ways in which, post-Wittgenstein, languages might be seen to be used.[10]

Documentary drama based on actual events and sometimes known as 'faction' is a small but significant part of British TV drama tradition. Two contentious instances in the 1980s, *Tumbledown* (BBC1, 1988) and *The Falklands Play* (script published 1987), documented by Geoffrey Reeves (in Brandt, 1993: 140–

61), reveal in their history of production – or non-production in the case of *The Falklands Play* – the contested nature of dramatizations of the 'factual'. Pursuing the elision betwen fact and fiction in the practices of viewing beyond this specific sub-genre, it is worth noting that a chance finding from a survey I conducted suggests that viewers are not always entirely clear which programmes present themselves as factual and which are fictional.[11] A drama series such as *Casualty* is scarcely distinguishable to some viewers' semi-attentive eyes from a documentary series such as *Jimmy's* based on an actual hospital, St James's in Leeds.

A considerable body of avowedly documentary drama – '*critical naturalism*' (1973: 86) in Williams's term – constructs fictional narratives based on specific aspects of the historical world though not on particular events. The most celebrated example of critical naturalism on television is Jeremy Sandford's *Cathy Come Home* (1966) shown in the *Wednesday Play* slot.[12] Sandford's play, in contributing to a debate about housing which resulted in Shelter, is one of the few dramas in any form that have had reciprocal impact on the historical world. That the effects of TV drama are not always overt, however, should not be read as indicating a lack of a more general effectivity. The irate responses periodically drawn by fictions which have a basis in actual events testify to their ability to contest the ground of dominant social assumptions.[13] Given that Establishment views claim to have immediate access to the facts, documentary drama which uses equivalently persuasive rhetoric to challenge orthodoxy can be effective in reorientating cognition. By retaining a commitment to the ethic of truth-telling, critical naturalists can call in question the 'discourses of sobriety' (Nichols, 1991: 3) on their own terms.

The objectivist, apparently unmediated, aspect of Naturalism passes, then, to documentary drama. Perhaps because, in the theatre, 'naturalism' remained the preferred term for work of verisimilitude, 'realism' and 'naturalism' became interchangeable terms for what here is called mimetic 'realism'. Turning, then, to TV drama realism, its characteristics seem to rest on that combination of mimesis and referentiality teazed out above. Drama which deploys mimetic conventions as a narrative strategy but makes no claim to refer to historical reality must be distinguished from those other realisms which do. The former

may be called fantasy realism. *'Fantasy realism'* is the basis of
'escapist' narratives in the Hollywood tradition, and becomes
flexiad drama in the looser narrative, or paratactical, structures of postmodern television (as in *Heartbeat*).

Realism's sustained tendency in television both to be referential and mimetically to make sense of the world is expressed
in this book by the term 'formulaic realism' to indicate that the
repetition of well-established conventions dominates the structuring principle (*Casualty*, for example). In spite of the conventional aspects, viewers are offered limited means by which
to negotiate their social reality. The criteria for the human
truth of the drama in this view are likely to be a perceived
correspondence with the way the reader sees and feels about
the world based on her own experience insofar as she is convinced by the plausibility of the world of the text in the broad
framework of the dominant realist-objectivist paradigm. The
range of complicit, negotiated or oppositional readings established by audience ethnographers comes into play since the
dominant viewpoint on offer, insofar as it is inscribed in the
textual structure, may nevertheless be rejected by detachment
from it. A range of engagements from different viewing positions is otherwise possible.

The sustained belief of many makers of popular programmes
that their constructions intersect with historical reality, that
they are taken to be both mimetic and referential, is evident.
Conventions are used to that effect. In the Realist novel full
description gave specificity to time and place, and apparently
random concrete detail served also to lend authenticity to its
constructed worlds. The environments of television soaps, series
and serials in contrast are physically constructed with varying
degrees of solidity. Phil Redmond, the originator of *Brookside*
(C4), was regarded as innovative in 1982 in rejecting the 'tired
conventions and flimsy stucco sets' (Gottlieb, 1993: 48) of the
soap genre, to use real houses in a real close for the environment of the drama.[14]

Redmond's stated aims for *Brookside* reveal, moreover, how
the solidity of the built environment was intended to authenticate the reality of the social world depicted:

I wanted to use the twice-weekly form to explore social issues,
and, hopefully, contribute to any social debate . . . From the

outset one of my main aims was to try and reflect Britain in the 1980s. . . . In 1982 I wanted to tackle the relevant social issues. Things like long-term unemployment, women's position in society, the black economy, the micro-technological revolution and its impact on both management and union structures within industry. Five years on, these issues are still a major concern to us, but the perspective has shifted slightly from the post-socialist society of the 1970s to the capitalist entrepreneurial ethic of the 1980s (cited in Gottlieb, 1993: 40).

These ambitions echo those of Naturalists such as Zola and the Goncourts who claimed to offer truer representations in their literary and dramatic experiments. With regard to the drama of his day, Zola argued that:

two formulas are before us: the naturalistic formula which makes the stage a study and picture of real life; and the conventional formula which makes the stage an amusement for the mind (1964: 155).

Additionally prefiguring modern controversies, the Goncourts were dismissive of mere entertainment. As Auerbach relates, they charged:

the public with corrupt and perverted taste; with preferring false values, pseudo-refinement, pruriency, reading as comfortable and soporific pastime books which end happily and make no serious demands on the reader (1953: 500).

Their challenge (one which might equally be addressed to Hollywood) anticipates those debates in modern popular culture over '*who defines reality* and *whose definitions of reality come to be commonly accepted as natural and true*' (Donald and Mercer, 1981: 70, their emphasis). The Naturalists frequently dealt in earthy matters which offended the respectable taste of the time. Correspondingly, *Brookside* has come to be the British soap most contentious in its engagement with social issues.

The concern convincingly to represent everyday life evident in Redmond's aims illustrates a continuity between late-nineteenth-century and late-twentieth-century drama. Notwithstanding Redmond's intentions, however, the dramatic format of soaps and its conditions of production and transmission militate against subtle portrayal of the minutiae of everyday life as found, for example, in Chekhov. There, 'thick description' (Geertz,

1993) sets character in a densely textured weft of personal, local, and broader histories, approximating 'agency in structure'. The competitive production context of a modern soap, in contrast, gravitates towards entertainment and away from slow, oblique unfolding of narrative.

The premisses of Naturalist drama listed above serve to point the differences. Because of its 'pre-watershed' slot in the schedules, *Brookside* cannot offer uncensored imitation of human behaviour. Frequently censured for being more daring than most, *Brookside*'s use of strong, street language on its inception came under the scrutiny of television's regulatory authorities. It was forced to temper its characters' expletives.[15] With regard to pace, the soaps (and other prime-time dramas) cut from high-point to high-point of intensity in the action as noted in the account of flexi-narrative. This selection of the intense moments of the drama – invited by the forces of cultural production outlined in Chapter 2 which demand that viewers' attention is 'grabbed' and held – does not afford the inclusion of 'the commonplace, the inessential, the irrelevant detail'. Where Chekhov suggested intense, internal conflict amidst the superficially unremarkable business of day-to-day living, soaps and series articulate everything at great pace on the surface.

The segmented construction of TV drama militates against everyday speech. A segment often ends on a 'punch-line', a witty remark or a barbed comment or a melodramatic revelation. Dialogue which reflects how people really speak is rare in TV drama since an inarticulate demotic precisely would not make sense as one disjointed utterance was overlaid on another. Because of the flexi-narrative pace, the characters are required to have and to articulate an unusual self-knowledge and self-awareness of their feelings and motives. In turn the verbal articulateness of the characters pre-empts the need for other televisual modes of exploration of character in society.

Besides the intention convincingly to portray ordinary life, what remains from the conventions of Naturalist drama is a style of acting and production which, except in rare examples,[16] does not overtly acknowledge the presence of the audience. The reproduction of real locations also remains as a convention though with variable success, as noted. Similarly, the employment of real properties and the wearing of authentic costumes, usually from contemporary life is retained.

Above all, the means of production tend to restrict the televisual vocabulary to the Mid-Two-Shot and the Close-Up, as recounted in Chapter 1, even in the more real (in the sense of non-studio based) locations of *Brookside* or *EastEnders*. This limited vocabulary may have the desired effect of drawing the viewer into the interpersonal relations, but at the expense of the placing of the characters and action in the broader sweep of socio-historical forces as desired, in their very different ways, by earlier realists such as Lukács and Brecht.[17]

Even where social issues are in play, they tend to be personalized rather than located in broader social or political processes. This difference from the Realism admired by Lukacs in the nineteenth-century European Realist novel is increasingly marked even in formulaic realism. As the diachronicity of history is called in question by a range of theorists of the postmodern, a sense of historical development fades also from television screens as period setting reduces history to heritage.

'Formulaic realism', then, would embrace most of the mainstream drama soaps, series and serials. They are mimetic – that is to say they conform to a familiar structural pattern – but in varying (mainly limited) degrees they retain referentiality to aspects of contemporary society. The shaping forces of their series' formulae and the conditions of their production tend, however, to preclude them from a fully convincing truth-to-life in the Realist tradition. They are usable stories which occasionally break the frames of their conventions to be highly usable, offering local, human truths in the terms of the (philosophical) realist paradigm.

To its critics, however, 'classic realism' as discussed above habitually distorts. It does not just reproduce reality, it makes sense of it. Indeed the essence of realism in their view is that it reproduces reality in such a form as to make it easily understandable. There is an intimation of a cooking of the case. Reality is not presented raw in all its contradictions, as in the intentions of the Naturalists: it is shaped through habitual human percepts, not as Realism's totalizing, explanatory account of the world, but simply for ready consumption by audiences. Ideology is deemed to be at work in Terry Lovell's formulation of it as, 'the production and dissemination of erroneous beliefs whose inadequacies are socially motivated' (1980: 50).

With these observations the heart of the matter may be

directly approached. In all that has been said above about Realism, Naturalism and modern TV realisms and naturalisms it is evident that it proves impossible for human beings to be strictly objective since they can never entirely transcend their subjectivities. As Thomas Nagel (1986) observes, however, it is a distinctive capacity of human beings to be able to stand outside their subjective position and see things from broader perspectives, even whilst they can never completely abandon their subjectivity. This feature allows humans to study and to represent the object world more or less 'objectively', even though the structures of language in which they formulate their percepts are ultimately shaping forces on the construction of that world. Unless the anthropocentric view is discarded – and in Nagel's view it is by no means the only possible perspective – human 'objectivity', embracing subjectivity, is the basis of human truth. Human percepts in this view are testable against, and may be modified by, a broader apprehension producing what is taken to be a more comprehensive model of the world.

Thus, through realist representations in TV drama, aspects of contemporary society may be explored. Representations constructed in human languages – perhaps particularly in symbolic formations such as TV dramas – can be tested against the viewers' experience in situated practices. It is on the basis of human intelligence and ability to take a more 'objective', broader view of the world that distinctions between fuller and more limited realisms ultimately rests, rather than on any claim about transparency of language and the ability neutrally to represent the historical world. The different discourses in play in any language inevitably contest regimes of truth. This book's critique of formulaic realisms is made in these terms.

TV drama's habitual realism, its seeming inability to engage in avant-garde experimentation with forms which more readily acknowledge the subjectivity of their visions, might be tentatively accounted for in terms of the cognitive assimilability of realism as an explanatory paradigm. Its modality corresponds to human beings' strong inclination to make sense of the world. In the form of narratives, the importance of which cannot be overstated in the context of human sense-making, stories told in the realist mode prevail in popular culture over more disturbing alternatives. If the world is unknowable, meaningless and chaotic, and one of the purposes of the arts is to construct symbolic formations reflecting this perception beyond the materialist-objectivist paradigm, then realism is outmoded. Antirealist strategies in the avant-garde arts of the twentieth century purport to challenge the positivist-determinist paradigm and to acknowledge subjectivity, drawing attention to the many (rather than a singular) ways of representing the world, or subsequently, from a poststructuralist position, indeed denying the possibility of representation. But television viewers, typically unfamiliar with avant-garde codes and conventions and contemporary critical theory, are confused by the lack of a sense-making frame and switch off.

In these circumstances, a dominant paradigm, particularly when settled in its representations into self-perpetuating formulae, needs a reflexive shake-up to prevent ossification. That is why the final category of realism proposed, critical realism (along with the rare examples of non-naturalism), is of the greatest importance. In the argument of this book it carries the highest value amongst realisms by offering the most usable stories in the foreseeable operational context of TV drama. Dennis Potter has made the point with clarity and force:

> Most television ends up offering its viewers a means of orientating themselves towards the generally received notion of 'reality'. The best naturalist or realist drama . . . breaks out of this cosy habit by the vigour, clarity, originality and depth of its perceptions of a more comprehensive reality. The best non-naturalistic drama, in its very structure, disorientates the viewer smack in the middle of the orientation process which television perpetually uses. . . . It shows the frame in the picture when most television is showing the picture in the frame (cited in Brandt, 1981: 27).

It is precisely because representations of reality are conventional, that they are shaped through human percepts in the realist mode (or indeed any other mode) that there is a constant danger, exacerbated by the institutional and other shaping influences noted in this book, of a reiteration of formulae.

A critical realism or naturalism has the potential to shake the too easy habits of cognitively assimilable formulae by addressing in the guise of authority a contemporary issue of ethical seriousness. In taking an unorthodox stance, it has the power to shock, to engage the audience's less common thoughts and

feelings if only those of outrage. This is particularly effective
if the drama's discursive position stands outside the Establishment. Indeed the case implicitly made in this book for restor-
ing something of the authority of writer/producers' supply-side
aesthetics with a distinctive vision rests not on a foundational
claim, but more pragmatically on the demonstrable ability of
some people to articulate fresh perspectives. The TV spaces for
risk-taking have diminished, however, as ratings discourse has
taken over.

Critical realism shakes, if it does not actually break, the frame
of TV drama's realist mould. Key examples will be discussed
in the following chapter. In the interim some brief, general
observations may be made. Potter speaks of 'a more comprehensive reality'. By this I take him to mean something akin to
the transcendence of a narrowly subjective viewpoint in Nagel's
sense of humans' capacity to stand outside their own local and
personal perspective. Without pretending to the absolutism of
objectivity, the concept of the broader view embracing many
perspectives affords us precisely Potter's sense of a more comprehensive world view.

A broad view, moreover, allows for human activity to be
treated as 'situated practices'. It affords connections to be made
between human behaviour and the social, historical and political conditions of life which inform it. As Inglis observes of TV
dramas: '[i]f they are serious, their business is indeed with the
hardship of situating agency within structure' (1988: 41). Formulaic realism, in contrast, tends to focus upon a narrow band
of human experience centred in institutionalized and individualized heterosexual relationships lent dynamism by a context
of contrived, melodramatic action.

An effect of the collapse of 'Realism' into 'classic realism'
has been to undermine any critical stance based upon the criterion of ethical seriousness and adequacy to the real. *Heartbeat*
and *Boys from the Blackstuff* become indistinguishable: both are
consigned to the MacCabe's amorphous heap of 'classic realist texts'. The restoration of a distinction between mimesis and
referentiality and a consequent broadening of the range of
realisms tentatively proposed here by way of illustration and
argument patently does not mark a return to positivism or a
notion of objective truth. It merely recognizes that the narrative frames in TV drama which serve a very large number of

human beings to negotiate an understanding of everyday life may be more or less varied or comprehensive in terms of a measure of human 'objectivity'.

Ways of seeing are always conventional and ideological but those of Realism, as established above, approximate most closely to the rational empirical view of the world which is Western culture's privileged, though not uncontested, form of knowledge. Fictional worlds might be taken to parallel the hypothetical models of scientists, which as Popper and others have shown are taken in a post-Einsteinian science to be no more than the best explanatory accounts of reality human beings can give at any one time, but falsifiable when tested against observation and experience.[18] In order that a limited range of formulaic conventions should not be mistaken for the Truth, it is vital, as in a self-reflexive science, that rigidifying ways of seeing are shaken frequently, as Potter advocates, to prevent them from becoming fixed. Non-realist strategies are, in Potter's view, the best means to achieve the shock of recognition that habitual views can be misprisions. Given, however, that realism has remained TV drama's dominant cultural mode for the reasons noted, a critical realism is vital.

As Guildenstern observes in Stoppard's re-working of *Hamlet*:

> All your life you live so close to the truth, it becomes a permanent blur in the corner of your eye, and when something nudges it into outline it is like being ambushed by a grotesque (1968: 28).

Formulaic realism is conducive to the permanent blur; critical realism is the agent of the grotesque.

IV

Finally, to frame a key question bluntly: assuming the existence of an object world, to what extent is it possible to perceive that world other than through the codes of a language? If, as in Wittgenstein's formulation, 'the limits of *language* . . . means the limits of my world' (1961: 57), what cannot be said cannot have meaning. To apply the question prosaically to TV drama: if a criterion of realist drama is truth-to-life, how is it possible to gain access to actuality to verify or falsify the truth of the drama's world other than through a language, a code parallel with – indeed with regard to realism, in the view of philosophical realists, identical to – that in which the drama is articulated? One answer, derived from the later Wittgenstein, would be to recognize the ways in which language is used and to acknowledge that linguistic utterances are not merely statements of positivist fact. The distinction between human objectivity and human imagination is then less firmly drawn.

There are different positions amongst contemporary theorists concerning the ontological status of the historical and fictional worlds. As Bannet formulates it, the matter of dispute precisely concerns where the line is drawn between fact and fiction:

> Objectivist theories generally hold that the line falls between different ways of employing language, and that they can determine which discourses are factual and which are fictional. Postmodern theory, on the other hand, places all discourse in the fictional camp by drawing its fiction/fact line between all of language and all of reality (1993: 113).

Naturalism and Realism tended towards the correspondence theory of truth which, according to Bannet, 'holds that discourse either has to duplicate reality or not and that discourse is fictional when it does not' (1993: 113). Realist drama's truth cannot ultimately depend, however, on a claim to duplicate reality for its worlds are imaginary, evidently fictional constructs. But the difference between TV drama's relationship to actuality and that between the news and the historical world appears to be a matter of degree rather than of kind, as established in the continuum from news through documentary naturalism to realism.

A resolution to this paradox of realism may be found in both/and thinking as indicated at the outset of this book. If the correspondence theory of truth is less strictly held, fantasy and illusion need not be set in mutually exclusive opposition to fiction and fantasy. Imagination and invention can be acknowledged as aspects of our understanding of 'the real'. To collapse the fact/fiction binary divide and take this view is to look at the continuum of realisms established above from the other end. Instead of placing emphasis upon the adequacy to the real of referential realist fictions, it is to stress the fictional elements of 'factual' programmes. It is not, however, like the postmodern semiotic idealists discussed above, to deny referentiality all together. Stories may be both taken as true and yet not mistaken for the Truth.

Critical criteria in terms of referentiality to the real established in Realism may thus be retained whilst fully acknowledging the element of fictionality, or constructedness through percepts, of the possible worlds of TV drama. As noted, if the constructed worlds of television are fictional in that they do not duplicate the historical world they must 'nevertheless 'fit' or at least intersect with something beyond themselves to provide knowledge of any kind' (Bannet, 1993: 113).

The possibility of cognition through responding with both feelings and the intellect to TV drama is thus acknowledged, with the 'fit' between the fiction and the actual worlds resting at times on referentiality. Alternatively mimetic but non-referential fictional worlds such as that of *Heartbeat*, for example, may be seen, by offering other possible worlds, to intersect in other ways with social actuality. They may even be taken by some viewers as a critique of the harsher world of historical reality, whilst others may use them as a flight from the present. What people do with the possible worlds in the fictional constructions of TV drama forms part of the discussion of Chapter 7.

In sum, the tracing of their genealogy reveals that the traditional premisses of Realism and Naturalism have been diluted and largely abandoned both conceptually and in institutionalized practices. At worst the two dominant uses of 'realism' explored above are flatly contradictory: Realism asserting truth-to-life in terms of probability and referentiality to the everyday; 'classic realism' endorsing mimesis as a set of conventions for story-telling but denying referentiality and probability. There would indeed appear to be some sense in John Corner's proposal cited at the outset of this chapter that the term 'realism' might better be abandoned, but that is no simple matter. Moreover, as the discussion above evidences, there are grounds for retaining the conceptual frame of realism notwithstanding the postmodern challenge (see Williams, 1994: 288). For the purpose of further discussion of critical realism in this study, I shall borrow in addition Bannet's term 'factitive fictions' (1993: 113).

As noted in Chapter 2, the commercial pressure to diversify

and extend the channels of television discourse tends towards the proliferation of dislocated signs with the possible consequences of a sacrifice of the traditional frames of sense-making, but without their replacement with a critical postmodernism. Moreover, in considering a text such as *Heartbeat*, Baudrillard's conception of the simulacrum seems apt. For, in its more extreme evasions, the mimetic spectacle of fantasy realism does indeed appear to have begun to replace seriousness under the sign of the real.

The increasing drift towards 'un-realization' may be stemmed, however, by recognizing that no language is neutral but accepting that there is nevertheless a dimension of referentiality in some fictional realisms. As long as realism remains the popular mode of TV drama, alternative views presented within the realist form – factitive fictions – offer the most usable stories pursuing the ethic of truth-telling to nudge human truths into focus. Improved technology and cinematic influence currently affords that possibility, though it may run counter to the tide of postmodern culture and its new affective order.

6 Framing 'the Real'

Oranges, Middlemarch, X-Files

'The truth is out there' (*The X-Files*)

I

The TV drama serials *Oranges Are Not the Only Fruit* (BBC2, 1990) and *Middlemarch* (BBC1, 1994) illustrate the case, opened in theory in Chapter 5, for critical realism in contemporary TV drama practice. As both serials are adaptations of novels of the same titles, their transposition to the screen serves additionally to bring out the influence of factors in the force field under discussion. George Eliot's thousand-page Realist classic, *Middlemarch*, is subjected to the dehistoricizing tendencies of popular television forms in postmodernity. Jeanette Winterson's own adaptation, in contrast, softens the fantasy frame of the novel to give the television version a more rooted grounding in televisual 'reality' to meet the audience's preference for habitual naturalism.

My final example, *The X-Files*, frames 'the real' differently by articulating a fashionable 1990s mind-set with regard to truth and knowledge. This may amount to no more than an entertaining play with the paranormal in the television sci-fi tradition of *Quatermass* (BBC, 1953), *Dr Who* (BBC, 1963) and *Kolchak, The Night Stalker* (ABC, 1974). But the series demonstrates interestingly another approach to blurring the boundaries between fact and fiction, consonant with that disposition to undecidability noted of the new social configuration. Whilst it is to an extent grounded in a recognizable world, *X-Files'* framing of 'the real' is more concerned with a disposition towards what might be regarded as real than the representation of an intricate weft of social life.

All three examples are factitive fictions, though each is very

different from the others. They retain, that is, a significant
element of referentiality to historical worlds. But the human
experience they treat is shaped in part by both the sense-
making frames of mimetic realism generally and by the specific
demands of the transitional postmodern moment in TV drama
production. All three appeal to 'quality' markets whilst espousing popularity and, together, the examples illustrate the *local*
(regional, UK) product (*Oranges*), the *national* flagship piece
with an eye to overseas sales (*Middlemarch*), and the North American, *transnational* product (*The X-Files*).

Marshment and Hallam have reiterated in the mid-1990s that:

> [f]or a text to be popular it must be both accessible and
> enjoyable [and] . . . in popular narratives realism continues
> to be the dominant form (1994: 145).

Each of the three examples deals with well-defined central
characters set in solid, identifiable locations inviting from the
audience credibility in their worlds as a basis for identification
and sympathy with character. Nevertheless, each blurs at the
same time, though in different ways, the fact/fiction divide. The
dramas employ a range of devices (musical, filmic, special effects, poetic, frame-shaking) which go beyond strict Naturalism
and the norms of TV formulaic realism to open up perspectives
at best eliciting an active and complex seeing from readers.

The two serials invite viewers to be detached and involved,
even to laugh and cry in the same moment, but neither ultimately allows sentiment to dissipate a critical perspective on the
contemporary historical world. *X-Files* draws viewers into its
narratives to chill and thrill ('Don't watch it alone'), but other
aspects of the series evince a reflective detachment, at least
gesturing at philosophical speculation.

The British serials invite an initial comparison and I shall
discuss them first before turning to *X-Files*. Both are set in the
regions of England, *Middlemarch* in the Midlands and *Oranges*
in a Lancashire mill town. Both are concerned with social re-
forms in the name of liberation from a stagnant and stultifying
tradition which offers itself as the natural way of life. In their
settings and major characters they thus reflect oppositional
strains of resistance to entrenched power. *Oranges*, particularly,
locates its anchor-point of view with a lesbian sub-culture under-
represented (until recently)[1] in British (let alone transnational)

television. Indeed, insofar as history is identified with the law of the father, *Oranges* invites an escape for young women from history in Jess's rejection of patriarchy, represented more in the church through the figure of the Pastor than by her virtually silenced adoptive father. *Middlemarch*, in contrasting parallel, illustrates the experience of an idealistic young woman frustrated, both sexually and politically, by a stultifying, hegemonic male order. Both television serials thus connect with the tradition of social realism identified as distinctive of the history of British TV drama but they also break from it, making no claims to documentary truth. They are imaginative fictions which intersect with aspects of their respective contemporary historical actualities.

The television version of *Middlemarch* transmitted more than 160 years after the period in which the novel is located, raises interesting questions of relevance to a (post)modern epoch. George Eliot, writing in the Realist mode, offers in her novel a reflective commentary on social progress in the nineteenth century. A similar referentiality, though differing in detail, is an important aspect of the TV drama from the point of view of Andrew Davies, the adaptor, but with reference to the 1990s as well as 1830s social context. There are resonances for Davies between Lydgate's frustrated attempts to introduce a health service to Middlemarch and the erosion of Britain's National Health Service in the 1990s.[2] More generally, as evidenced in the rise and fall of Bulstrode, there is a correlation to be drawn between the hypocrisy of moralizing financiers today whose material success, like that of their nineteenth-century predecessors, is sometimes based on moral graft and corruption. But, as the discussion below reveals, a range of forces in the production and reception of *Middlemarch* in 1994 militate against the television text as social critique.

Nevertheless, both *Middlemarch* and *Oranges* potentially have something to say about contemporary politics, sexual or civic. *Oranges* confronts more overtly a mainstream audience in sympathetically representing a lesbian perspective and thus giving a voice to a historically marginalized group. Both television serials, however, pick up on their source novels' interrogation of the yet dominant viewpoint of Western society – that of the caucasian, heterosexual, male, middle class.

Above all, each serial situates agency in structure, dealing with the experience of individuals whose lives are threatened to be constrained and diminished by social forces. They thus challenge social conventions, political orthodoxies and habitual ways of seeing in the name of freedom for the typical individual imbricated in resistible, and possibly mutable, social forces. Whilst the main characters, that is to say, are individuated and realized dramatically, the focus of interest is not solely upon their distinctive psyches but also on their representativeness of a social group or class. Thus *Middlemarch* and *Oranges* treat seriously issues concerned with the lives of ordinary people in the socially extended tradition of realism, and draw viewers into their possible worlds to make them care about the characters. But, in so doing, neither is lacking either in entertainment value nor a range of perspectives to invite a complex seeing.[3]

Both serials achieved critical acclaim but were also relatively popular. *Middlemarch* achieved five million viewers on average per episode. In full awareness of the challenging nature of *Oranges*, Jeanette Winterson was more pleased by its 'street success' than by critical accolades (see 1994: 81). Neither *Middlemarch* nor *Oranges* approaches the 13–15 million audience for *The X-Files, Heartbeat* or *Casualty* but they demonstrate that critical realism can attract a very significant audience. In the space available it is not possible to give a full account of the two serials. The aim here is to bring out through analysis of selected extracts some family resemblances which distinguish critical realism from the other realisms and naturalisms delineated in Chapter 5, and to convey a sense of why factitive fiction of this kind may yet be the dramatic form offering the most usable stories with an ethic of truth-telling in television.

II

The story of *Oranges Are Not the Only Fruit* concerns a young girl, Jeanette in the novel but Jess in the screen version, who has been adopted and brought up by a dynamic evangelist, listed in the script simply as Mother. The narrative traces Jess's unconventional upbringing in an otherwise typical Lancashire mill-town of the 1950s with a life that revolves around the small group of mainly elderly women that gravitates towards the influence of Mother in the sect, and the Pastor whom she reveres.

The scenes are very short, indeed as short for the most part as any flexi-narrative. The difference, however, is that one story, that of Jess's childhood and adolescence, is the focus; indeed Jess appears in virtually every scene. Thus, whereas in flexi-narrative characters tend to be two-dimensional and narratives to be fragmented and undeveloped, *Oranges* develops and rounds the characters of Jess and Mother, tracing their relationship over a decade.

In finding she has a sexual preference for women as she matures, Jess is brought openly into conflict with the rigid moralism and religiosity of the sect. In one of the most powerful scenes in the TV serial version, Jess is the subject of a kind of exorcism purporting to oust the devil who has inculcated '*Unnatural passions*' (Winterson 1994: 128) in her. This experience in which she is bound and gagged by the Pastor – assisted by Mother and the other women – to be prayed over for three days causes her considerable confusion. She does not finally break with her home, however, until a second affair with Katy, whom she meets on a mission in Blackpool. Fearful that she and Katy might be subject to further oppression, she moves in to Elysium Fields, the funeral parlour run by the renegade Cissy with whom she finds part-time work to support herself whilst she takes the entrance examinations to Oxford. The narrative ends with Jess's success in gaining admission to the university and a way out of her restrictive environment.

In adapting her novel for the screen, Winterson was engaged in another fictional treatment of the facts of her own upbringing. She has acknowledged that the basis of *Oranges* is autobiographical but denies the work is an autobiography and directly challenges those who would reduce novel or screenplay to empirical fact.

> Of course it's true that I was brought up by Pentecostals but I have drawn on a number of influences and experiences in creating my story. And it is my story, not my life, in spite of the deafening cries of 'autobiography' and questions such as, 'Were you tied up and gagged?' (1994: 81).

A particularly interesting feature of the adaptation for the screen in the light of the realist tradition of TV drama texts, however, is Winterson's perception that some of the anti-realist devices of the novel would need to be abandoned. She 'knew that real changes had to be made to [her] experimental, in many ways anti-linear, novel to render it the kind of television that would bring viewers in off the streets' (1994: 72–3). In particular, she drastically reduced the frame of 'fairy tales and allegorical passages . . . [which] worked as a kind of Greek Chorus commenting on the main events' (1994: 72). In so doing Winterson is drawn – albeit gently and from a distance – by the Realist and Naturalist impulse to articulate everything through the mouths of the characters and to suppress other compositional devices. Winterson is aware, however, that adaptation is a matter of transposing as best as possible the perspectives inscribed in the devices of the novel into the established conventions of TV drama. She realizes that:

> [t]he camera, with its silent ability to offer other dimensions to what appears to be happening, works as a mute Greek Chorus. The power of the image means that you don't always have to spell it out (1994: 72).

In sum, Winterson understands that in the medium of television there is a need to work within the framework and conventions of the dominant realist paradigm but that TV drama is not restricted in this mode to an empiricist 'factuality'.

At the level of historical fact she reports that, intertwined with elements of her own upbringing, there are aspects of the imaginary which may or may not draw on actuality:

> Characters who never existed, never could exist, jostle alongside some that did. I don't know how much people believe of all this. What I do know is that it is the fusion of fact and fiction, the conscious deliberate merging of different realities and unrealities, that makes *Oranges* so compelling (1994: 82).

Winterson thus recognizes in the practice of her adaptation the theoretical conclusion of Chapter 5: that the hard line which people would like to draw between fact and fiction is artificial, the delusion of a positivist science that would reduce all knowledge to empirical fact on the one, positivist hand and the tendency to treat everything as fiction on the postmodern other.

In making the screeenplay Winterson is explicit, moreover,

about the need to 'offer a consistently surreal world view to make up for the flights of fancy and the suggestiveness of language that [she] felt could not be included' (1994: 72). She relates that a favourite passage in the novel was effectively an essay on the differences between history and story-telling. Winterson needed to:

> dissolve and scatter [the authorial intrusion] throughout the three episodes. The characters are always telling stories, to each other, about themselves, even to themselves, and set against this is the notion of history, objectivity, fact. In virtually every scene there are two definitions of reality at work (1994: 72).

Indeed it is this aspect of the TV serial, amounting to a technique of construction, which invites complex seeing. For although *Oranges* is centred in Jess's point of view, the perspective is neither singular nor exclusive. It is precisely this feature, moreover, which gives the lie to the notion posited by MacCabe and the 1970s conventionalists that the 'classic realist text cannot deal with the real as contradictory' and that it 'ensures the position of the [reading] subject in a relation of dominant specularity' (1974: 24) beyond contradiction. For, as Christopher Williams notes:

> narrative forms and narrative discourse are frequently questioning and very frequently in conflict within and between themselves (1994: 280).

MacCabe's notion that a metadiscourse subsumes and controls all the other discursive articulations in as complex a structure as a film or TV drama simply fails to take account of both the range and flexibility of the uses of realist conventions and reading practices.[4]

A remnant of the allegorical and fairytale frame of the novel is evident in the fantasy sequences which open each episode of the TV serial. The first and third episodes feature fairgrounds and the second the interior of the sect's church. All three involve elements of the grotesque as characters familiar to Jess (and subsequently to the audience) appear distorted or masked. The first sequence located in an old-fashioned steam fair finds all the major figures from the sect riding horses on the merry-go-round. From the camera's and Jess's point of view, their grinning faces merge with the exaggerated teeth, curled lips and flared nostrils of the merry-go-round horses. Small Jess (the child played by Emily Aston) drifts to the fortune teller's tent where she is told, 'You'll never marry and you'll never be still' (Winterson 1990: 85). In another distorted pre-figuration of the action, Jess (the adolescent played by Charlotte Coleman) is confronted by a hooded and masked figure of Melanie (to be her first lover) in a carriage emerging from the tunnel of love. Jess '*gets into the carriage which disappears into the tunnel*' (Winterson 1994: 85; emphasis indicates directions).

The haunting quality of this fantasy sequence, setting the 'reality' of the fictional world at a distance, is sustained through-out the series in the music track drawing on the sound of a steam organ which in its hollow reverberations and syncopated rhythms echoes the sense of seeing the world otherwise as if in a house of distorted mirrors. From the outset it is thus signalled that an alternative, slightly ironic, perspective is on offer and the music gently but persistently reminds viewers of it.

In the discussion of realism and naturalism in the previous chapter no mention was made of music, for in strict Naturalism only diegetic sound is admissible. In film and television practice, as noted in Chapter 1, however, a non-diegetic, music sound-track has become so much an accepted convention that it tends to be 'overheard' (as in overlooked) by audiences. Typically in mimetic realist convention it is intended that the music should be unobtrusive as it serves to underscore the emotion of the dramatic moment, but – as Brecht's collaborator, Kurt Weill, was aware – music can operate, like Winterson's Greek Chorus, to comment on the action.[5] In *Oranges* the music track precisely does not close down the possibilities of the incident but acts as Brecht envisaged in his 'Epic Opera' (1964: 38) as an ironically humorous commentary on the action to invite a critical distance and awareness in viewers of a range of ways of seeing.

Besides the devices of fantasy and the use of music, Winterson deploys a number of TV drama naturalist techniques of com-pression of time and space to achieve the effect of disjunction in continuity. In shifting from the penultimate to the final scene in Episode Two, for example, she deploys a common device of bringing in the sound cue of the following scene over the end of the concluding scene. Where this device is typically used to mask the edit, however, Winterson uses it with a twist.

Barred from seeing Melanie after the exorcism, Jess never-theless sneaks into her house at night and into her bedroom and bed. The scene ends:

JESS: Make love to me.
MELANIE: I can't, I can't.
JESS: Well, I'll make love to you. Let the sin be mine.
[*They start to make love*]
PASTOR: [*Voice over*] A soul redeemed for Jesus.
            INT. PARLOUR DAY
PASTOR, JESS, MOTHER, MAY, MRS GREEN, WILLIAM *is handing around cups of tea*
PASTOR: Don't you feel better Jess?
MOTHER: She does, you can tell.
MAY: She looks her old self again, eh Jess?
                              (Winterson 1994: 144; emphasis
                                 indicates directions).

The technique is effective in terms of television narrative com-pression but the transition from one scene to another is made to resound with the kind of multiple ironies which ultimately lend *Oranges* its distinctive tone. Jess is mocking the religiosity of the sect when she says, 'let the sin be mine' but the words are relocated in the spiritual context by the Pastor's voice-over. His observation, however, 'a soul redeemed for Jesus' operates on one level as a comment on Jess's and Melanie's love-mak-ing, as if conferring Jesus's seal of approval. His following words in the parlour, however, are on the surface a self-satisfied allu-sion to the exorcism he has conducted but are readable in the context as Jess feeling the better for her night with Melanie. Mother's and May's platitudes serve only to confirm the sense that – quite the opposite of their reading of the situation – any visible improvement in Jess arises from sexual satisfaction rather than from the exculpation of the devil. If Jess is her 'old self again', it is the self of the physical lesbian lover not that of the transcendent, spiritually 'elect'.

Putting music to another use with the kind of irony evident above, Winterson has considerable fun with hymns and gnomic biblical utterances. At the opening of Episode Two, prefiguring its action, perhaps, the congregation are heard singing 'While I Was Sleeping Somebody Touched Me'. Towards the end of the episode, as Melanie and Jess innocently enter the church to meet their denunciation after spending a night together at Elsie's house, the Pastor is reiterating one of his habitual prayers: 'Some are sick and some are sad and some have lost the joy they had' (Winterson, 1994: 137). In the murk of the subsequent events of the exorcism, an irony resounds from these words raising the question who exactly is sick and what quite is the lost joy. Winterson thus deploys to effect the principle of montage with one image, verbal or visual or both, projecting forward on to the next or backwards on to its precedent to change it and create additional perspectives. It is through a combination of techniques such as these that Winterson creates the space which affords, indeed invites, complex seeing from a fairly simple linear love story.

The soundtrack, and dialogue in particular, remains important to television in the face of a semi-attentive audience, as noted in Chapter 1. Much of the key information is still carried in the dialogue of popular TV dramas, almost as if they were radio plays. It will be apparent, however, that Winterson is demanding much more active attention from the audience in the play of visual image against music track or verbal utterance. Not only does *Oranges* confront through its subject matter, but its techniques in addition challenge the reader to respond to the various levels of meaning set in play.

Primarily a novelist, Winterson resists the postmodern drift away from a literary theatre tradition, from a verbal to a more visual culture, and the commercial drive informing the consumption of spectacular fragments in flexiad drama. She notes of formulaic realism, furthermore, that '[t]oo many writers, in all media, struggle for realism and all they get is naturalism; flat unapproachable situations, language so long dead it doesn't even smell anymore' (1994: 74).

The celebrated 'good ear for dialogue' in the Naturalist recording of the surfaces of life can, at its best, lend documentary conviction to a constructed world. Particularly in the case of dialect it can have a dynamism and vitality. As noted, however, what passes for naturalistic dialogue in much formulaic realism is 'caption-speak', utterances which – quite uncharacteristic of people in actuality – articulate their inner lives and concerns in pithy cliches. In contrast, the acceptance of the shaping force of tropes in a realism which does not insist on the distinct 'fact' of how people speak from the 'fictional' constructs of language

affords the vitality which Winterson admires in the dialogue of
Pinter and Bennett (see Winterson, 1994: 74).

Winterson's humorous word-play echoes that of the popular comedy writer/performer, Victoria Wood, who, like Alan
Bennett, draws on the ideolects of the North of England simultaneously with warmth and detached amusement.[6] The accuracy
of their observations is not a matter of dull empiricism but of
local truths expressed in a colourful vernacular. A few examples
from *Oranges* illustrate Winterson's exploitation of the distance
between pretensions to spiritual grandeur and the banality of
the parochial by the simple device of juxtaposition. Referring
to Pastor Spratt who inspired her conversion to the faith at a
Glory Crusade, Mother says:

> He was on his way to hot places like Africa but he came to
> us and to Wigan first (1994: 90).

Conflating the material everyday with the transcendent spiritual, Mother tells Jess who is seeking somewhere warm to
nurture her hyacinth bulbs for the school competition, 'You
don't need an airing cupboard when you've got Jesus' (1994:
96). In another example of the principle of verbal montage,
Mother is feeling sorry for herself in Birtwistle's cafe:

> MOTHER: I'd be thankful for my graveside. I need something
>   to put an end to my sorrows. Goodbye Cissy.
>   [*Exit Cissy*]
> MAY: Have a Horlicks.
>   (1994: 122)

These examples of the wit and humour in Winterson's vibrantly
realist, not dully naturalist, dialogue, tap into a vein of 1990s
popular humour as noted. Thus, although *Oranges* is in part
associated with the high cultural form of literature,[7] its popular discourses lend it broader accessibility.

There may be something peculiarly British, perhaps English,
regional even, about such writing and the humour derived from
it. It is grounded in those residual, rooted cultures which it is
the tendency of postmodernity to dislocate. It is hard to imagine
comprehension – let alone a positive reception – of *Oranges*
in America, for example. The serial, and my estimation of it,
implicitly poses questions about the drift to transnational production at the expense of regional, if not national, TV drama.

Further to illustrate the difference between routine and mechanical representations of human experience in formulaic television and the critical realism of *Oranges*, I turn finally to the latter's treatment of sex and violence. Both feature in *Oranges*. Physical violence figures primarily in the exorcism scene which itself has sexual, even sadistic, overtones as the Pastor straddles Jess to hold her down and bind her. The sexual relationships of Jess with Melanie and then Katy, in contrast, are directed to convey an innocence of awakening passion and shot – in the case of the first nude encounter – sensitively in the glow of firelight. There is no coyness about the camera, however, and lust is not denied by a soft-focus sentimentalism. In Jess's second physical relationship which Katy instigates, the writer's directions make this point clear. The two young women have returned from a night of – for Jess unaccustomed – fun at the fair (not a fantasy steam fair but with echoes of the fantasy sequences). They are outside Katy's family caravan but there is nobody within:

KATY: Well, good night then.
[*She steps forward towards* JESS *and gives her a hug. It's a very tight hug.* JESS *pulls back and looks at* KATY. *It's very close, face to face. Slowly* KATY *moves to kiss her;* JESS *hesitates then joins in. No hurry about this shot*]
(1994: 152; emphasis indicates directions).

The sexual moments are not routine and mechanical, heterosexual encounters. That they are between two women in itself places them outside of television's norms, but they are additionally charged by the context setting agency in structure. Jess has been seen to be physically as well as mentally tortured by and for her sexual preference. Her social world is generally sexually repressive but draws on specific heterosexual cultural 'norms' to castigate Jess who, it is alleged by Pastor, has 'taken on a man's appetites' (1994: 157).

Jess's sexual behaviour, which is not static and mechanical but develops from an innocent initial exploration with Melanie to a fully conscious choice implied by the hesitation in the extract above with Katy, is an example of situated practice. Her sexual preference is set against Mother's own sexual repression and the deflection of her sexual energies into religious zeal.

This dimension is subtly portrayed but evident in the TV serial. The relation between religiosity and sexuality is pointed early in Mother's account of her conversion at the Glory crusade:

> The preacher looked just like Errol Flynn but holy. [*she sighs.*] Yes, a lot of women found the lord that week (1994: 90).

The physical attraction of Pastor Spratt for Mother is substantiated by her continuing to have his photograph by her bed. In contrast her sexual relationship with her husband is non-existent: in her naivety Small Jess probes the, to her, odd feature that 'When you're in bed he gets up and when he gets up you're in bed' (1994: 95). Mother does not want to talk about it. Her agitation when 'Next door are at it again' (1994: 115) reinforces a sense of repression (or transference) of her sexuality following her one-off physical relationship in Paris with Pierre in her youth (1994: 130–1). Espousing a conventional puritanism, she equates sexuality with sin and she sees worldly pleasures as a deflection from life's purpose. In spite of the singularity of her religious zeal and the humour directed at her, Mother is thus drawn by Winterson as a rounded character, the multiple dimensionality of which is well brought out by Geraldine McEwan's performance in the serial.

Oranges may gain its primary credibility as a TV drama in constructing a credible world with believable central characters in accordance with the realist paradigm, but it gains its critical resonances from its metaphors, its departures from a dull, flat and mechanical naturalism or formulaic realism. *Oranges* rescues the 'sin that dare not speak its name' (1994: 137) from its denial by omission from public discourse.

Oranges are the only fruit offered to Jess in her childhood. In hospital, Jess observes:

> I wouldn't mind a pineapple. I've been eating oranges for sixteen years. It's unnatural (1994: 129).

'Not oranges' thus comes to stand for 'otherness', for sexual otherness explicitly in terms of Jess's preference for the female gender but implicitly also for the cultural otherness beyond evangelical Christianity and the bounds of a repressive patriarchy and parochialism. In being one of a very few TV dramas openly to treat a physical lesbian relationship – and explicitly nude at that – the serial broke new ground. Its impact is dependent in part upon referential realism since it aims to establish lesbian experience as an aspect of the historical world. For this reason, Winterson cuts back, as noted, the allegorical and fairy-tale elements of the novel. She retains, however, sufficient devices in her factitive fiction to afford complex seeing of a possible world which might possibly be the world some human beings inhabit.

Lack of space precludes a full discussion of the reception of *Oranges* but two key points might be drawn from the account of Hilary Hinds (1992). The first concerns the lesbian relationships, the potential shock of which was to some extent defused in press response, according to Hinds, by the de-centring of the issue from the series. Instead of stressing the otherness of lesbianism, emphasis was placed by commentators upon a liberal humanist reading which sets Jess's sexual preference against the rich tapestry of human experience, almost implying it is something she will grow out of. Secondly, the difficulty for viewers of identifying with Jess, whose point of view as noted is central to the piece, was facilitated, in Hinds's account, by an accident of the history of the series' transmission. The first transmission fell shortly after the death threat to author, Salman Rushdie, issued in an Islamic *fatwah*. The public reaction to religious fundamentalism, subsequently mediated in the British press as an extremism which threatens the freedom of speech, lends justifiability to Winterson who, an author like Rushdie, must in a liberal democracy be seen to have the right to express her view. In terms of response to the series, the context of opposition to religious bigotry tended to draw sympathy for Jess in a negative reaction to the religiosity of the sect. When coupled with the pre-publicity for the serial which drew on the critical success of the novel and located the serial as an authored drama in the 'serious' Wednesday night slot (presumably harking back to *The Wednesday Play*), the transmission drew less reactionary opposition than it might otherwise have done.

Whatever the justifiability of Hinds's account, the point is reaffirmed that textual meaning – though texts are disposed to communicate a preferred view – is not fixed. Besides variable viewing positions, accidents of the history of transmission can lend aspects of a work more or less symbolic significance.

III

The dramatization of George Eliot's novel *Middlemarch* on BBC1 in the Spring season of 1994 brings into sharp focus a range of issues central to this book. These include: (dis)continuities in dramatic form and narrative tradition; the debate about the codes and conventions of television realism in relation to 'adequating the real'; questions of canonicity and ethical seriousness as criteria of value; and the capacity of 'serious' television drama to succeed aesthetically or commercially in the (post)modern production context.

In screening *Middlemarch,* the BBC extended its tradition of adapting the classics of English Literature for the small screen by taking on a work dubbed by A.S. Byatt 'the greatest novel in the English language' (in BBC, 1994: 5). Produced by Michael Wearing and with a screenplay by Andrew Davies, the serialization had a budget of six million pounds for the 300 minutes running-time of its six episodes. By any standards of TV drama production *Middlemarch* was expensive to make, as befitted its status as a flagship production for the BBC at a time when the future of the institution was in question. Such funding is made possible by the world sales potential of a prestigious British period drama with established actors such as Robert Hardy, Peter Jeffrey, Michael Hordern and Patrick Malahide to draw the audience. Motives other than profit might, however, inform the serialization. For, in a number of respects, the *Middlemarch* project surpasses in ambition and audience reach 'BBC classic drama' which, as designer Gerry Scott observes, 'used to be a studio production, mainly broadcast on Sunday afternoons at children's tea-time, and seen largely as being educational' (BBC, 1994: 30).

Middlemarch, in its contrasting novel and television serial forms, offers an excellent example for discussion of linguistic codes and conventions. Two issues are of particular interest in the context of this study: constructed mythologies (in Barthes's sense[8]) seeking to naturalize themselves as 'reality'; and the relative decline in (post)modern TV drama of a sense of history. The theoretical question of the facility of languages, and of the Realist form in particular, to 'adequate the real' has a particular contemporary relevance to the televisual dramatization of classic literature. For if a television serial could afford unmediated access to the past, it would be possible for the viewers to adjudge the quality of life and its ethical seriousness or otherwise in comparison with modern society. There is, however, no possibility of such unmediated access since all reconstructions cannot but be constructions ideologically shot through with modern ways of seeing.

There is, then, a primary question of the ability of the written language in the form of George Eliot's novel to give a full account of English society in the 1830s which it consciously professes to do. Questions then follow about the capacity of any language to recreate – as opposed to construct – myths of the past in visual and verbal imagery. Even assuming positive answers about the capacity of the written word or the medium of television, the ability to translate George Eliot's one-thousand-page prose fiction into a televison drama serial of six fifty-minute episodes would remain for consideration. The issue of adaptation as translation will be the focus of this discussion.

As established in Chapter 5, the conventions of Realism are homologous with the methodology of empirical science in that an attempt is made to transcend the subjective point of view to take a broader, more objective view of the world. As Nagel has noted, however, objectivity and subjectivity are themselves relative to different fields of enquiry:

> A standpoint that is objective by comparison with the point of view of one individual may be subjective by comparison with a theoretical standpoint still farther out. The standpoint of morality is more objective than that of private life, but less objective than the standpoint of physics. We may think of reality as a set of concentric spheres, progressively revealed as we detach gradually from the contingencies of the self (1986: 5).

A Realist novel such as *Middlemarch* advances percepts of how the social world operates, paralleling the hypotheses of science about the physical world. In some respects like a sociological study, it documents in detail its observations of lived experience in support of its way of seeing. The range and breadth of *Middlemarch*'s coverage of provincial town life in the 1830s approximates to a more objective view than is possible in a first person narrative. With regard to human intercourse, for example, an attempt is made to embrace both the inner and the outer perspectives of the characters and their lives, as it were the physical reality and the subjective experience of it.

Whilst Nagel acknowledges that the idea of objectivity 'applies to values and attitudes as well as to beliefs and theories' (1986: 5), the novel might be seen, in relation to his concentric spheres, to take the standpoint of morality, less objective than the physicist but well outside the personal. In contrast with the presumed scientific objectivity of Flaubert,[9] however, the authorial commentary of *Middlemarch* evidently presents the personal views of George Eliot (Mary Ann Evans) throughout. But, unlike the selfconscious mode of the writers of postmodern fiction, the viewpoint is not reflexively acknowledged. The relative suppression of point of view is important in varying fictional modes in terms of their apparent truth-claims. Though ultimately, as Nagel points out, 'we can't forget about those subjective starting points indefinitely: we and our personal perspectives belong to the world' (1986: 6).

In the dramatization of the novel, the viewpoint of the novelist and dramatizer, following the conventions of TV drama's realism, are suppressed. The world of Middlemarch is presented apparently unmediated, thus authenticating its presumed objectivity. It is not until the summary at the very end of the serial, when the later histories of the characters and George Eliot's observations on the significance of the lives of ordinary people are recounted over the visual images (in the voice of Judi Dench as George Eliot), that the authorial voice is overtly heard. This does not mean that the viewpoints of either George Eliot or Andrew Davies are absent from the serial – indeed there are interesting conflicts between them – but that their perspectives remain unacknowledged in accord with the conventional aspect of critical realism.

The process of dramatization for screen of a weighty and densely textured novel inevitably means selection, condensation and most significantly transposition from the medium of the written word to that of visual images with a soundtrack, bound, moreover, by the conventions of television drama. Inevitably in that process of translation Davies both reads (in Barthes's sense) and rewrites *Middlemarch* in part from his own point of view but with an eye to George Eliot's way of seeing. The notion of fidelity to the original, so often raised when a film or TV serial is made of a novel, is misplaced precisely in its failure to recognize that the process of dramatization is one of translation between languages which are not wholly commensurable. It reveals, furthermore, something of a characteristic 'high cultural' reification of a work implied in the conception of aura which, Benjamin famously notes, mechanical reproduction displaces.[10]

To take a specific example where the difference of viewpoint between Davies and Eliot informs the serial, Davies reads Eliot as being unable to resist revealing her views of characters even to the detriment of her narrative. She reveals, he argues, too much antipathy to Casaubon even before he appears in the novel such that his attraction for Dorothea is almost incomprehensible. Similarly, Davies feels that George Eliot cannot bear her readers to like any of her characters more than she does and that she is severe with characters such as Will Ladislaw and Rosamund Vincy whose physical attractiveness and shallow natures afford them, as she sees and presents them, too easy a life.

Davies's attempts to redress the balance – or tell the story from his point of view – were not entirely successful. Whilst his writing of a weighty and intelligent political speech for Ladislaw to deliver on Brooke's husting served successfully to lend a depth to his character – which Davies perceived to be necessary to make him worthy of Dorothea – his attempts conversely to lighten Casaubon prior to the marriage were to some extent foiled by Malahide's performance. The actor played his own reading of George Eliot's authorial viewpoint portentously against the grain of Davies's intended dramatization.

With regard to the process of translation, a televisual way of seeing and story-telling informed changes to the language and narrative structure of the prose fiction novel. Thinking in filmic language, producer Michael Wearing saw Middlemarch – and Lydgate's arrival in it – in terms of the iconography of a Western: Lydgate as the pioneering individual, the outsider riding in to town to make his mark. Thus the re-working of generic tropes may be seen to endorse Baudrillard's sense that media languages recycle themselves in a loop divorced from any historical reality. This kind of thinking also brings out the way in which the balance of a novel can be shifted by the very nature of translation between mediums governed by differing generic conventions.

The two stories centrally informing *Middlemarch* are those of Lydgate and Dorothea, two young idealists committed to progress through social reform. In the novel the two narratives are given roughly equal weight, Dorothea's if anything taking precedence. In the serial, however, it is Lydgate's story which seems stronger. The reason for this might be accounted for simply in terms of the different media. People who do things and make things happen suit the characteristically action-driven plotting of drama – particularly in realist forms – much better than thinkers, whose contemplations are more adequately expressed in the verbal medium of the novel which affords time and space for reflection. In the narrative, Dorothea is frustrated by being a woman constrained by social convention and by her repressive husband from actively engaging in projects. There is literally little she can do. In contrast, Lydgate, with the liberty of masculinity, is afforded the opportunity to visit his patients in and around the town, open a new hospital and engage in his practical medical research. This difficulty is emphasized by television producers' conception of an affective order and viewing conditions which takes as too slow the kind of pace of cutting which might afford reflection on the part of the audience. A tension between the demands of (post)modern television and the measured reflection demanded by the density and complexity of George Eliot's novel is played out in the process of dramatization.

Taking up Micheal Wearing's perspective, the title sequence – cut at sufficient pace to suggest a progressive dynamic – does show Lydgate approaching Middlemarch aboard a stagecoach. He observes the building work of the railway on its outskirts and merely remarks, 'the future'. Lydgate's bright disposition suggests a man ready for action in contrast with some of the more sleepy rural imagery of the shepherd driving the sheep with his dog and the slow traffic of carts in town. The music underscores this juxtaposition, increasing in tempo as Lydgate arrives on the scene. The serial's first sequence proper also involves horse-riding though, ironically in the light of the comments on action versus reflection above, featuring not Lydgate but Dorothea.

Whereas the novel opens with a discussion of religion which

might have yielded visual imagery but would scarcely have provided a dynamic opening likely to hook the casual television
viewer, Dorothea's horse-ride with her sister through the woods
affords cinematic dynamism with tracking shots and action
Close-Ups inter-cut to establish both character and location in
a visually interesting way. Making a further contribution to the
economy of condensation from weighty novel to the television
serial, the ride attempts in addition to solve a problem of the
characterization of Dorothea as Davies wished to construct her.
He recognized that the incidents of the narrative afforded
opportunities to bring out her spiritual and intellectual zeal but
that the passionate dimension of her nature – in Davies's view
a repressed sexuality – was more difficult to convey through the
plot action. The horse-riding sequence was intended to imply
Dorothea's wilful suppression of a potent aspect of her personality. Women riding can connote an active sexuality through
the associations of physical exertion and close sensual proximity to – and perhaps control over – a powerful animal. The
heat of the chase was intended to throw into relief Dorothea's
immediate announcement as she dismounts that she will give up
the activity. That the sequence may not entirely have conveyed
such an implication does not negate the point of the illustration,
namely that an attempt was being made to translate an aspect
of Dorothea's character which is dealt with obliquely in authorial commentary in the novel into a mainly visual language.

Another aspect of transposition affected by the differing
mediums is the mode of story-telling. Although *Middlemarch*
was originally serialized for publication by George Eliot, its intertwined narratives needed restructuring for a television version.
Where the novel traces one story across a considerable span
before moving to the next, the conventions of television drama
– accelerated in pace in developed TV practice as illustrated –
demands a much faster cutting between shorter narrative segments. The danger of this pacey mix when a number of stories
are being told is that it gravitates towards the soap format.
Segments are inter-cut so rapidly that no one narrative can be
developed with any subtlety and viewers are afforded no time to
engage deeply with in emotional terms, and/or reflect upon, the
experience depicted. That this is a tendency rather than formally
determined, however, is evidenced below and in Chapter 8.

Whilst the serialization of *Middlemarch* avoids the worst super-
ficiality of soaps in terms of representing the textures of lived

experience, it does suffer to an extent from the traction of the range of forces noted which tend to pull George Eliot's densely textured and reflective fiction into the action narrative mould of modern TV formulaic realism. Furthermore, the central couples and their personal relationships, particularly that of Dr Lydgate and Rosamund Vincy, tend to predominate. As a consequence, formulaic realism's disposition to efface history to focus on de-contextualized personal relationships in the present moment comes into play. The broader historical context (two years prior to the 1832 Reform Act) of *Middlemarch*, the novel, whilst evident in traces, is minimalized in the television version. It remains in the narrative of Brooke's pretensions to stand for parliament, in Lydgate's wish to open the hospital and in Dorothea's reforming zeal. But formulaic realism's privileging of clearly – because two-dimensionally – drawn characters, and action over complexity and reflection, exacts a cost in the television adaptation of *Middlemarch*. The loss is precisely that of situated practice. The reforming zeal of Dorothea and Lydgate comes to seem more a matter of quirks of personality than part of an historical tendency since their personal relationships, with Casaubon and Rosamund respectively, are made in their immediacy to seem the very stuff of life, in the manner of soaps and popular series.

For all the influences recounted above involved in the re-shaping of *Middlemarch* from page to screen, some features of the experience of reading the novel are successfully transposed and carry its capacity, in Wittgenstein's terms (see below), to make its object stand still for apprehension and reflection.

A great strength of George Eliot's novel in suggesting the textures of experience is her ability to convey the complexity of motivation. At its best the dramatization is comparably successful. The moment of Lydgate's visit to the Vincy household with a message for Mr Vincy when his conscious mind, had it been fully engaged, would tell him that in working hours Vincy would be at the warehouse, illustrates that success. As he perhaps unconsciously expected, Lydgate finds Rosamund, whom he suspects has fallen in love with him, alone and unhappy in her passive predicament of awaiting his move. In a trice he finds himself kissing away her tears and engaged to the Mayor's daughter without ever consciously making a decision about his relationship with Rosamund.

The serial's capacity to convey the complexity of such moments was aided by fine performances, in particular from Douglas

Hodge as Lydgate. Comparable moments show him in Close-
Up reacting at his wife's bedside after Rosamund, having rejected his specific advice, has fallen whilst riding and suffered
a miscarriage. The mixture of anger, pity and love for his wife,
sorrow at the avoidable loss of their child, frustration at that part
of his marriage which strikes him as folly are all conveyed by
subtle televisual 'face-acting' caught in a series of reaction shots.
The complexity arises here from situated practice: Lydgate's
positive social dynamic in the tide of a progressive history is set
in tension with his equally powerful private passions which are
undermining his project. The depth of emotion evoked arises
from a felt complexity within – and potentially through empathy
beyond – the diegesis. Screen time constructed through a series
of inter-cut looks and glances affords viewers a more profound
engagement than is characteristically offered in formulaic
realism.

To succeed in affording viewers time to respond to and
reflect on emotional and intellectual complexity, the rhythm
of the editing of *Middlemarch* is at such moments very much
slower than that of a typical soap or popular series. An example
is the sequence in which, having deferred a decision overnight
on bowing to Casaubon's will by agreeing to follow his bidding
in the event of his death, Dorothea seeks to join her husband
on the following morning in the garden where he is reading
only to find him slumped dead over his books. The thoughts
and emotions that might be running through her head are
complex. Her marriage has been miserable and not at all what
she consciously anticipated in terms of her spiritual and intellectual development or, unconsciously perhaps, in terms of sexual
satisfaction. She recognizes however that Casaubon, despite his
apparent emotional rejection of her, has had a frustrated inner
emotional and intellectual life of his own. Physically spurned by
her husband, she has felt an attraction to Will Ladislaw though
she is not as yet – at least consciously – aware of the strength
of her feeling. In one sense Casaubon's death is liberating for
her; in another it is a great loss and sadness. A complex web
is George Eliot's central metaphor for the book as a whole and
each of its parts. It is an apt metaphor to describe Dorothea's
feelings at this moment, and the lingering camera demanded
that viewers reflect on its complexity.

In modern TV screenplay terms the sequence which treats

this moment is very slow. Two minutes at the end of the episode are afforded to Dorothea from her entering the garden to the fade to black and the credits at the end of the episode. Almost half of that time is taken up with a Close Two-Shot, foregrounding the top of her deceased husband's head, but showing Dorothea full-face to camera speaking just a few words slowly and softly in a fruitless effort to rouse him as the truth of the situation slowly dawns on her. This is an exceptionally long time for a TV camera to linger on inaction involving no further plot information or dialogue. It demands an active and imaginative response from viewers to engage with the complex web of Dorothea's thoughts and feelings. It is this aspect of the series which, with some success, attempts to retain the textures and moral seriousnesss of the novel, whatever the motivations of the production overall and the difficulties of the transposition of codes. The weakness of the dramatization, as the discussion above of its better moments illustrates by contrast, is that the focus has ultimately been shifted from the broader historical and intellectual context of the action of the novel on to the interpersonal romantic relationships.

There is real value, in the terms advocated in this book for the engagement of deeper feelings for other human beings in a world which tends to desensitize, in the way those relationships are treated. The characters are drawn more fully than the stereotypes characteristic of popular format TV drama. The complexity of the characters' motivation; the sense conveyed that the interplay between mind and body, decision and action is elusive and that the notion of interest-free, rational action is thus in question; the demonstration that the best-intentioned of actions can result in unhappy effects; the sense conveyed that social circumstances constrain human potential – all contribute to an imaginative viewing experience increasingly rare in the TV drama schedules. It is in this kind of TV drama that the emotional aspect of the ethic of truth-telling comes into play. For a human truth – in marked contrast with a positivist, instrumental truth – is established through a mixture of thought and feeling, albeit in accordance with recognized norms of plausibility and credibility.

The demands consequently made on viewers to watch intently and actively to work out the implications of the internal drama because they are obliquely presented mainly through visual images unsupported by an explanatory dialogue is in marked contrast to the often over-written popular formats in which, at worst, the dialogue fully articulates the motives of two-dimensional characters, and the visual images merely reinforce the words. The slow pace affords, as noted, time for a mixture of thoughtful and deep emotional responses. In short, there is some potential in the dramatization of *Middlemarch* for the kind of rich reading experiences offered by the novel. The forces of modern TV production and reception have tended, however, to pull the serial towards the narrative structure of a soap and, furthermore, to an over-emphasis on love interest. It is unjust to say that the dramatization has reduced the novel to a soap, but equally unjust to claim it has translated the novel fully into the television medium.

It remains briefly to place the dramatization of *Middlemarch* in its historical moment. The production by the BBC at a time when its Charter was under review, and when the justifiability of its very independent existence as an institution had been called in question by government ministers, might appear to bear the traces – if only of guilt by association – of serving to (re)construct and popularize a national heritage tradition allegedly inscribed in literary and dramatic high culture. The effective, if unintentional, reassertion of a perennial 'English-ness' in *Middlemarch*, the serial, thus has political resonances in the mid-1990s. The title sequence is interesting when viewed from this perspective. Carved in Roman capitals in stone with gold in-fill, the graphic depiction of 'MIDDLEMARCH' is underscored by measured orchestral soundtrack which strongly evokes the 'England' connoted in the music of Vaughan Williams.

As Andrew Davies acknowledges, one reading of the serial – notwithstanding the context of its historical setting just prior to the 1832 Reform Act – serves to remind a modern audience of a time when Britain was confident of its values and people knew where they stood – subservient to their 'betters'. Much of the action of the plot develops through time to restore misfortunes and redress injustices: Bulstrode's downfall leading to Fred Vincy's ultimate success, for example. When set against visual imagery of the countryside which evokes the 'Englishness' of Constable, the serial – through the very quality of its composition and its technical facility with lighting and photographic apparatus – is lent a sense of national geographic permanence.

Indeed, at worst, the skeleton of the narrative might be taken to illustrate that the zeal for reform, differently pursued by Dorothea Brooke and Will Ladislaw, is no more than a diversion from the true course of their lives, their personal relationship in love.

At worst, following postmodernism's dehistoricizing tendency, the history of George Eliot's *Middlemarch* becomes the heritage of the BBC's *Middlemarch*. The past is dislocated and, in place of history, 'free-floating signifiers' are attractively packaged and recirculated. The work and expense to reconstruct the environment of Middlemarch, stressed in the pre-publicity, serves less as empirical realism to authenticate that dynamic process of historical formation valued by Lukács in the historical novel, than as spectacle. It may even serve to reify a reactionary sense of endurable 'English-ness'.

Period drama is increasingly seen worldwide to be the area of British television expertise. Indeed the 'quality' status accorded British television rests in part on the longevity of British (European) cultural traditions. The established reputation of the canon of English (European) Literature is augmented in its television version by valued features of more recently established traditions. The dramatization adds actors with international reputations but exhibiting a peculiarly British acting style. Britain provides in addition a wealth of historic locations. There may also be general associations of cultural myths such as those of stability, democracy and fair play.

High production values are demanded for spectacular imagery. Foremost this entails shooting on film with a budget comparable with that of modern feature film production. Money is needed to find and restore locations 'authentically' and to construct a world which ultimately convinces, not by a history grounded in human experience, but by the depth and richness of its textures. In a medium where landscape is restricted, the sumptuous interior settings and costumes are in themselves a feature of popular spectacle on television.

To raise money, the BBC wearing its new commercial livery took full advantage of pre-publicity in all available media to build an audience for a popular project with 'high art' associations – ideally suited to the taste of the new social confugration. Following the broadcast of the series, an educational 'resource pack' (jointly prepared with the BFI Education Department) was produced on a commercial basis for educational institutions to extend interest in the series and potentially to prepare a young audience for future BBC period serials. To amass the budget necessary for a production of this kind, however, world sales – and probably co-production money – are needed, and these have implications for the product.

Attractive imagery of 'the past' is required for the American market, but there must be no dirty fingernails to puncture the myth. In the account above of the dramatization of *Middlemarch*, the tension between the *mise-en-scène* as historically grounding context and as heritage backdrop may be seen in play. When contemplating the implications of the ethical seriousness of a television dramatization such as *Middlemarch*, the pleasures taken by some viewers which militate against a critical consciousness can be neither underestimated nor overlooked.

IV

The X-Files offers in Dana Scully (Gillian Anderson) a woman striving for identity and independence against traditional constraints like her predecessors, Jess and Dorothea Brooke. Scully, too, feels the centripetal force of a heterosexual, bourgeois culture based on marriage and the home in tension with her desire for a career. She faces the both/and 'post-feminist' challenge to sustain a career whilst finding time for the romantic and family relationships she feels she would like to develop. In a notable reversal of traditional gendering, however, Scully is presented as the efficient, rational scientist in contrast with her male partner, Fox Mulder (David Duchovny), who, besides his belief in the paranormal and much which is inexplicable in rational-scientific terms, is obsessive about his work by way of a boyish enthusiasm rather than a macho pursuit of power. Indeed Mulder's quest for information concealed from him is only in part the traditional detective's dogged pursuit of truth since there is also a 'Boy's Own' sense of adventure and readiness to believe what mature adults dismiss as nonsense. He does, however, have a more personal interest in the paranormal. Having watched helpless as a small boy as his sister, Samantha, was abducted by aliens, Mulder not only believes in realms beyond the scientific-rational norm, but is convinced there is a major international government cover-up of the truth that is 'out there'. In 'Anasazi', a frustrated Mulder argues that, 'conventional wisdom, outward convention, and science offer us no answers. Might we not finally turn to the fantastic beyond the realm of science?' Initially Scully is appointed precisely to monitor Mulder's vagaries and, perhaps even to debunk the X-Files project. Whilst, then, Duchovny's traditional film-star good-looks and Anderson's conventional attractions (including Monroe-esque parted lips) afford the narrative suspense of a possible romance between the protagonists, any relationship between them is complex, mixing a possible professional antagonism with a working need for an unusual degree of sympathy and trust. The series thus gently challenges essentialist gendering and this constitutes its first blurring of boundaries.

Another concerns narrative structure. In accord with the now familiar tension between the audience's residual desire for narrative sense-making (at least as perceived by production executives) and the (post)modern television medium's inclination to resist closure in order to provide an endless fictive experience, *X-Files* blurs formal boundaries, though not by flexi-narrative means. In many respects, most episodes follow a traditional plot/resolution format, though, in the nature of its concern with inexplicable phenomena, *X-Files* militates against easy sense-making. In selling the idea of the series, producer Chris Carter found himself in conflict with Fox executives who wanted the endings made more explicit (see Lowry, 1995: 20). Unconsciously hinting at reception theorists' formulation of poststructuralist reading dispositions, a frustrated Carter argued, 'There's no sense to make! You make the sense for yourself' (cited in Lowry, 1995: 20).

Nevertheless, a range of devices have been employed in *X-Files* to offer some kinds of closure whilst resisting tying up all loose ends. In most episodes, the particular narrative enigma posed is resolved, though the explanation of the paranormal dimension of the story remains unaccountable. Indeed, following the two-part story, 'Colony' and 'End Game', in which groups of alien clones (including multiple Samanthas) have infiltrated earth and await an opportunity to inherit the planet when human beings finally forfeit their ethical claim to a right to dominate it, scientific rationalism is very clearly affirmed. It is as if the conviction of the story-telling – well produced in shady lighting with fast-cut sequences of Close-Ups of objects (or parts of wholes) distorting the physical world and with impress-ive special effects – is such that the programme makers (or distributors) felt impelled to end on a note of reassurance. As the comatose Mulder pulls through his encounter with an alien hit-man, Scully, at his hospital bedside, observes in voice-over:

> Many of the things I have seen have challenged my faith, and my belief, in an ordered universe. But this uncertainty has only strengthened my need to know, to understand, to apply reason to those things which seem to defy it. It was science that isolated the retro-virus Agent Mulder was exposed to. It was science that allowed us to understand its behaviour and, ultimately, it was science that saved Agent Mulder's life.

The rhetorical emphasis on science as our hero stirs, along with Scully, shot in softly-lit Close-Up, showing a special caring for her partner who has apparently sacrificed his sister to save her life, positively reaffirms scientific-rationalism and human psychological norms. But, in the series overall, reassurance of this kind is held in undecidable tension with an inclination to the non- or supra-rational.

There are other potentially on-going threads of narrative (besides the development of the relationship betwen Scully and Mulder) as in the instance of the 100-year-old genetic mutant, Tooms, who rises from the dead to feast on five human livers every thirty years. More plausible, perhaps, are the recurrent appearances of the mysterious agents 'Deep Throat' and 'X' who seem to be on Mulder's and Scully's side, but who cannot wholly be trusted. Similarly, Mulder and Scully's relationship with their boss, Asst. Director Walter S. Skinner, is fractious since Skinner at some times (as in 'End Game') goes out of his way to help them whilst at other times he summarily obstructs their investigations.

In short, Carter's primary interest in filling a niche in the schedules created by the absence of a crime/horror mix was modified as he became increasingly aware 'that people wanted shows about the characters and their lives' (cited in Lowry, 1995: 25). Thus *X-Files* has developed into a hybrid crime thriller/ horror series/serial narrative form with a dash of soap romance, offering both the pleasure of closure and the hook of continu-ity, but avoiding flexi-narrative fragmentation by focusing on a single story in each episode with space for the Scully/Mulder relationship slowly to develop.

The context of *X-Files'* episodes is grounded in a TV drama referential realism. Locations, dates and times are typically inventoried in titles and voice-overs, in the tradition of Realist specificities. The episode *Space*, for example, is located at a NASA rocket-launching pad. News footage lends authenticity to the events. The images, both of the interiors of mission control and the exteriors of rocket launches and landings, are those familiar from television coverage of actual missions. Interiors feature large, open-plan, windowless rooms whose occupants sit at computer terminals in serried rows facing a big-image screen. Individuals, shot in Close-Up, talk into head-set microphones in coded, but familiar, language ('OTC to control'). Moments of achievement – a successful launch for example – are celebrated by 'buddy-bonding' applause, and whooping as the high tension of possible failure is released.

Such empirical grounding is ironically necessary to lend conviction to the paranormal aspects of *X-Files*, in the case of the episode *Space*, the demonization of Lt.-Col. Belt (Ed Lauter) by a spectral force which inhabited him on a space walk. Brief flashbacks in dream or memory – the two are not clearly distinguished – reveal glimpses of a white-suited and helmeted spacewalker, his face, visible through the plastic visor, contorted in terror as he yells, 'It's coming at me'. A dark grey, over-size but quasi-human visage bears down on the camera placing viewers momentarily in the position of Belt in his darkest hour. Similar special effects subsequently in the episode dissolve Belt's face with that of the incubus and show it coming and going like a whirlwind in quasi-human outline. All this is done with style and conviction, subtly deploying electronic technology to impressive effect. The clues to narrative sense are only gradually revealed and narrative tension is also sustained by other means.

Apparent sabotage to the shuttle awaiting launch, which Belt seems unwilling properly to investigate, is revealed to Scully and Mulder by Michelle Generoo of ground control, whose fiancé is captain of the craft. Leading Scully and Mulder back to base, Michelle's car is mysteriously overturned. Then, following a tense, but ultimately succesful launch at the second attempt, the shuttle is physically struck by an unidentified force. Only the voice of the shuttle occupants is heard.

Driven by production constraints and an increasing under-standing of horror/thriller story-telling, Carter has learned that having frightening events happen off-screen is most effective, drawing as it does on the viewers' imaginations (see Lowry, 1995: 27). The emotional tension of the episode is fed through Michelle who ultimately has to talk the shuttle down in a pre-mature and unplanned landing as Belt finally succumbs to his incubus and has to be restrained and hospitalized. Mulder's intuitive insight into what is going on leads him to interrogate Belt fiercely, at risk of the Lt.-Colonel's life, to reveal his sole knowledge of how to bring the shuttle into land without implo-sion. In the proverbial nick of time, the information is relayed to Michelle who thus brings her fiancé safely in to land.

It will be evident that much of *X-Files* as demonstrated by this episode is the standard stuff of a well-told thriller. The enigma-resolving deduction is even made by the white, male profes-sional hero, though it is Scully who has first suspected Belt and looked sceptically on Mulder's idolatry of the former space-man. The plot cannot, however, be reduced to a simple battle between the forces of good and evil for Belt is shown ultimately to have been struggling not only against his incubus alter-ego, which sought to destroy the mission but also with his need for it to succeed in order to avoid giving Congress an excuse to cut the budget. The demons, it is suggested, are both within and without.

The political context of the pressure on Belt is the nearest this episode comes to situating agency. A marked difference between *X-Files* and the two serials discussed in this chapter is that the thriller fiction elements tend to be privileged over the series' referential grounding in common human experience, though the development of Scully and Mulder's characters and relationship, noted above, offsets them. A feature of *X-Files*, figured in its title, however, is the sense it conveys of political, and specifically governmental, forces, concealing unpalatable truths about the paranormal or the inexplicable in rational terms. The series builds on the infamous Roswell (New Mexico, 1947) incident in which alien beings allegedly descended on an American airbase only to be destroyed along with all evidence of their visitation. In the episode specifically evoking Roswell, 'Deep Throat', a military husband returns to his wife after a prolonged and unsatisfactorily explained absence, apparently himself physically, but mentally much changed. Dimensions of his brain appear to have been wiped as if it were a computer hard-disk capable of continuing to function in spite of the deletion of some of its memory-bank.

X-Files thus intersects with contemporary life in resonating with mistrust of politicians and the disposition, arising from the broad questioning of Enlightenment rational-scientific certainties, to espouse all kinds of alternative mind-sets from new age psychic powers to Eastern mysticism. The opening up by fast communications of a variety of cultural outlooks has supplied disillusioned Westerners with a host of alternative frameworks of belief, albeit dislocated from their primary cultural grounding. The very idea of an impartial truth is similarly undermined by increased awareness of the packaged mediation of information, if not outright media distortion (*pace* Baudrillard). The popularity of *X-Files*, then, is partly accountable in terms of its 'proffered conspiracy theories alleging government atrocities' (cited in Lowry, 1995: 27). Deep Throat was, of course, the name of the informant in the Watergate scandal which much influenced producer Chris Carter.

Given its resonance with the search for new identities and the undecidability of the new social configuration sketched in Chapter 2, *X-Files'* broader popularity is equally as unsurprising as the disproportionate number of young educated viewers evidenced in the Nielsen ratings. There is amongst this latter group a cult following which may amount to more than emblematic T-shirts and microcultures of 'X-philes' who communicate with each other (and the series' producer) on the InterNet and hold conventions, both virtual and actual. There have been several cult television series mixing sci-fi elements with politics, *The Prisoner* and *Star Trek* being notable examples. But the distinctiveness of *X-Files* in its historical moment is its mode of address, typified in the cool but not uninvolved disposition of its protagonists and the measured whistling of its titles' soundtrack evoking a sceptical detachment but in circumstances which ultimately may commmand belief in defiance of rational plausibility. *X-Files* balances scepticism – verging on outright rejection – of rational sense-making advocating a quasi-mystical alternative, with re-ssurance of scientific rationalism, both explicitly – in Scully's words cited above – and through its narrative structures. Its critical realism – following (post)modern culture's increased recognition of the importance of fantasy and the psychological as dimensions of actual human experience – emphasises disposition over empirical, social grounding. As a factitive fiction, its emphasis is more on the fantasy than the (empirical) factual, but in a way which poses questions about how the two relate in human ways of seeing.

V

The very best TV drama – in the scale explored in this book – makes you think. It stops viewers in their tracks, drawing their attention away from the knitting, the newspaper, the distractions of domesticity, to command attention. After the event, it plays on people's minds. By coming from an angle different from the regular perspective, by framing things just off-centre, it demands that viewers see something afresh and perhaps to recognize that their accustomed mythologies are inadequate accounts of the world. To talk of art with regard to the everyday medium of television may seem highfalutin'. But, as Tilghman records:

> Wittgenstein spoke of art as the view of the world *sub specie aeternitatis* in which the object becomes a world in itself. . . . the work of art selects an object, a scene, a situation, and makes that object stand still and be contemplated. What it is that art can make still is most importantly human life. It displays to us *humanity* and in that way shows us the meaning of life, that is what it is to be a human being (1991: 176).

TV dramas may be artworks in Wittgenstein's conception, as the examples above, in their different ways, illustrate. In a primarily entertainment medium, there are inevitably forces other than artistic in play, as this book demonstrates. The commercial impetus evident in the production of *Middlemarch* illustrates the current tensions of a culture in transition. But 'art' may signify a broad category of texts sharing family resemblances and, as symbolic formations, TV dramas have the potential to show what cannot be said. They may illuminate the significance of human life, not for all time, everywhere for all people, but for a period of time within a culture, and possibly beyond it. Works of critical realism are particularly usable stories since their strategy is to construct convincing worlds to draw viewers

in. But, through a range of small but significant devices of dislocation, they avoid reduction to a dull, formulaic naturalism.
In their commitment to the ethic of truth-telling, they do not
reinforce mythologies but invite examination of them.

In comparison with *Oranges* and *Middlemarch*, *X-Files* is limited
in terms of situating agency within structure, though it is referential to the contemporary, as demonstrated, in its framing
of the real. It illuminates human life not by suggesting the complexity of the social web, as in *Middlemarch*, or the difficulties of
expressing 'deviant' sexual preference in a homophobic society, as in *Oranges*, but by articulating an uneasy undecidability
in contemporary culture inclining towards alternative ways of
seeing.

The continued production and/or transmission on British
television of a range of quality factive fictions testifies to sustained diversity and quality. But the pace of life in postmodernity and fast-turnover flexiad postmodernisms militate against
moments of stasis for contemplation. As long as televisual realisms remain popular, however, factive fictions in the critical
realist tradition retain the utmost potential for cognitive and
affective reorientation. In accordance with the rule of diversity,
it matters if such drama gets squeezed from the schedules.

7 The Public Stock of Harmless Pleasure

Pleasures, Meanings, Responsibilities

> It is not enough to know the *ensemble* of relations as they exist at any given time as a given system. They must be known genetically, in the movement of their formation (Gramsci, 1971: 353).

I

British broadcast television follows American in becoming increasingly a medium devoted to entertainment. All aspects of television presentation involve excesses of sounds and images. Even the more evidently factual and informational programmes – the news, current affairs, documentaries – have developed a range of presentational devices to attract interest in a context where competition for viewers is increasingly fierce.[1] This competition, moreover, is not just between one programme or channel and another, but between broadcast television itself and the other attractions of expanded 'infotainment' in the home.

To attract an audience, broadcast television must compete in the leisure/pleasure market-place. New technologies of production and reception, as noted in Chapter 1, remain in development to this effect. There can be no doubt that the range of possible pleasures afforded by television in general, and indeed any one specific programme, has increased exponentially in the history of the medium. Besides wider choice and technological improvements, it is now a commonplace in Media Studies that members of the plural audience use television's polysemic texts in a number of ways, taking and making a range of meanings and pleasures from them (Morley, 1986 and 1992; Fiske, 1987). In broad terms this rich potential is to be applauded. But there may be losses as well as gains in the economy of these developments. In the force field explored in this study, a culture of consumerism extends its influence to shape dramatic forms and images in some ways rather than others.

Of particular significance in the postmodern economy of pleasures is the pace of circulation and intensity of short-term gratifications. Discrete moments of pleasure replace each other in rapid turnover. In contrast with the profound and durable effectivity of art more traditionally conceived, the postmodern aesthetic preference is for the attenuated but ebullient. In television drama it is the fast-cutting of narrative fragments from hot-spot to hot-spot which draws an audience rather than the tempered, exegetic build-up over time to a climax and resolution of more traditional narrative forms.

The dazzle of glamour and style in the look of television, moreover, increases in importance as the intensity of each moment is designed to catch or keep the eye. Vibrant sound is omnipresent in this regard.[2] A reflectionist marxism might see this as the very 'cultural logic of late capitalism' (Jameson, 1993: xv ff). It is at least homologous with time–space compression which accelerates the pace of life from modernity to postmodernity particularly by means of electronic communications.

In the general celebration of polysemy and pluralism, a critical perspective – from which some interests are seen to remain served more than others – is frequently forgotten by commentators. But this book avowedly takes an interrogative stance. Thus, at the risk of dressing myself in the bizarre attire of a Malvolio[3] to deny others the simple enjoyments of 'cakes and ale' in the pursuit of a crabbed and misplaced virtue, I want in this chapter to explore – and raise some questions about – the accumulative pleasures of an alleged democracy in consumerism.

Firstly, the functioning of an economy of multiple pleasures in television as articulated in ratings discourse must be brought out. As long as large numbers of people regularly watch the dominant flexi-narrative and flexiad forms, production companies rest content that they are giving the public what it wants, namely pleasures in entertainment. But the unproblematic notion in ratings discourse of a simple, pleasurable fulfilment of popular needs proves on reflection, to be more complex than at first appears.

Apart from speaking in the name of an absent audience as noted, ratings discourse has tacitly espoused the ideology of individualist populism, dominant in the 1980s. Adorno, the sternest critic in the 1930s of an emergent culture industry based on popular pleasures, remarked:

> it is claimed that standards [of the culture industry] were based in the first place on consumers' needs and for that reason were accepted with so little resistance. The result is the circle of manipulation and retroactive need in which the unity of the system grows even stronger. No mention is made of the fact that the basis on which technology acquires power over society is the power of those whose economic hold over society is the greatest (in Adorno and Horkheimer 1979: 121).

As I write, the tussles over which UK (or transnational) channels should hold the broadcasting rights for major 'national' sporting events – centred on Murdoch's apparent attempt to corner the entire market for his satellite channel, BSkyB – serve perhaps to bear Adorno out. Moreover, without dismissing popular pleasures as summarily as Adorno – particularly in recognition that what people do with television must be offset against any influence it may have on them – it can be acknowledged that pleasures and desires, far from being purely natural phenomena, are themselves constructed in social history. Indeed, that history must be taken into account in any analysis of pleasure.

The 1980s saw a rapid expansion of market research used as the foundation for knowledge-claims about people's needs and desires. Drawing, sometimes disingenuously, on the important democratic principle that people must be allowed to speak for themselves, apologists for deregulation and policy-making through market mechanisms allege that their methods prove that they are giving 'the people' what they want. The validity of such assertions, however, must remain in considerable doubt.

With regard to television audience research, Ang has demonstrated that the producers' view of the audience rests on untenable assumptions. These are based on the 'construction of a set of binary oppositions (production versus consumption, 'sender' versus 'recipient', institution versus audience' (1991: 23) which leaves producers in 'profound ignorance, or at least in great doubt, about the precise ingredients of their success or failure' (1991: 27). In short, for all the research and audience analysis undertaken, producers are never quite sure why viewers like or dislike their programmes. Their understanding is itself founded on a conception of audience's passive pleasure in reception which is brought into question by the very dynamics of a plural audience reading programmes from several perspectives.

More fundamentally, the location of the site of pleasure in the sovereign individual who today responds to the market research questionnaire may itself be placed both historically and ideologically. It is particularly traceable to Bentham and James Mill who, in their scientific theories of utility, proposed the regulation of pleasure in the processes of consolidation of a capitalism which required a controlled economy of work, conceptually and spatially distinct from leisure/pleasure (see Mercer, 1983). The individualization and privatization of pleasures, then, develops with an industrial economy underpinned by a framework of regulated social practices and ultimately by legislation. Indeed, Foucault (1984: 206–13) has made much of the wholesale ingestion of self-regulation under the surveillance of Bentham's 'panopticon' where isolated individuals feel themselves to be constantly subject to the observation of an unseen eye.

Besides the construction of the dualisms, work/leisure and constraint/pleasure, consonant with the regulatory requirements of industrialization, Bentham and Mill contribute the notion of the instrumental measurement of aggregated individual pleasures. Pleasure in the Benthamite formulation is, moreover, an apparently transparent phenomenon. Thus, the basis of what eventually emerged in the 1980s as Thatcherite and Reaganite individualist populism is established. To make specific to television this broader context, ratings discourse as a means of justifying populist product rests on an unacknowledged historical conception of aggregated individual pleasures which it places beyond question.

In the following discussion, in contrast, pleasures are avowedly conceived as 'situated practices'. Pleasure is not taken at face value as an innocent aspect of a harmless entertainment industry. The constraints of individualization, privatization and domestication of human experience will be weighed against the more readily available pleasures of postmodernity, but not in a mechanistic, utilitarian scale. The various needs which TV drama fulfils and its processes of pleasure and meaning formation will be brought out in what Sparks has called the 'production and reproduction of social life in everyday transactions' (1992: 42).

Since the means by which most people have some opportunity to partake of the profusion of postmodern pleasures remains that of paid employment, a work/leisure model may still obtain in popular consciousness, if less in work practices as conditions of employment change. Furthermore, since a (philosophically) realist disposition on the part of readers remains widespread and realist forms remain predominantly popular, the pleasures thereby generated merit initial discussion. Sustaining, then, at first a dualist model in which work and leisure are sharply differentiated in an industrial context, immersion in leisure may be figured as an an escape from the rigours and constraints of rationalized labour. Pleasure derives, as Colin Mercer reads Bourdieu, from 'a wholehearted and unself-conscious involvement in a cultural event, form or text' (1983: 84).

Quite contrary to the postmodernists, Bourdieu accounts for popular participatory pleasures not in terms of 'semiotic productivity' (Fiske, 1992: 37) but by way of involvement in narrative texts as follows:

> The desire to enter into the game, identifying with the characters' joys and sufferings, worrying about their fate, espousing their hopes and ideals, living their life, is based on a form of *investment*, a sort of deliberate 'naivety', ingenuousness, good-natured credulity ('We're here to enjoy ourselves'), which tends to accept formal experiments and specifically artistic effects only to the extent that they can be forgotten and do not get in the way of the substance of the work (Bourdieu, 1992: 33).

Bourdieu's account of pleasure, then, leaves little room for popular appreciation of any of modernism's formal aesthetic invention, let alone postmodern play. It does, however, offer an explanation of the residual preference – perhaps dominant even yet – for mimetic and referential realisms in popular television drama, and serves as a qualifier to overstatements of postmodern reader's 'enunciative productivity' (Fiske, 1992: 37).

In aesthetic matters, however, Bourdieu makes a sharper distinction between working-class taste and that of an educated elite than his own account of social reformation implies. Indeed, a limitation of his 'findings' lies in their tendency to reify the social formation. As Daniel Miller points out, '[w]orking class people are reduced to a relationship of immediacy from which they cannot escape' (1987: 156). Under postmodernity, new, less common or rigidly formulated, habits of work and social life afford varied patterns, and a more diverse range, of leisure pursuits. In the broad terms of Chapter 2, the relative asceticism of Fordism with its standardized production of functional goods gives way to the diversified profusion of flexible accumulation. A culture of austerity dissolves into a culture of contentment as personal pleasure in consumption – particularly of services and leisure pursuits – is legitimated and vigorously encouraged. The sharp work/leisure distinction becomes blurred, and a more complex account of pleasure is required.

Where previously value was located in the production of material goods to meet 'real needs', the pleasures of consumption of all kinds are promoted in the postmodern economy.[4] The keyword is 'fun' and, in order to maximize consumption potential, fantasy displaces responsibility. According to Bourdieu, we might recall from Chapter 2, the role of cultural intermediaries in promoting the new affective order is taken on by the new petite bourgeoisie which itself emerges in the concomitant social reformation of postmodernity.

With regard to aesthetics, there is progressive potential in the extension of aesthetic pleasures available to all in aspects of everyday life, not just constrained to prescribed leisure time. Moreover, there is an apparently democratizing tendency in the aestheticization of everyday life in contrast with a conception of art reserved for an elite in exclusive, specialized spaces. Indeed, the blurring of the categorial distinction of the 'great divide' between art and popular culture is a key feature of postmodernism, proliferating pleasure sites. The shopping mall vies with the art gallery as a space for aesthetic experience. The sheer diversity produced by a global economy – drawing on the different tastes and cultures of the world – offers a profusion of pleasures in goods and services to those with the means to buy. The social extension of pleasure through expanded commodity and service production in postmodernity's electronic economy echoes that transformation of experience offered through the industrial revolution. The democratic impulse in material and sensual satisfactions of that earlier epoch is vastly extended.

But, as suggested at the beginning of the chapter, there may be debits as well as credits in the balance sheet of this economy of consumerist pleasures. Again a historical view of the formulation of conceptions of pleasures is illuminating. An ambivalent attitude to pleasure, emergent in the early nineteenth century, has been documented by Trilling (see 1980: 57–8). He locates it in Keats. It is an ambivalence between a politics directed towards pleasurable fulfilment in increased affluence and 'a stern and even minatory gaze' (1980: 59) of the artist at all that affluence implies. The Romantics' general advocacy of abandonment to pleasure, the will, as Keats put it, 'to burst Joy's grape against his palate fine' (1953: 751) does not stretch readily to the pleasures of commercial commodities. The Romantics' predilection for 'natural' pleasures – Wordsworth's preference for the Lake District over the industrial city for example – comes into conflict with the pleasures of commodification.

Trilling's identification of a 'point in modern history [when] the principle of pleasure came to be regarded with . . . ambivalence' (1980: 58) is accompanied by another insight pertinent to the construction of pleasures in postmodernity. For, in his recognition that extended commodity production and the accompanying social transformation demands a rethinking of pleasure, he notes:

> an influence to be observed in the growing tendency of power to express itself mediately, by signs or indices, rather than directly, by the exercise of force (1980: 55).

Indeed it is precisely the obfuscation of the ensemble of power relations in the conflation of luxury commodities with signs of pleasure that instigated the crisis in the Romantic critical aesthetic. The Romantics' advocacy of abandonment to pleasure in the face of the instrumentalizing controls of Bentham could not readily embrace the pleasures of the products of capitalism's regulated industrial system. Moreover, the sense identified by Trilling, in which power is masked in the dazzle of the sign of pleasure in luxury goods is sustained from this moment of ambivalence in the early nineteenth century through Adorno's critique of the culture industry in the 1930s on to Debord's figuration of the 'society of the spectacle'.

Pleasure, then, would seem a less simple concept than the advocates of a postmodern leisure economy wish it to appear. Emotionally and psychologically, as Freud famously observed, there is a 'beyond the pleasure principle'. There is more to life, one might say, than the maximization of personal pleasures, not simply in terms of the barriers imposed by 'the reality principle' but with regard to the human psyche. Taking up the Romantics' ambivalence about the satisfactions to be gained from different kinds of pleasures, moreover, we might, whilst teetering on the edge of cliché, reiterate the commonplace that excesses of some pleasures – material goods for example – do not seem synonymous with human happiness: 'I don't care too much for money; money can't buy me love!'. It is musings such as these which lead in the penultimate chapter of this book to a direct discussion of cultural value. In the interim, having identified a deficit column, we should not overlook the more positive conceptions of the postmodern pleasure economy.

Where liberty in modernity (in the wake of the Romantics) is located in a space for critical negation and resistance to commodification, in postmodernity, in contrast, 'it is in the sphere of consumption . . . that many will seek to express their sense of freedom' (Tomlinson, 1990: 6). Indeed, in a wholly commodified world there is nowhere else to go. In this context particularly, however, the sense of *post*modernity as a development of modernity is evident. In a shift from a model of production for basic needs to a capacity for mass-produced consumer goods, Fordism gradually gave rise to an understanding that the definition of 'real needs' in terms of subsistence is inadequate. Aspects of the irrational in desire for symbolic goods and services overtakes the rational equation of 'real needs' and their satisfaction.

As Simon Frith, writing of the development of radio in the 1930s, has observed of this transition:

> The very idea of a 'luxury' was becoming suspect, could no longer be confined to bourgeois commodities. The problem was that if new inventions, new goods, could create their own need (no-one needed a radio before it was invented) then the concept of need itself had to be re-thought. 'Real' needs were based on obvious material problems (food, shelter,

warmth). 'Superficial' needs, by contrast, appeared to reflect irrational choices: why did people pick out one fashion rather than another? One sort of washing powder? One tune? Tastes and preferences became a matter of expert investigation. . . . Advertising was the symbol of mass culture as the manipulation of desire (1983: 122).

In a post-industrial society, the marxist labour theory of value is called further into question relative to surplus value created by microchip technology and the concomitant increase in pleasures produced in the consumption of symbolic commodities. Furthermore, the labour theory of value is not readily applicable to, 'the nature of "mental" work and of nonphysical, nonmeasurable "commodities" of the type of informational bits or indeed media or entertainment "products"' (Jameson, 1984: xv). Fantasy, the irrational symbolic in desire, thus comes to figure much more widely in postmodern space offering considerable potential for pleasures genuinely experienced. The antisocial tendencies of the irrational emphasized by Adorno have tended accordingly to be overridden, though they remain of concern.

In addressing this shift, moreover, theorists have proposed a possible meeting of a resistant politics of pleasure with the symbolic in popular culture through a rethinking of both the conception of needs, as indicated by Frith, and that of a rigid distinction between production and consumption. The alleged loss of fixity in the relationship between signifier and signified characteristic of accounts of postmodernism affords space for a rethinking of consumption as production.

Barthes, for example, takes the loosening in the factuality of language to afford a productivity in play in the gap between signifier and signified. The postmodern textual bricolage, in this formulation, invites constructive play through its pluralism of juxtaposed discourses without harmonious resolution. Insofar as such a principle of construction informs the texts of popular culture – and Fiske (1992) sees it as characteristic – a conjuncture may emerge between pleasurable play and a politics of resistance.

Language becomes a battleground for Enzenberger's semiotic guerrilla warfare.[5] Against the fixity of meaning proposed in capitalist production, the argument goes, stands the process of 'semiotic, enunciative, textual productivity' (Fiske, 1992: 37) and thus a range of diverse pleasures in diverse styles. More moderately, in Mercer's formulation, the popular can be articulated to a critical aesthetic 'at once democratic and socially managed, as contested and controlled, as a structured balance of forces rather than as a con trick' (1983: 88).

Combining a theory of articulation with poststructuralist theory of subjectivity, an account may be offered of production-in-consumption in terms of a radical democracy (Grossberg, 1987; Mouffe, 1988). The first aspect stresses what people do with television as contrasted with its effectivities working upon them. The opportunity is emphasized for readers to harness the kaleidoscope of dislocated signs and codes to new ends. Such an active disposition is lent support by postmodern philosophy's anti-foundational formulation of a subjectivity, not fixed and essential, existing in the same way in every practice, but multi-faceted and constantly under (re)construction.

Abandoning the unitary subject of liberal individualism, postmodern subjectivity is conceived in terms of:

> a decentred, detotalized agent, a subject constructed at the point of intersection of a multiplicity of subject positions between which there exists no a priori or necessary relation and whose articulation is the result of hegemonic practices (Mouffe, 1988: 35).

With regard to television viewing, this conception might be contextualized particularly in relation either to viewing habits (semi-attentive and fragmentary) and/or the paratactical structures of postmodern texts (inviting a process of bricolage production-in-consumption), and/or that breakdown of a fixed relationship between representation and referent (creating space for textual play).

Particularly where there is visual and other stylistic excess, even referential texts lend themselves to a range of meanings and pleasures. As Grossberg puts it, moreover:

> [i]f not every meaning is a representation, and not every text has representational effects, it may also be true that texts may have effects other than meaning-effects, and meanings themselves may be involved in relations other than representational. That is, the connection between a particular cultural

practice and its actual effects may be a complex multiplicity of lines and articulations (1987: 36–7).

Whilst it has aspects of radical democratic potential through the empowerment of viewers to make meanings or take pleasures, however, this way of thinking, taken to extreme, advocates an indiscriminate commitment to the popular contemporary. In an apparent distortion of Gramsci's notion that people may make history but, not in conditions of their own making, an uncritical postmodernism overlooks the weight of traditions, both positive and negative. Popular culturalists find radical potential in all aspects of postmodernism. In talking up the contemporary, however, they tend to efface both history and consequence.

Even assuming that the account above of production-in-consumption of popular culture is tenable – and the residual realisms (textual and dispositional) of TV drama qualify, if they do not actually contest, the assumption – two issues remain. The first, as noted, concerns the critical force of postmodern play in relation to variant textual strategies. Put bluntly, the question is whether some postmodern texts rather than others invite a creative/critical disposition of segments of the audience not already so disposed by their marginal social position.

The second – to be discussed in Section II – raises the problem of justice which postmodernism's abandonment of Enlightenment axioms tends to overlook. In demonstrating their allegiance to subordinate social groups by emphasizing popular creativity in 'textual productivity', commentators such as Fiske accept that the industrial texts in which fans 'participate' carry little cultural capital. But in championing what is done by some with industrial texts, Fiske overlooks the 'realist' disposition of the popular audience (as demonstrated – albeit in too rigid a frame – by Bourdieu). His position also leaves unchallenged the inequities in the distribution of both cultural and economic capital, at worst celebrating the inventiveness by the economically and culturally disadvantaged in re-making a cake with the crumbs discarded by the wealthy in actual, or semiotic, orgies.

Whilst Fiske acknowledges some of the contradictions both in his position and in cultural practices, he ultimately espouses a semiotic, consumerist democracy which does nothing to advance a democracy of citizenship (see 1992: 46–7). His account of popular culture offers symbolic, psychological empowerment – by no means unimportant in people's everyday lives – but perhaps at the expense of political empowerment involved in challenging and changing structural inequities and related injustices at the political level. I shall return to this problem.

Taking up again, meanwhile, the idea of textual play, a semiotic overload is a feature of postmodernity to which television has itself contributed. As Grossberg notes, '[t]elevisual excess takes many forms – visual excess, stylistic excess, verbal excess, imagistic excess (1987: 43). The proliferation of channels and the resultant 'surfing' arising from an inability to settle on any one programme, together with the bricolage and paratactical principles of construction where narrative is less important than the style of the images and surface is all, suggests at first sight a resultant non-sense. For sure, the sense-making frames of realism are precluded from postmodern texts in perpetual process. But as Collins has pointed out, the productivity-in-consumption of active readers demands that new meanings are made in a more or less conscious awareness of the constructedness of television programmes. As he summarizes:

> This absorption/secondarization process involves the manipulation of the array by texts operating within it – television programs (as well as rock songs, films, best sellers, and so forth) that demonstrate an increasingly sophisticated knowledge of the conditions of their production, circulation, and eventual reception (1992: 332).

Empowerment through play rests, then, on the interplay between a textual self-consciousness (texts which draw attention to the devices of their composition) and the newly flexible and active subjectivity. It assumes, a consciousness, to cite Mouffe again, that, 'we are in fact always multiple and contradictory subjects, inhabitants of diverse communities . . . constructed by a variety of discourses and precariously and temporarily sutured at the intersection of those subject positions' (1988: 337). It nevertheless remains arguable as to whether the intertextual play of texts and a flexible subjectivity is unrestrainedly liberating or whether the inability to make sense of a bombardment of signs leads in Collins's phrase, to a 'disempowering apathy, in which no image is taken at all seriously' (1992: 336).

Indeed the dominant excess of (post)modern television, emotional excess (Grossberg, 1987: 43), would seem to militate against any kind of critical articulation. As Grossberg puts it:

> Current TV's most powerful annunciation is emotionalism. . . . It presents an image of an affective economy marked on the one side by an extreme (postmodern) cynicism ('life is hard and then you die') and, on the other by an almost irrational celebration of the possibility of winning against all the odds [lottery fever in the UK, for example]. . . . It is almost as if, in various ways, viewers get to live out the emotional highs and lows of their lives on TV, as if they just want to feel something that strongly, no matter what it is (1987: 43).

Amidst this welter of emotionalism dislocated from any historical context, the radical democracy achievable through flexible subjectivity would seem unsure to say the least. It is not so much that the feelings repressed by the rationalization of modernity have been freshly liberated, but that they have been substituted by a contrived emotionalism. An active and critical disposition is assumed in the new social formation despite that the dominant affect of the new order would appear to be isolated emotional intensities.

John Caughie offers a tempered summary of the debate:

> The argument, then, is that television produces the conditions of an ironic knowingness, at least as a possibility, which may escape the obedience of interpellation or cultural colonialism and may offer a way of thinking subjectivity free of subjection. It gives a way of thinking identities as plays of cognition and miscognition. . . . Most of all, it opens identity to diversity, and escapes the notion of cultural identity as a fixed volume. . . . But *if it does all this, it does not do it in that utopia of guaranteed resistance which assumes the progressiveness of naturally oppositional readers* who will get it right in the end. It does it, rather, with terms hung in suspension . . . : tactics of empowerment, games of subordination with neither term fixed in advance (1990: 55, my emphasis).

Whatever spin is put on these formulations, then, it is evident that the allegedly innocent pleasures people experience are constructed in social histories. Indeed Mouffe acknowledges that postmodern philosophy's:

absence of foundation 'leaves everything as it is,' as Wittgenstein would say, and obliges us to ask the same questions in a new way. Hence the error of a certain kind of apocalyptic postmodernism which would like us to believe that we are at the threshold of a radically new epoch, characterized by drift, dissemination and by uncontrollable play of significations (1988: 38).

Whilst, then, there may be potential in the play of signification of a postmodern aesthetic, its powers of liberation cannot be assumed in advance. The extension of the range and reach of pleasures in postmodernity does not in itself resolve the questions posed by Adorno's critique of the culture industry, though the historical circumstances in which Adorno wrote and which coloured his judgements no longer obtain in quite the same way. Nevertheless, questions about pleasure must still be asked, albeit in a new way under new circumstances.

Precisely because subjectivities are constructed in history and open to a range of discourses, pleasure or unpleasure is by no means a simple matter of political correctness. Moreover, people get pleasure from processes in which they know they are consenting to forms of domination. Sentiment, regret, nostalgia, desire, ambition and identification play a significant role in the economy of pleasure. Thus, as Miller remarks:

a Romanticism is based on the assumption that populism is right simply because it comes from the mass populace, and ignores the clear ability of mass movements to favour antisocial politics such as fascism, or self-destructive private practices. At a lesser level, this Romanticism may lead to an undifferentiated treatment of popular culture as intrinsically positive . . . , an attitude which leaves no room for the principle of discrimination (1987: 207).

From a critical perspective, then, an open textuality may invite creative play, but there can be no simple assurance that the playfulness of active readers will be free from entrenched reactionary attitudes. In these transitional and uncertain circumstances, critical textual strategies, both realist and postmodern, are still required in the medium of TV drama to encourage a critical disorientation of habitual ways of seeing. Not everything can be left to 'semiotic, enunciative and textual' productivity:

textual composition matters, whether the principle of construction is realist or postmodern.

It is no longer meaningful, however, to force a wedge between
the pleasures of popular texts and social responsibility or meaning along traditional political fault-lines. As Barthes puts it:

> on the left, because of morality (forgetting Marx's and Brecht's
> cigars), one suspects and disdains any 'residue of hedon-
> ism.' On the right, pleasure is championed *against* intellec-
> tuality, the clerisy: the old reactionary myth of heart against
> head, sensation against reasoning, (warm) 'life' against (cold)
> 'abstraction' (1976: 22).

The various dualisms of pleasure/order, leisure/work, individual
/society, production/consumption are increasingly inappropriate conceptual tools in postmodernity. Taking again a both/
and approach, in contrast, a way forward in pursuit of a critical
aesthetic can be discerned without either espousing wholesale
an unrestrained populist hedonism or adopting the dismissive
stance of an Adorno in his blanket condemnation of popular
culture. It is a matter of thinking the two, popular culture and
aesthetic value, together rather than merely asserting the one
over the other in a fixed hierarchical relation. Above all, by
recognizing the necessity for politics and ethics to be imbricated
with aesthetics in the breaking down of rigid categorial distinctions, discriminations can be sustained in accord with the ethic
of truth-telling.

II

The processes of the global market which facilitate the hedonist
profusion in postmodernity have drawbacks. A range of anxieties, insecurities and dislocations accompany the increased access
to pleasures generated by technological, economic and social
reformation. New patterns of employment break up rooted
communities and their traditional cultural specificities. Insecurities accompany the disruption of established forms and sense-
making frames. A loss of a sense of place, of history, of subject
identity can be frightening equally as it can be liberating or
exhilarating. An information overload can disorientate. Anxieties may arise from the very impulse to be continually up-beat

on the road to the postmodern funhouse which not all, in any case, are eligible to enter.

Those Westerners unemployed as a result of electronic and technological efficiencies or peripheral Fordism, for example, are left with inadequate financial means; those with newly-found jobs in industries relocated in 'developing' countries often work in bad conditions on low pay. Anxieties are generated globally by the need – induced by omnipresent advertising and image-making – to fund the partaking in the pleasures on offer in the market-place of postmodernity. Credit facilities may have displaced the ethic of debt avoidance but not the demands to keep up with the repayment instalments.

Besides anxiety, is the problem of justice. Whilst the challenge of both/and thinking creates space for progressive possibilities, the elusive undecidability of some postmodernist thought leaves it equivocal about political and economic liberation. Meanwhile, an increasing gap opens up between the wealthy and the poor in developed economies, and large parts of the 'developing' world are left without the basic needs of food, shelter and clean water. Post-colonial theory may offer a warrantable critique of the erstwhile certainties of Western Enlightenment in this con-text (see Bhaba, 1993), but a democracy of consumer pleasures is not the same as a democracy based on an equitable distri-bution of material wealth and political power. Herein lies the difference between an abstract, rational conception of citizen-ship and a sensuous abandon to pleasures in a consumerist democracy.

Whilst, then, there can be no denial of the increased value of the symbolic and the extended spaces for personal desire and pleasures in postmodernity, the new revisionist celebration of televisual and consumerist democracy is overly enthusiastic. At worst it becomes affected by the rhetorical trend pacily to talk up the contemporary. It is notable in this respect that post-modern thought effaces depth models to privilege surface and the dislocated signifier. The formerly fundamental issues of political power and distribution of wealth in relation to it are by-passed in postmodernist revisionism, not resolved.

The devolution of the aesthetic into everyday life has pro-gressive potential, but the tendency to aestheticize every aspect of human life can still mask human reification and commod-ification or plain human suffering. The categorial boundaries which separated aesthetics from ethics and politics in the Western tradition of autonomous art must also be collapsed if everyday life is to be aestheticized. Ethics and politics must once again be seen to be imbricated with aesthetics to avoid the negative and nihilistic tendencies of wholesale aestheticization (see Chapter 9). This is the residual lesson of Adorno's stringent critique of commodity capitalism.[6]

It is with the fears, anxieties and dislocations of postmodernity, and the pleasures of TV drama's mollifying *divertissements* and sense-making frames, that this section is concerned. Beyond psychoanalytic accounts, not all pleasures are evidently to do with sexual or textual play. In the domestic context the desire for escapism and consolatory meanings is an important aspect of television's economy of pleasure. Cultural reassurance and facilitating the assimilation of social change are key functions of TV drama and, in an effort to understand the range of forces in the field shaping contemporary schedules, account must be taken of them.

The dislocation, fragmentation, anomie noted successively by Baudelaire, Benjamin and Berman (see Berman, 1993) to be characteristic of modernity continue, and are exacerbated, in postmodernity. Whilst postmodernism encourages the abandonment of holist attempts to make sense of the world, human beings have at least a residual – if not an inherent – disposition for patterning, at least to the extent of trying to make sense of their own, increasingly privatized, lives. In this context, a demand is created for some stability, however illusory. In television, the medium which as noted serves increasingly as the interface between the public and private spheres, pleasure is taken in the consolation of traditional sense-making frames. As reported by Dorothy Hobson, the plea of many viewers is that television drama might '[g]ive us some stability in our lives. We have enough change forced upon us in our lives no more is needed' (1982: 146). Indeed, respondents took pleasure in representations of 'life as we'd like it to be at times' (Hobson, 1982: 147) even though they recognized that their call was for escapism. This residual need, however it might be questioned from the point of view of a progressive, democratic – let alone more radical revolutionary – politics is deep-seated and has a significant influence on both television schedules and the internal structure of programmes.

Formulaic realism thus serves to some the function of a welcome cultural reassurance precisely in its tendency to make sense of things. The patterns of the texts fulfil the expectations they create; the enigma is resolved. Moreover, through familiarity with fabular forms, as MacCabe puts it: 'we know what is happening but we don't know what will happen, but we know that we will know what will happen' (1976: 99). In such narratives the complexities of referential critical realism are sacrificed to followability. The very reiteration of familiar pattern in which the status quo is challenged but order is ultimately restored may contribute to a feeling of security and well-being as a necessary antidote to the dislocations of the contemporary. As Neale puts it, '[e]ach genre . . . engages and structures differently the two basic subjective mechanisms which any form of the balance involves: the want for the pleasure of process, and the want for the pleasure of its closure' (1980: 26).

The scheduling regularity of TV soaps and series has a ritual function. Genre knowledge may thus be fitted to domestic habits by viewers and schedulers alike. In an economy of anxieties and pleasures, as Neale observes, 'genres institutionalise, guarantee coherence by institutionalising conventions' (1980: 28). Thus, for example, drama such as *Heartbeat* is recognized to be suitable for a family slot on Sunday evening. At this time particularly viewers do not want to be confronted with a disturbing critical realism but prefer to rest secure in the affirmation of membership of a community whose troubles are readily solved by human agency, and in the knowledge that nothing embarrassing in front of the children will appear on the screen. Recognition of television's displacement of church on Sundays should perhaps be accompanied by an acknowledgement of the quasi-mysticism of Sunday evening programming.

TV drama, in the conventions of mimetic realism, has a long history in popular television of facilitating the assimilation of social change because of its tendency to naturalize its representations. It is a matter of what Barthes (1977: 165) and Bourdieu (1992: 166) term the 'doxic' and, just as with hedonist individualism, it is not an innocent pleasure. Doxa, received truths, are a feature of traditional societies with a consensual way of seeing the world. In fractured societies, competing classes or groups vie as noted for the power to assert their view of the world as the 'natural'. Indeed, in spite of the claims of postmodernists of the non-viability of grand narratives, Bourdieu perceives an 'underlying complicity' or 'consensus within dissensus' (1992: 183) lingering on into postmodernity. Elaborating on Bourdieu, Sparks suggests furthermore that, 'if elements of doxa survive in differentiated societies then television is likely to be one of the spheres in which they reside' (1992: 51). The domesticity of the medium both lends itself to the familiar and an affirmation of order. Television narratives are adaptable in embracing new social developments in their representations and, even when new formations are treated superficially or comically, they nevertheless serve to introduce, to assimilate and ultimately to establish as natural the configurations they depict. Thus the doxic is not immutable, even where social change is limited, since new circumstances nevertheless arise.

The fashionable (Barthesian) 'mythologies' of 1990s Britain offer a particular form of cultural reassurance. It resides in idealized British period settings, evident from *Heartbeat* to *The House of Eliott*, and from *Middlemarch* to *Miss Marple*. In addition, the rush of 'aga-sagas', narratives set in English middle-class, village domesticity such as those of Joanna Trollope, derive from a wish for the affirmation of a knowable community. The more established middle classes, disturbed by the multiple dislocations of the Thatcher years, seek solace in constructions of a rural idyll in a form of nostalgia and are curiously satisfied with heritage simulacra as illustrated with regard to *Heartbeat*.

Significant reference to a more objectively and less prettily documented history is typically effaced. The casting of the 'characters' makes them all – to greater or lesser degree – visually attractive. Even the villains are metonymically stylish and there are few dirty fingernails. The *mise-en-scènes* for popular series draw on values and lifestyle imagery. The Oxford of *Inspector Morse* (ITV), for example, overlooks the (now redundant) motor industry to foreground the colleges, stately homes, stone farmhouses and rectories of the vicinity. The buildings stand for a constructed notion of a solid burgher Britishness, the fading of which – carried in the pained disenchantment with modernity of the hero, Morse, himself – is inscribed in the dominant tone of regret for *temps perdu* evoked in the series overall. Morse's 1950s Jaguar is a metonym of pre-industrial craft culture, a world of real walnut dashboards and real leather upholstery. His passion for opera is, similarly, a statement of a class allegiance to a refined high culture, critical of an allegedly dehumanized commercial and industrial world.

The drift in the 1970s, away from the social realism in the drama of crime of the 1960s (see Sparks, 1992: 26–7), might be seen as the beginnings of an intermittent but extending response in TV drama to an actual world which is becoming increasingly fragmented and incomprehensible. Sparks has accordingly observed that:

> the increasing distance of the sphere of dramatic action from public experience affords greater dramatic licence, more schematic narratives, more action and less contamination by the equivocations of the real (1992: 27).

The effacement by convention and codification of the murkier aspects of actual human experience allows the richness of the colours and textures of the imagery to show through to offer sensual gratifications. Even where the darker sides of human life are treated, an aesthetic of cinematic production values casts a beautifying gloss on proceedings. A catalogue display unhindered by social anxieties offers sumptuous costumes, antique furniture, attractive pre-industrial settings, appealing soundtrack. In some respects, these possibilities of pleasure are not new. Film – more than television historically – has never prevented viewers from choosing their pleasures amongst the stars, the photographic beauty, the score and so forth as an alternative to engagement in the narrative. With improved technology, television can offer textual qualities actively encouraging the abandonment, even in formulaic series, of narrative followability and fixity of meaning, though interest in incident, at the level of what is going to happen next remains relatively high.

Indeed, many series and serials, remain referential and TV drama (in Britain at least) continues to treat human unhappiness in 1990s, albeit mainly as a mechanism of disequilibrium, a mainspring of the many narrative crises. Series set in hospitals or other social institutions dominate the British schedules. From a practical makers' perspective, hospitals, health centres, fire stations, lifeboat houses and police stations afford contexts for groups of characters plausibly to come together in a society which is in reality highly privatized rather than communal. Because such places deal with people in exceptional moments of their lives – times of trouble, injury, birth, death and illness – they afford dramatic incidents, in the vernacular sense of exciting because unusual.

Above all, however, such series offer opportunities for human agency. The doctors, nurses, lifeboat operatives, fire officers, police and detectives make effective interventions night after night and week after week. They are able in the context of a conventionalized narrative structure to achieve positive outcomes. The constraints in social life of the reality principle over the pleasure principle are effectively dissolved in such referential, formulaic drama, producing a new vicarious pleasure of dissipated frustration for viewers whose agency is more constrained in social structure than that of their fictional counterparts in dramatic structure.

The cultural reassurance approach to understanding the popularity of formulaic realism is not, however, to resurrect the exorcised ghost of the cultural dupe passively consuming the ideology inscribed in TV dramas. Television viewers are active on a number of levels. The very pixels which make up the television frame must be scanned – and in that sense constructed – by the human eye to yield a picture. The conventional jumps through time and space in the most standard of popular TV dramas demand that viewers make connections, and viewers have become increasingly more skilful in this respect over time. As David Puttnam observes, '[i]t is *amazing* how fast the audience are [*sic*], how little plot and explanation they want. In fact after a while they resent explanation. They enjoy interacting and picking up hints.'[7]

Furthermore, as Umberto Eco has demonstrated, 'every text is made out of two components: the information provided by the author and that added by the Model Reader' (1979: 206). He also points out that:

> it is impossible to explain what happens at the level of the reconstruction of the narrative structures (*fabula*) without resorting to deeper structures, that is, *world structures* (systems of individuals along with their properties and mutual relations) with different imputed truth values (1979: 210).

Thus, Eco proposes an active interrelationship between ideology, in the sense of people's ways of seeing and understanding the world, and the fabular or formulaic text. The understanding of any particular example of a formulaic TV drama will be intertextual in terms of a familiarity with popular generic forms such that the kinds of inferences made by readers to make sense of the text will draw on their experience of structures learned in their repetition. As Eco puts it, 'the reader activates one or more intertextual frames to take his inferential walks and to hazard forecasts apropos of the course of the *fabula*' (1979: 209).

Some viewers no doubt feel affirmed, reassuringly located in their sense of self-identity, by television's formulae. This self-identical subjectivity may well be, as Mercer has observed, 'complicit with particular pleasures; [and] these pleasures are themselves complicit with specific political relationships' (1983: 99). The various discourses of pleasure imply, however, that there may be no singular 'good life' but a plurality of possibilities. Thus, some viewers may take comfort from knowingly indulging in escapism; others, more aware of codes and conventions, may take pleasure in feeling smart that they can predict the narrative outcome, and experience a sense of reassurance in the process. Formulaic realism then, besides being polysemic, is polyplacatory.

The interplay between the mind-set of viewers and principles of textual composition, both established in culture, is the crux of the matter. Indeed the extent to which deconstructive strategies in accord with the new affective order have permeated into popular consciousness lies at the heart of the debate figured in this book about the relative 'activity' and reflexive consciousness of contemporary television viewers. More open textual structures are demonstrable, but it may be that viewers select those fragments which allow them to make a satisfying sense of things. As Eco observes, 'it is easier and more pleasurable to read co-operatively than to "code switch"' (1979: 22). As television literacy increases, moreover, new conventions can, as noted, be readily assimilated into the realist paradigm. Thus, the extent to which readers resist television's disposition to sense-making to engage in intertextual play must remain an open question pending further developments and additional ethnographic research. More people in the new social configuration fall within economic groups attractive to television schedulers and perceive themselves to be part of the expanded middle classes, the mainstream. If oppositional resistance, textual and political, is demonstrably stronger at the social margins, the mainstream

television audience, notwithstanding the diversity of its membership, is likely – in its embourgeoisified domestication – to
be more susceptible to preferred reading positions. Comfortable in the world, they have no desire for disturbance: to them
dehistoricized idylls make sense enough.

III

A hierarchy of pleasures is constructed – though with differing
valences – in all fractions of society. Distinctions of worth are
widely made and never free from interest. Where middle-brow
taste for affirmation and reassurance produces, in Barthes's view,
the text of mere pleasure 'linked to a comfortable practice of
reading', the text of bliss:

> imposes a state of loss . . . discomforts (perhaps to the point
> of a certain boredom), unsettles the reader's historical, cul-
> tural, psychological assumptions, the consistency of his tastes,
> values, memories, brings to a crisis his relation with language
> (1976: 14).

It is not necessary fully to embrace Barthes's sexual-psychoana-
lytic account of pleasure to argue that disorientation to critical
effect might be taken to be the nub of a critical aesthetic.
Since, taken overall, the force field of influences on television
production gravitates towards the comfortable affirmation of the
dominant group, opportunities to promote a critical aesthetic
in TV drama might seem severely inhibited.

As with many of the issues addressed in this study, however,
a simple binary division is unhelpful. It is not a matter of being
either a 'cultural dupe' or a Barthesian textual surfer, riding the
waves across and against textual dynamics. In Chapter 8, I shall
suggest, with reference to *Between the Lines,* that a popular series
can invite critical response by small but significant departures
from formulae. Textual construction has effectivities, though
the impact of any text must be weighed against the tendency
of narrative and ideological closure and the seamless flow of
television programming to militate against critical reflection.
The potential of formulaic series, through cross-referencing in
multiple plotting, to bring out critical perspectives thematically,
for example, has already been noted.

But this is not to propose a textual reductionism to a singular meaning inscribed in authorial intention. Even in the scepticism about the new revisionism expressed in this book, meaning is by no means seen to be fixed in the moment of televisual production, and due allowance is accordingly made for the production of meanings in consumption. The argument is rather to acknowledge that the text may have some force in the processes of the production of meanings and pleasures. It is not to reassert the outright authority of the text, but to invite acknowledgement that – even where postmodern self-reflexivity is concerned – some texts more than others are conducive to a critical disposition.

At a time of cultural transition, a question arises about the extent to which the multiple narratives and dynamic imagery of flexi-narrative or flexiad drama might amount to a multiple coding which encourages active readings through play in the spaces of an open, *lisible,* textual construction.[8] The distinction, drawn provisionally in Chapter 4, between a critical postmodernism and the less careful bricolage of discourses in *Heartbeat* will be revisited in Chapter 10 to explore this issue more fully. The principle of diversity requires a wide-ranging television schedule. But, if a new affective order is to emerge without loss in terms of the criteria for TV drama of value set out in this book, that is to invite people to think and feel more, textual strategies of a critical postmodernism will need to be developed alongside those of critical realism.

Pleasures, however, are neither excluded from nor under-valued in this project. Just as it is recognized that there can be fun and entertainment in the context of a responsible television industry, so commercial interests are noted to be not always at odds with those of a progressive society. Increasingly constructed as private consumers, however, contemporary television viewers may lose the freedom or willingness to make any collective sense of the world. In a world alleged to lack truth or centre, there is – for some – nothing to be done but revel in the ludic postmodern mode: knowledge can only be local, 'truths' merely relative. But, as many commentators are coming to recognize, a need remains for some ethical commonality to address universal problems such as damage to the ecology, inequities of global markets and injustices.

The argument of this chapter has sought to demonstrate the

advisability at least of keeping the conversation open between not yet exhausted traditions and not unambiguously radical innovations. My interest, in both senses, in this book overall is to argue for the retention of those kinds of TV drama which have the potential to expand horizons and invite critical engagement with the programmes and with the world to which directly or indirectly they relate. A market approach to TV production will not assuredly lead either to diversity or critical aesthetics. They can only come through argument initially from outside the industrial context, and central to those arguments must be the advocacy of a space for critical strategies in popular television culture.

8 Diverse Innovations: Radical 'Tec(h)s'

NYPD Blue, Between the Lines, The Singing Detective

> ... kitsch in a national theatre and an intensely original play in a police series. The critical discriminations are at once important and unassumable in advance (Raymond Williams, 1975: 12–13).

> We're not interested in formulas. They're boring. . . . what we've set out to do is to make entertainment for grown-ups (Tony Garnett, executive producer *Between the Lines*).[1]

I

Police and detective fictions have an established history in popular story-telling in all modern forms of narrative expression. They have been a mainstay of television since its early years and, along with soaps, continue to dominate the schedules in the US and UK alike. As with the other examples of TV drama discussed in this book, the styles and forms of presentation of detective fictions have varied considerably over time. They are now designed to offer a range of pleasures over and above narrative suspense and closure, often being commercially inclined in some directions rather than others in (post)modern production. To bring out some critical distinctions, this chapter explores three TV drama detective series – each innovative, but in different terms, and accordingly likely to have different effectivities.

The most celebrated postmodern television detective series is undoubtedly *Miami Vice*. As it has been discussed elsewhere (Buxton, 1990; Grossberg, 1987) however, I note it here simply as a marker which cross-refers, in its principles of construction, to *Heartbeat*, though the dramas are very different in surface style. Indeed style is everything in *Miami Vice*, for, as Grossberg summarizes, it is:

> all on the surface. And the surface is nothing but a collection of quotations from our own collective historical debris, a mobile game of Trivia. It is in some ways the perfect televisual image, minimalist (the sparse scenes, the constant long shots etc) yet concrete (consider how often we are reminded of the apparent reality of the scenes). The narrative is less important than the image. In *Miami Vice* the cops put on a fashion show (not only of clothes and urban spaces, but of their own 'cool' attitudes) to a Top-40 soundtrack (1987: 29).

Indeed, as in *Heartbeat*, the music is unrelated to the narrative and used for its discrete appeal, typically in *Miami Vice* dubbed over a car chase and used as a regular insert whatever the context of any particular storyline. I shall pick up on the idea of a 'pure' television in my discussion of *Twin Peaks* in Chapter 10. Having marked in *Miami Vice* a limit position of postmodern style in the detective series, however, I begin with a look at a more recent innovative, American series, *NYPD Blue*.

II *NYPD BLUE*

I say 'innovative' but, besides its new stylistic features, *NYPD* is in a tradition reaching back to *Hill Street Blues*. Steven Bochco, the producer responsible for both, moreover, is also behind *LA Law* and the short-lived – but interesting in the context of innovative detective series – *Cop Rock*.[2] The family resemblance between these dramas is their slick televisual weft of plot and character. It is the combination of apparently fast-action, narrative in a glossy (high production values) style with a range of characters in a 'work family' whose personal lives are to the fore. Bochco's productions sustain the notion of 'quality' television noted in Chapter 2. Indeed when, in the perception of its American fans, *LA Law* fell short of standards of character development and the series allegedly became repetitive with mediocre writing (see Brower, 1992: 172–4), letters of complaint flooded the NBC network.[3]

In *NYPD*, Detective John Kelly (David Caruso) and his partner Detective Andy Sipowicz (Dennis Franz) (I refer to the first
series of *NYPD* before Jimmy Smits replaced Caruso in the lead
role) are the focus of a work family in the 15th precinct of the
New York Police Department. Unorthodox on occasion in their
methods like many a TV detective hero, they are nevertheless
typically devoted to their work and the cause of justice. They
are moral crusaders not mechanistic enforcers of the law. Kelly,
unattached and thus available for a sequence of affairs, supports alcoholic divorcee Sipowicz, whose unerring reliability
as a work-buddy is assured in return. When Sipowicz's drinking threatens both his job and his tenuous relationship with
DA Silvia Costas, Kelly is, in the current expression, 'there for
him'.

'Rockin' Robin', the episode to be discussed, was shown
twice in the UK, as the final episode of the first series (18 June
1994) and as a trailer to the new series (16 January 1995).
Indeed on-going narrative, sustained in *NYPD*'s flexi-narrative
form alongside closure within the episode of some narrative
strands, spanned the six-months gap. One of Kelly's colleagues
and an ex-lover, Janice Licalsi, is facing trial for the murders
of mobster Angelo Marino and his driver, committed at the end
of the previous series. Kelly, despite the fact that he begins a
new sexual relationship in the episode, is sufficiently concerned
about Licalsi to arrange for a top lawyer to take on her case and
persuade her to abandon her guilty plea.

This sense of general human concern and mutual respect,
transcending particular interpersonal or sexual relationships,
is the underlying communitarian ethic of Bochco's productions.
In the midst of a mesh of high-tension narratives – one concerned with a homosexual murder and another with Sipowicz's
renewed attempt on an inspired hunch to rescue the abducted
small daughter of a local car-dealer – Lieutenant Arthur Fancy
returns to the office with the results of his wife's pre-natal scan.
He is able to announce that he and his wife are 'having a boy',
and the team all crowd around him to view the print-out image,
remarking on the baby's evident 'little thing'. Thus a traditionally domestic and 'feminine' concern, the stuff of soaps, is
seamlessly interwoven, in the 'new man' 1990s, with more traditionally recognizable police series features such as murders,
abductions, car-chases and shoot-outs. The former boundary

between macho male, public action and sensitive, privatized domestic life is blurred, if not obfuscated, whilst pace and style are sustained.

In its public sphere setting of police department life in New York with only occasional scenes given over to close interpersonal duologues (in bars for example), it is remarkable that the series sustains such a personal feel. It does this largely through exchanged looks and glances, often on the stairs in the precinct or in the thick of an, inevitably armed, raid. Relying on modern viewers' sophisticated reading skills, *NYPD* extracts maximum conviction from minimal visual information transmitted at speed. The pleasures of the series' devotees may even rest partly in the sense of achievement in gleaning so much texture of life from such pacey fragments.

Besides its particular mix of content, *NYPD* is distinguished stylistically from its predecessors. It adopts a pseudo-documentary camera style, the single camera – apparently hand-held though stabilized by steadycam – defying the conventions of shot/reverse-shot editing by panning between speakers in a duologue. So slickly controlled is its movement, however, that the result has more the feel of a breathless, excited immediacy than the slightly leaden conviction of the hand-held documentary camera. Indeed, its 'searching' for its subject, evident in a tendency slightly to drift past, only to return to, centred framing can be disconcerting to the point where some viewers find it difficult to watch. In the titles sequence, besides a fast editing rhythm, the restless tilting and panning of the camera over people and locations tends to disturb by disrupting normative technical codes.

Whilst this camera style may draw the attention of some viewers to the devices of televisual construction, to others it may lend a quasi-documentary authenticity to the drama. The camera style works together with a low-key naturalistic acting style in which the demotic dialogue is spoken at a level so low that it suggests the actors are unaware of the camera. In this way a documentary 'authenticity' is sustained simultaneously with the editing rhythms of action-adventure.

In tension, however, with a sense of a single documentary camera capturing the action as it happppens (implying the impossibility of reconstructing the living moment) is an almost art-house cinematic poetry. In 'Rockin' Robin', a leitmotif of touching hands and hugs serves to bring out thematic links between the various narrative strands and the series' ethos of mutual support, of people being there for each other amidst a street-wise cynicism. Thus there is 'bonding' at both televisual and social thematic levels. The camera lingers on the joined hands of the abducted girl and her father as they are reunited, a shot echoed in a moment between Costas and Sipowicz when she refuses his gift until he has control of his drinking. Kelly hugs Sipowicz for being 'lucky and good'. The episode concludes with a sequence in soft-focus silhouette of Kelly in bed with his new lover, underscored by a mellow oboe refrain. *NYPD* thus offsets a tendency to sentimentalism with an innovative (for America particularly) nudity in sex scenes, prominently figuring Caruso's humping bottom. However, a visually sensitive treatment, reminiscent of art-house depiction of physical encounters, is tastefully deployed to soften any potential 'offence'.

Besides its stylistic features, then, *NYPD* innovates by sustaining character development and the work-family ethic in previous Bochco productions, and pushing back boundaries on explicit sexual content. It does not, however, set its agents in the broader structure of New York or more broadly American public or political life. Its communitarian 1990s ethos, including a multi-ethnic mix in its casting, also challenges some traditional gender boundaries. But it simultaneously reaffirms traditional representations: all the women featured are conventionally attractive, if not actually glamorous, and the male caucasian leads remain ultimately tough-minded and independent. *Between the Lines* in UK is prepared to be more challenging to its audience.

III *BETWEEN THE LINES*

According to James Saynor, *Between the Lines* is 'essentially a *Hill Street Blues*-style, post-leftist cop show' (1993: 11). But in addition to drawing significantly on the Bochco stable's American 'quality TV' 1990s production values, *BTL* reflects that 1960s British critical realist tradition which Tony Garnett is credited with initiating. Without marked development, 1960s British realism would not in itself resonate with the dominant values of the 1990s – production or ideological. An adjustment without wholesale compromise results in a blend of postmodern television's pacey dynamic and glossy production values with vestiges of 'serious' social analysis.

Given the intensifying commercial context of TV drama production, *Between the Lines* may not have been made without the path-breaking *Edge of Darkness* (BBC2, 1985), which demonstrated that co-production financing does not necessarily entail a bland product. The distinction of both series is their use of established popular film and television genres with a radical edge achieved by small but significant deviations from formulaic narrative and product moulds. Both gain popular attention by drawing on not only the detective genre but also the thriller and the western. Consonant superficially with the traditions of patriarchy in police series, they offer (in common with the other series under discussion here) conventionally attractive and interesting caucasian male protagonists as the agents of moral quest beyond the confines of the law. Both involve: head-to-head conflict between powerful people; thriller intrigue about what exactly is happening; car chases and shoot-outs. In addition each uses a strong soundtrack for a range of functions including commentary on the action.

Both series break the standard detective mould in refusing a heavily indicative narrative and ideological closure to leave the impression that no one agency (governmental or individual) is fully in control of events. Furthermore, they place agency in structure to bring out the relations between systems and individuals. In their consideration of the forces of social power, both *BTL* and *Edge* suggest that political expediency rather than the greater good is the driving force of establishment institutions. The social positions and values of the central males are accordingly called profoundly into question. Elements of narrative resolution are held by these means in tension with a number of loose and open ends. With regard to institutional production context, it should be noted, *Edge* would not itself have been made without an eye to the American market, the casting of star-rated American actor Joe Don Baker in a leading role clinching the funding.[4] In turn, Garnett has recognized the contemporary context of TV drama production in shaping *BTL*.

In his early years, Garnett had little time for popular formats. In 1970, he observed that, '[t]he odds are against original work being done in serials' (cited in Saynor, 1993: 11). But by the

1990s when the single play (shot on film) had given way to a different kind of film product, Garnett remarked that:

> [t]here's an element in television today that has the smell of art-house preciousness about it, where people are making one-off films which they hope will win awards at some film festival. I've never wanted to come out humming the lighting. That's one reason why I wanted to plunge back into the world of the popular series, where there's still large audiences (cited in Saynor, 1993: 11).

In producing *BTL*, then, Garnett has been both manouevred into, and actively interventionist in, the popular series. Making drama in the dominantly popular form and drawing on its narrative and cinematic conventions as well as the currency of its production values, he has nevertheless sought to remain subversive.

Between the Lines, like *Edge of Darkness*, resists the formulaic mould of UK series such as *The Bill* (ITV Network), even though J.C. Wilsher (who has written 35 episodes of *The Bill*) was *BTL*'s initiator. For, whilst *The Bill* varies a little from episode to episode, its stock characters and standard narratives characteristically fit more or less tightly the formula of TV drama's version of classic realism. Each episode treats an incident of crime or social concern and customarily the disruption of narrative and social equilibrium is restored by the end of the episode. An additional narrative interest is provided by the interrelationships between the various officers at Sunhill police station. Little is learned, however, of their private lives beyond the station. They are observed in the system of police bureaucracy but typically not situated in the broader socio-political sphere.

In marked contrast with the overall brightness of Sunhill and its extraordinarily high crime resolution rate, Garnett invites the audience to read between the lines with reference to law and order in contemporary Britain. The series is avowedly referential: all those involved in the production 'insist that it is entirely based on the reality of what goes on in Britain today'. As Garnett puts it, '[w]e deal in fiction and try to tell the truth'.[5] The setting of the series in the police Complaints Investigation Bureau (CIB) means, as he wryly notes, that, 'we can have corrupt police officers on the screen every week' (cited in Saynor, 1993: 11). Besides redressing a representational one-sidedness in mainstream formulaic police drama, Garnett contrives in addition to call Establishment power in question as many of the *BTL* stories involve the intervention of the Home Office or MI5. Thus the dominant sense of the police's concern to pursue truth and justice as the highest priority is under-cut by a context which frequently shows justice to be frustrated.

The locus of principled judgement is Detective Superintendent Tony Clark (Neil Pearson), placed centrally in the drama as the preferred figure for reader identification and bearing the stamp of the popular police hero, a moral crusader not merely a law enforcer. In one episode, for example, Clark firmly establishes the culpability of a 'bent copper' but is prevented from proving his case owing to the reluctance of his superiors to confirm evidence which might lead to the police being called into disrepute. In another to be discussed, Clark's pursuit of justice is literally thwarted by the intervention of MI5, when the shooting in a Territorial Army barracks turns out to have been set up by undercover agents.

Garnett's series thus draws on a device, popular in the police genre, of placing the incorruptible detective at odds with the institution for which he works and to which he commits his life. A sense is also created by this structural device of a moral superiority of the protagonist which, besides inviting the sympathy of viewers, serves as a relief valve against the constraints of law enforcement in a highly administered society. Characteristically used, as for example in *Inspector Morse*, this device is ultimately conservative serving to release tensions created by manifest injustices. Having little power to find redress in an administered world in which the legal system is at best bureaucratic and expensive to engage in, individual viewers may find solace in vicarious identification with those agents who appear to be able directly to do something. Hence in part, perhaps, the broad popularity in popular televison and film of assertive individualism in the thriller, western and police detective genres. Deployed by Garnett, however, the device is more enlightening than consolatory, subversive even, since *BTL* locates the cause of the frustration back with the Establishment: the police hierarchy, MI5, the government itself, even international capitalism. Frequently, the narratives in *BTL* are resolved to the extent that Clark and his team are certain of their case, but action to bring to light their findings or to secure justice is prevented, and the clarity of resolution muddied by a vagueness as to which forces are at work, and how and why they operate, to serve their own purposes. This sense of political conspiracy or confusion – in different episodes one or the other is greater – is likely to leave viewers, in marked contrast with *The Bill*, asking questions rather than feeling that their acculturated sense of an ordered, comprehensible world is reaffirmed.

A feature of the second series of *BTL* which differentiates it from the standard cop series, is its treatment of the central characters and its flouting of conventional screen relationships. More than most formulaic police dramas, *BTL* finds space amidst the investigative action for the private lives of its characters. With regard to protagonist Tony Clark, the second series abandons the bed-hopping sexual adventurousness of the first. Whilst previously a dimension of immaturity and insecurity was seen to inform Clark's promiscuity, the second series risks the loss of appeal afforded to macho male heterosexual identification by a philandering television hero. Francesca Annis is cast as Angela Berridge, a married Home Office mandarin older than Clark, with whom he becomes obsessed after an initial affair. The series thus retains an element of conventional female attractiveness and heterosexuality but places more emphasis on Clark's complicated and confused attitude to women. Whilst she enters a sexual relationship with Clark, Berridge is not as interested in him as he is in her, and there is even a suggestion that she allows herself to be seduced only in order to pursue professional interests. She has no intention of abandoning her family, and Clark is consequently left, evidently lonely, pursuing her in the guise of a lovelorn, romantic suitor. The stereotype '[r]andiest 'tec on telly'[6] of the first series is revealed in the second to be a much more complex human being.

In another daring challenge to social and televisual conservatism, Maureen 'Mo' Connell (Siobhan Redmond), the female member of Clark's three-person team, is revealed to have a female sexual partner. Hints of a lesbian inclination are evident in the first series in which she lives with a man, but it is not until the second that the full lesbian relationship is revealed in terms of explicit physicality. In the world of policing, typifying macho male values both on screen and in the historical world, the idea of openly representing bisexual or lesbian women is risky. *BTL* takes the issue literally head-on, with Mo shown in

Close-Up kissing her new partner with sexual hunger. In a subsequent episode, she brings her partner to the police social, affording opportunities for immediate shock and confrontation of the issues on the part of both her peers and professional superiors.

Similarly under-cutting and calling in question stereotypes, Harry Naylor (Tom Georgeson), the third CIB team member, represents superficially the experience-hardened, slightly world-weary, committed professional police officer. Naylor has accessible contacts throughout the world of the police force and its criminal couterpart simply by having been around a long time and having played by the unofficial rules of the game. A heavy smoker and drinker, he shuns the sharp-suited image of Clark, and growls his bluff insights into the investigative process. But the second series also looks beyond this stereotype to represent a broader personality. The established gruff, no-nonsense image is under-cut by the revelation that Naylor's hobby is ballroom dancing with his wife to whom he is devoted. It gradually emerges that Joyce Naylor is suffering from cancer and is unable to get immediate treatment under the NHS. Harry 'moonlights' to work with a private security firm to raise the money for private health care. Another topical political issue is thus raised in passing (compare *Casualty* in Chapter 2).

Further to illustrate the exploration of character in the context of a cop series, the episode of 23 November 1993,[7] entitled 'The Great Detective', serves to show how *BTL*, in the midst of a tense drama of power conflict, can embrace telling moments of the personal lives of its main characters. The central narrative involves the investigation on a charge of corruption for a second time of Chief Supt. Trevor Dunne, a highly successful Metropolitan detective, much admired in the ranks. It emerges that he has indeed convicted falsely a former informant and known criminal, Peter Hoskins, whom he could not lawfully convict of a brutal murder on available evidence. Throughout, a sense of Dunne's natural justice is set against the letter of the law and the visual imagery reinforces the value loading of the episode. Dunne is featured running with enthusiasm a boxing club for young lads, whilst Hoskins is shown – shot in Close-Up and from a low angle – to be a bear of a man with a tendency to unprovoked violence. Even Clark is somewhat reluctant to challenge such a legend as Dunne, and in one scene at the boxing club, Clark and Dunne spar together, man to man, as it were, in a clean fight. Ultimately, however, clear videotape evidence of Dunne 'taking a drink' from Hoskins leads inexorably to his downfall, which he takes with dignity.

In typical *BTL* mode, however, the videotape evidence – withheld from the earlier inquiry and thought to have been wiped – has been passed circuitously to Clark by the Metropolitan Police Commander Sparrow who is envious of Dunne's record and jealous that the ranks address Dunne as 'the guvnor' rather than himself. As ever in *BTL*, justice and truth are murky concepts never free from personal or systemic interest. Clark's immediate superior, Chief Supt. Graves, who has initiated the investigation into Dunne, turns out to be a protégé of Sparrow's.

Cut into this main story, however, are several sequences of the protagonists' personal lives. By means of brief verbal exchanges and looks and glances between them, a texture of relationships is constructed which grounds the high action narratives in a representation of lived experience. Early in the episode, Mo is seen emerging late at night from a pub with Kate, a female friend and colleague who is lodging temporarily with her. Walking and talking about their careers in the force, they are propositioned by young men kerb-crawling in a BMW. When the young men fail to respond to her firm but lighthearted rebuttals, Mo flashes her police identity and the men, shocked, speed off crashing into some boxes as they go. The ensuing dialogue says much in a few words:

KATE: That was brilliant. Did you see his face? (*in imitation*) 'Bollocks'. I tell you it's worth staying in the job just to get rid of wankers like that.
MO: Well you know, it's the wankers *in* the job that really bother me.

Besides affording humour to give the drama overall a texture of light and shade, the retort picks up on tensions between Mo and her two colleagues. In an earlier exchange in the office, Mo has challenged Harry's patriarchal manner in addressing her as 'darling'. In addition she is at odds with her male colleagues in not sharing the adulation of Dunne whom she sees simply as a 'bent copper'. Having seen the videotape evidence, she differs from Clark and Naylor in thinking it should be referred immediately to their superior. The boys are playing for time but Mo does not share the male bonding.

These moments precede the scene where, unable to sleep, she enters Kate's bedroom. Following a brief verbal exchange about their mutual restlessness in which Mo takes a sip from Kate's mug of coffee, the two women kiss – at first gently and then with more passion. The two-shot is in Close-Up. Arriving bright-eyed at work the next day, Mo reports the videotape's existence to Graves, much to Clark's annoyance. It remains unclear whether she has gone behind her colleagues' backs, however, for Harry supports her when, in the face of Clark's anger, she protests that Graves demanded that she tell all she knew. But Harry has his own agenda.

Having discovered that the videotape had probably been supplied by someone in the force, he has returned overnight to the office to retrieve – and presumably destroy – the tape. Dunne, it transpires, is his ex-boss and he retains loyalties. Clark, however, knows of this affiliation and, suspecting Naylor, intercepts him at the office. Thus even between the close CIB associates, largely at one in pursuit of truth and justice, all kinds of personal interests are in play. They serve as weft to the dramatic texture. Mo's lesbian relationship – more overtly revealed subsequently in the episode – is woven into a number of dealings with male sexual assertiveness and aggression. Similarly, Harry's 'moonlighting' and Clark's partial success in his affair with Angela Berridge are played off against Mo's evident sexual fulfilment.

In a final sequence of juxtaposed images, Harry shuffles into the security firm's yard, Mo kisses her new lover hungrily, Clark sits alone after closing time in an empty hotel bar, evidently stood up by Berridge, and Dunne is confined in his cell. Melancholic strings play over the sequence in an explicit invitation to sympathize on different levels with each of these unconventional anti-heroes. The juxtaposition, with only musical comment, invites critical reflection as the credits roll.

Thus the unconventional use of a three-hander team of investigators, rather than the traditional detection partnership of a Holmes and Watson, Morse and Lewis or Kelly and Sipowicz, is augmented in its disorientating strategy by character development. The location of the characters in a broader personal and wider political context, moreover, militates against the ahistorical and asocial individualism which typifies formula film and television heroism. In retrospect, Garnett felt that his early television success *Cathy Come Home* was politically soft because it offered a middle-class audience a locus of compassion through identification with the central figure.[8] In *BTL,* he uses that traditional naturalist viewer–reader identification to draw viewers in, only to challenge their expectations and shake their frames of reference.

Likewise to this end, he sets up a traditional villain figure in Dakin, the ex-policeman turned freelance security professional who frequently plagues Clark's efforts to unmask the truth, only to reveal as the second – and indeed the third – series progresses that the skullduggery in play is not simply the result of the ruthless self-interest of a particular individual. For Dakin is also ensnared in the complex web of the Home Office, MI5, the sometimes lawless agents of international security and the twilight world of illicit arms dealing. Thus, as Saynor has observed of Garnett's earlier work with Loach and Jim Allen, there is:

> some sort of deep-level, sad empathy with the agents of oppression – mine-owners, politicians, welfare officials, army people – who were treated without maliciousness. They were more like objects of pity trapped in a foggy purgatory on the wrong side of the class struggle. It was by creating an imaginative understanding of these boss-class factotums that, paradoxically, the system could be thrown into sharpest relief as the only available culprit (1993: 13).

Going further than *NYPD*'s communitarian work family, *BTL* avoids simply personalizing the political and social issues. It thus invites a questioning of systems and structures, but it does this in the aesthetic of the 1990s glossy television series. The explicit class politics of *The Big Flame* (1969) and *Days of Hope* (1975) have moved somewhat with the times and the documentary drama characteristics – hand-held camera, long takes, 'natural' lighting, dialogue improvised by non-professional actors, unrefined sound – have given way to fast-cut sequences constructed for the aesthetic effect of a stylish filmic 'look'. But viewers are not left 'humming the lighting' as the drama has not been politically gutted. Selective examination of a second episode further illustrates its innovative features.

The titles sequence of *BTL* is a stylish collage of images running for thirty seconds. Its rapid inter-cutting of more than ten key images, including some of sex and violence, parallels the titles to most mainstream popular series in serving as an audience hook. All the shots are shadowy and set at night giving a feel of undercover, thriller action. There is constant movement and the images are largely in Close-Up. The musical soundtrack initially features a melancholy single guitar picking out the strain of a lament. As the pace of the action increases, however, a clarinet brings in the orchestral accompaniment which is gradually foregrounded, emotively crescendant, with a stronger rhythmic pulse.

The episode of 2 November 1993,[9] entitled 'Some must watch . . .', continues in similar vein to the titles with a three minutes and twenty seconds long sequence of visuals cut to a music soundtrack which in this instance is reminiscent of orchestral Vivaldi. The only verbal sound is police orders in the action sequences and a voice-over of one of the characters on the telephone which provides limited contextual information. The scene is a North London suburb early in the morning as people make their way to work. An establishing shot of a flower stall and pavement bustling with commuters is wiped by a van moving from right to left across the screen. The camera follows panning slowly from right to left to reveal in soft focus the painted sign of a 'Territorial Army Centre'. This emerges to be the location of the key action. From a Mercury telephone van parked alongside, several men take out a pair of very extended stepladders to scale a high wall topped with barbed wire. Prior to this a man with tortoiseshell spectacles is glimpsed from behind in quarter profile as a shift of differential focus brings him briefly into vision. He is watching something intently. Another, younger man is also seen to be observing from a window opposite the TA Centre. The pace of the action accelerates – against the bustling but serenely controlled mood set by the music – when the young man realizes that there is a break-in to the TA enclosure. He is patently on surveillance and his hasty phone-call requesting uniformed police back-up reveals him to be a Special Branch officer, Inspector Pollock.

The following action sequence is a standard police/military 'silent approach' as Pollock and his team, weapons drawn, stake out and enter the premises. The camera is not quite in the hand-held, rapidly mobile, pseudo-documentary style of *NYPD*, but it pans back and forth as if seeking the flashpoints of the action. Once inside, Pollock's team find themselves in a large hall where a man in brown overalls is in a doorway, his back to them. Under the tense shouts of 'Armed police' and 'Armed police, drop it', the man turns with a gun-shaped, electric drill in his hand. Shots ring out and in the middle distance blood spatters over the door behind the man. As he falls to the ground, the camera picks out, slow motion and in Close-Up, falling paint brushes, nails and other tools as the Vivaldi-esque music soundtrack weaves to a resolution.

In this account the mix of thriller, police detection with a stylish, even high art, aesthetic (the soundtrack, art-shot slomo, manipulation of differential focus) is evident. The lack of dialogue for such a length of time shows, moreover, the influence of cinematic story-telling rather than a studio-bound, literary theatrical tradition still evident in lower budget productions like *The Bill*. Whilst the style reverts to a more standard fare of dialogues (in offices, restaurants, cars), formal meetings and police interview scenes as the investigation of Clark and his team gets under way, the cinematic 'look', in terms of lighting and carefully framed shots, is retained to sustain high gloss production values. A number of exterior shots on the Thames bankside, in New Scotland Yard and outside Whitehall are intercut to reinforce location. Throughout, however, the production values are not merely enjoyed for their own sake – though they no doubt afford viewing pleasures – but they are played off against other features of the series.

The plot of the episode is very complicated and indeed difficult to unravel on one viewing. Unlike *Miami Vice*, however, this is not because the narrative is subjugated to superficial style, but to convey a complex, murky world. The 68-year-old man shot dead by Inspector Pollock in Crouch End TA Centre was working it transpires for MI5, but not as an agent so much as a handyperson planting bugs on its behalf. The break-in to the TA Centre was by MI5 which had deliberately created a breach of security in Special Branch to justify its bugging – and other harassing – of that arm of the police force on the grounds that its security is lax. Inspector Pollock had been working undercover with a man called Hodges, a corporal in the TA who had been approached by a terrorist organization (implicitly the IRA) with a view to buying weapons to be stolen by Hodge from the well-equipped TA Centre weapons store. But Hodge, it emerges obliquely through Clark's investigations and Home Office refusal to take the matter further, is indeed an MI5 plant, set up merely to implicate and embarrass Pollock and make the Special Branch appear leaky. Audio-tapes have been obtained through further bugging in supposedly secure places, and photographs of Pollock and Hodges have been taken by the man in the tortoiseshell spectacles whose identity is never fully revealed in the episode – though his spectacles are glimpsed several times.

This plot is an ideal vehicle for *BTL*. Besides affording the tangled complexities of a good thriller, it allows the series to probe the integrity of the seat of government figured in the title sequence, and by implication – rather than clear whodunit exposition – to convey that expediency rules in a petty, internecine power feud between MI5 and Special Branch. Indeed every institution featured appears to be at best incompetent and at worst dangerously out of control. The consequent lack of an accountability, central to a well-functioning democracy, is thus pointed up in the episode.

All sides, including Clark and his team, are embroiled in the farrago. Thomas Wenleigh, the under-secretary at the Home Office who steps in on behalf of the Minister to try to avoid the affair hitting the headlines and implicating the government, insists that any contact with the press must have his approval. Nevertheless, MI5 deliberately leaks information denying that the shot man is one of their agents. Angered at the imputation that a police officer has blunderingly shot an innocent man, Clark – with the approval of the Head of CIB – counters with his own leak to an ex-lover, Molly Cope, who works for *The Guardian*. In the midst of this confusion, observations of a politically interrogative nature are frequently made in the dialogue. As noted, however, of Garnett's earlier television productions, the political barbs are made all the more effective by showing the mingled yarn in all social groups. Clark here, for example, operates on dubious terms parallel with those of MI5.

Nevertheless, there is enough mud in circulation in *BTL* for some of it to stick, inviting critical questioning of contemporary social power structures. Indeed in the denouement of this episode, an expediency which suits the government is explicitly pursued in the place of truth. Hounded by Molly Cope to do something in response to the official television news whitewash of the incidents at the heart of the episode, Clark intercepts Thomas Wenleigh on his way to work in Whitehall. Initially Wenleigh genially suggests that 'truth is an abstract romantic concept', but when Clark admits to being a romantic of that turn, Wenleigh puts to him a hypothetical circumstance. It involves a police officer who breaches the Official Secrets Act by leaking to an attractive young woman journalist information of a sensitive nature, with 'important implications for national security'. Wenleigh points out that, should a tape of the telephone conversation be brought as evidence in this hypothetical situation, the police officer concerned would not only lose his job and all pension rights but that he and the young lady in question would be likely to serve many years in prison.

Thus with telling irony pointing a political lesson for anybody willing to learn from it, the episode ends in one of its keynote terms with Clark 'shafted'. Truth (in terms that Nietzsche, Derrida and Foucault would doubtless approve) is challengingly revealed to be the rhetoric of the most powerful agents in a social structure. Once again, a Garnett production manages to point the finger of suspicion at systems rather than merely at individuals.

It is by the range of means illustrated above that Garnett and his team of writers and directors create a cop series with the production values of the 1990s, but with a human and political edge. By adhering to his long-standing insight into systems and structures of power, he retains the important element of setting agency within structure. In mingling this weft with the warp of a cop show, the *BTL* team harness the pulling power of a linear detection narrative to the density and complexity of both thriller intrigue and political and personal power relations. In bringing the narrative to a close, nothing is resolved. The agency of the detective protagonist discovering the truth is repeatedly thwarted by systemic expediency. In both drawing upon and subverting the framework and imagery of popular formulaic drama, *BTL* draws the audience in and takes it somewhere else. In Dennis Potter's phrase it 'disorientates smack in the middle of the orientation process'; in Garnett's terms it provides, 'entertainment for grown-ups'.

IV   *THE SINGING DETECTIVE*

My final example for discussion of radical tec(h)s goes back a decade to 1986, a moment just prior to the election for a third term in Britain of Mrs Thatcher's Conservative government. Dennis Potter's *The Singing Detective* raises like no other detective series the nexus of key questions about transitions at the core of this book. As a firm believer in the potential of TV drama to engage a 'common culture', Potter stood nevertheless for an uncommon, non-naturalistic, studio-based TV drama. He also stood against the consumerist drift of 1980s culture and the shift in TV drama from electronic theatre to film, both of which the 1990 Broadcasting Act were effectively to secure. And yet, as Cook (1995) has documented, the controversial success of *TSD* in Britain ironically brought opportunities for Potter in the commercial sphere of American film. This success raised Potter, as Cook puts it, 'from "distinguished television playwright" into genuine "television *auteur*"' (1995: 245). Although he could not ultimately withstand the move to film and an attendant shift in the power-relations of drama production from the writer to the director (see Cook, 1995), Potter temporarily reclaimed in *TSD* the status of playwright as author.

Whilst a series such as *Moonlighting* plays with the codes and conventions of the detective series to entertain a sizeable audience, and *Twin Peaks* self-consciously disrupts whilst simultaneously reaffirming the detective genre, ultimately for a limited, 'cult' audience, *The Singing Detective* confounds categorization. It is a non-linear, multi-layered metafiction which challenges conventions and pushes against boundary distinctions, and yet, I shall argue, it is not postmodern, at least not in terms of textual form as characterized in this book. An audience averaging 8 million over the first three episodes – and rising to 10 million after the publicity over the 'forest adultery scene' – suggests an appeal beyond an elite 'high culture' audience of perhaps 3 million for something 'arty' on Britain's Channel 4 or BBC2.

In drawing upon the detective fiction genre, paying *hommage* stylistically to film noir, and using 1940s popular song, *TSD* is a text in popular traditions. And yet the visual, narrative and thematic complexities of the piece have other resonances. Cutting sharply and repeatedly from discourse to discourse and narrative to narrative, as it does, as well as disrupting the time and space frames which make for the comfortable viewing of formulaic realism, *TSD* might alternatively be characterized as an *avant-garde* artwork. Given the retention, indeed building, of an audience of 8–10 million, it may be that Potter achieved in *TSD* his aim of a challenging but popular TV drama. Indeed, as Cook summarizes, 'Potter's democratic faith in the ability of television drama to cut across socio-economic hierarchies of class and education seemed to find justification' (1995: 243).

The series centres on a writer of detective fiction, Philip Marlow (no final 'e') in hospital suffering (like Dennis Potter himself) from painful flaking skin from head to toe, a symptom of psoriatic arthropathy. Immediately the text is multi-layered in the *doppelganger* play between fictional character and real author. I shall return to the implications of this 'play'.

Developing, meanwhile, a thumbnail sketch of the piece, another dimension of Marlow's narrative is articulated in flashbacks to his childhood. Central is the sexual encounter between his mother and his father's best friend, Binney (the 'forest adultery scene'), witnessed by the young Philip from his treetop in the forest. The events in the flashback correspond to events in the present hospital 'reality' involving Marlow's wife and an affair she is having (or Marlow imagines she is having) with Finney, a film screenplay writer and producer. This leitmotif is also echoed in the novel, written by Marlow and titled *The Singing Detective*, visualized at yet another level of the series' narratives, perhaps locatable in Marlow's mind as an adaptation of his novel into a screenplay. Marlow's novel is coincidentally being read by one of his fellow patients at the level of hospital 'reality'. The events of this Chandleresque detective fiction involve further illicit sex and cold-war intrigue culminating in the death by drowning in the river of a Russian prostitute.

This last figure echoes the drowning in the Thames of Philip's mother, and also Marlow's wife. It is taken by some commentators to be an image of the return of Philip Marlow's repressed knowledge of the active, predatory sexuality of his mother (and perhaps women in general). Indeed, throughout Potter's work a refrain may itself be 'detected' of masculine fear (and perhaps suppression by imaginary elimination of) the feminine 'other'. Indeed, Potter has, at worst, been charged with misogyny on this account.

It is beyond the scope of this book to discuss fully these

aspects of Potter and his work (see Cook, 1995), but it should be noted that Potter's TV drama, like it or loathe it, addresses the tensions in the social codes of patriarchal culture as they are manifest in works of fiction. Where *NYPD* progresses a little in its representations of the 'new man', and *BTL* invites a questioning of doxa by deploying recognized codes and conventions only to take them somewhere else, *TSD* delves beneath the surface representations to the codified psyche. Its disturbances can thus resonate at a profound emotional or psychological level whilst its distanciation techniques make for a play of ideas approximating to the rational critique Brecht hoped to encourage throught the devices of *Verfremdung* (estrangement or making strange).

The extent of narrative complexity is evident in the above attempt briefly to describe *TSD*. For convenience, Bondebjerg (1992) has labelled the three main narrative strands *the crime plot* (Marlow's novel), *the therapeutic plot* (Marlow's illness and ultimate recovery), and *the socialisation plot* (the account, set against British postwar history, of Marlow's past life), and I shall borrow his terms here. But he recognizes that the plots cannot be clearly distinguished from each other. Whilst, moreover, there is ultimately a kind of resolution to the plots in that Marlow recovers sufficiently to walk again and to leave the hospital, the various structural confusions and formal ambiguities militate against a sense of closure.

A reading which sees the series as a journey of discovery (Hunningher, 1993; Cook, 1995) whereby Marlow plumbs the depths of his psyche to discover the root cause of a mental condition which in turn gives rise to his physical skin condition, comes closest to a resolution of the enigma. If the answer to the 'whodunnit?' lies in an oedipal complex in Marlow's psyche and its purgation with the assistance of psychotherapist, Dr Gibbon, then all the narrative strands lead, as Potter put it, to 'the man in the hospital bed'.

In this view, the various layers of the text, apparently disparate in the narrative exposition, finally cohere in modernist vein in Marlow's consciousness. As Cook remarks:

> in keeping with the modernist sensibility . . . the decision to root a view of the past in the experiences and imagination of a writer protagonist, emphasises the fact that, far from being

an objective assessment, any perspective on history can only ever be *subjective* (1995: 217).

Viewed in this way Potter has articulated in a TV drama series a consciousness in which objective events in the historical world, both public and private, are mediated, necesssarily, through a mind. If this is the achievement of *TSD*, then it illustrates Potter's theory of disorientation 'smack in the middle of the orientation process'. Against the flow of TV drama, it does not set up normative expectations and then disorientate viewers by taking them somewhere else (as, for example, in *BTL*), but functions quite differently from the various realisms as discussed in this book.

Right up to the final moments of *TSD*, fractures in all normative, sense-making frames are designed to leave a doubt in the mind of even the viewer most keenly disposed to make all ends tie up. Firstly, the moment of Marlow's catharsis is undercut by 'Into each life some rain must fall', the music over-dub of Ella Fitzgerald and the Inkspots to which Marlow and Dr Gibbon clumsily dance together, mouthing the words of the song. More dislocating in the pseudo-denouement, however, is the transgression of the small-time, fictional detectives who feature in the *crime plot* – one large one small like a comic double-act – when they burst from their assigned fictional narrative frame on to the hospital 'reality' level of the *therapeutic plot* to confront Marlow A (their author) with the poverty of their anonymous roles. Marlow B, the jazz-singing fictional detective, likewise invades the hospital space, however, and, by design or accident, literally effects the death of the author, Marlow A, by shooting him in the head. Marlow A is nevertheless subsequently released from hospital alive, and apparently better if not yet well, the next day.

Correspondences between the narratives strands are marked by a range of devices. Some actors play multiple roles. Patrick Malahide, for example, plays three: Binney, the spy in the detective story, Mark Binney, who seduces Philip's mother, and film producer, Finney, who steals both Marlow's screenplay of *TSD* and his wife. Michael Gambon is both the bedridden Philip Marlow and the visualized jazz-singing version of the detective in his novel. This again suggests a further correlation between author and fictional character as, provocatively, between Potter and Marlow. But a neat schema of explanatory correspondences is refused. The parallels in the narratives' drownings, between Philip's mother, Marlow's wife, Nicola, and the Russian prostitute are not similarly reinforced by a single performer playing the parts. The numerous pairings and triplets, in antithesis or parallel, between characters serve to draw attention to the text as fictional construct, even as more familiar technical codes and conventions provide bearings on the TV drama. They function like the many other devices which overdetermine narrative moments or break the narrative mainframe (if the *therapeutic plot* can be so called). Some of the various 1940s songs serve, as Hunningher suggests, to bind the narratives (1993: 248), but equally others serve to break the frame. Thus, *The Singing Detective* is familiar enough generically to sustain the interest of a popular audience, but sufficiently defamiliarising to disorientate, 'smack in the middle of the orientation process'.

Whilst *TSD* looks like a self-contained, modernist, fictional construct from one angle, it also intersects with the historical world in ways which qualify a sense of it as an self-referential structure. The events of Philip Marlow's life are grounded in British post-war history. As Cook establishes, '1945 is not just the period setting of Marlow's novel but also the year of his childhood to which he keeps returning in memory' (1995: 214). There is tension between the modernizing world of the metropolis, rebuilding post-war, and the quaintly antiquated, forest world of Philip's upbringing. The social dislocation attendant on this historical transition is carried in the character of Philip's mother who, coming from London, is bored by the outmoded way of life in the forest and frustrated by its entrenched familial hierarchies. It is Philip's father's inability, or unwillingness, to challenge forest mores which leads to Mrs Marlow's dissatisfaction with her husband and in turn to her affair with Binney and Philip's trauma in witnessing it. In short, it leads ultimately to 'the man in the hospital bed'. In this account of the narrative strand a linear, causal chain of events typical of classic realism is evident. In addition, the referential grounding of contemporary social history in a recognizable form is another aspect of the series which sustains accessibility and a degree of followability. Realist conventions – mimetic and referential –are thus mixed with popular and modernist codes to these ends.

That there is a superficial correspondence between these

central narrative events in *TSD* and the trajectory of Potter's own life, moreover, has led some commentators to offer biographical readings of this (and Potter's other) fiction (see Cook, 1995). My interest here in the relationship between fact and fiction is not, however, in whether the events of *TSD* actually happened in Potter's life but in his avowed exploration of the blurring of any clear distinction between 'fact' and fiction. The compositional strategy of *TSD* which, for reasons of accessibility or otherwise, embraces those noted aspects of linear narrative understanding and a sense of closure (comprehensibility and followability), ultimately collapses the distinction between its narrative levels of 'reality' and fantasy, as we have seen. There is a potential fusion between Potter (as author), his doppelganger, Marlow A (detective fiction writer), and his counterpart, Marlow B (jazz-singing detective). Though shot dead by Marlow B, Marlow A emerges from the hospital curtain, dressed and ready to be taken home by Nicola. Thus the series' closure is simultaneoulsy an opening for textual play, but of a kind which invites not free association but a serious reassessment of the categorial distinction between fact and fantasy.

A both/and thinking is invited and it reverberates like an after-shock through the empirical, ethical and epistemological bearings we have in the world. Marlow's rational detection of the cause of his ills is demonstrably shot through with repressions in his psyche. If he has found liberation in reflecting profoundly on his past in a kind of regression therapy, the conclusive outcome remains fragile in that it is as disturbing as it is consoling. The challenge to TV drama's linear plausibilities based in doxa breaks mind-sets as well as narrative frames. The certainties of ethical distinctions excoriating the feminine (Mrs Marlow) to privilege the masculine (Philip's father), with all the attendant cultural associations of patriarchal hierarchy, are confounded. Philip, the 'wannabe' detective as omniscient narrator must ultimately come down from the moral highground of his tree into the murk of the quotidian. In all dimensions, clear categorial distinctions are collapsed into both/and.

In *TSD*, Potter achieves his aim through a controlled confusion of narrative time and space, the very form of his fiction holding in suspension the facets of several contradictions, not separated out but as they inhere in each other. The production history provides a telling clue in this respect (see Cook, 1995:

221). Director Jon Amiel had thought to shoot the visualized novel in black and white to emphasize its *noir* style. But Potter objected that this device would too clearly demarcate levels of fiction (the crime plot) and fictional 'reality' (the therapeutic plot) which were not discrete. A positive contribution made by Amiel in respect of blurred boundaries to the production over-all, however, was his script editorial comments which led Potter to redraft the entire series just prior to shooting. This had the effect of strengthening both a strand of narrative clarity leading to possible emotional release (for both the protagonist and readers), but, more significantly even, an interplay between the psychological/emotional and Potter's tendency to the rational/intellectual. It is this last which allows *TSD* to show that the 'objective realities' constructed in mainstream television fictions are shot through by subjectivities which remain unacknowledged.

Potter's TV drama has always sought to shake or break the frame but with varying degrees of success. In *Pennies from Heaven* the device of over-dub on popular songs, on Potter's own reflection produces 'a piece on one leg' – interesting but not going anywhere; accessible but limited in its innovative scope. *Blackeyes*, alternatively, draws attention to the implication of the author in the ideology of his fictional constructs patently enough, but to do so has such a dense palimpsest of metafictional devices that, in TV drama viewing terms, even the most ardent Potter devotees have difficulty in getting a purchase on the piece at one viewing. But in *TSD*, Potter's deftness with innovatory techniques allows him to tread the margins of the popular and the avant-garde, not with precarious balance but with assured footing.

Potter is by no means policing the boundaries, however, between the codes and conventions of the avant-garde and those of popular culture. Indeed, it is the multiple coding which invites the 'postmodern' tag (as in Jencks's, 1989 conception). Hunningher picks up on Potter's belief that the TV play should draw its vivacity from other genres and programme styles in asking of *TSD*, '[i]s this a Chandleresque thriller, a psychological drama, a hospital soap?' (1993: 236). There are elements of all, as well as facets of social realism and the musical. But *TSD* is no paratactical bricolage with narrative strands or free-floating signifiers simply left unresolved to play against each other. There may be open ends in *TSD*, but the series follows a strong compositional principle evident in the series' stylistic excess and the self-consciously over-determined structural parallelism noted.

Although Potter deliberately set out to 'break up the narrative tyranny', nudged by Amiel he nevertheless recognized the audience's need for answers in his final draft. Thus, Potter's concessionary acknowledgement of detective fiction's generic tendency towards closure and the audience's need for potential answers in TV drama, militates ultimately against the conception of *TSD* as postmodern fiction in the formal terms of a *Miami Vice*-style paratactical bricolage of surfaces. Or, as Bondjeberg summarizes:

> Potter has learnt from the postmodern condition not to respect the discourse of the great divide.... He is thus undermining the elitist side of the *avant garde* project without losing the critical dimension, and without surrendering to easy notions of postmodern commercialism and nonsense (1992: 178).

Indeed, in products such as *Miami Vice* and *Heartbeat* at the limits of the consumerist approach to the making of TV drama in the late 1980s and 1990s, the faith of Potter in a thought-provoking TV drama with appeal in a 'common culture', noted above, has apparently been either lost or betrayed. In Cook's view, 'Potter demonstrated decisively with *The Singing Detective*, a mass television audience could enthusiastically embrace a multi-narrative serial drama structured in non-linear fashion' (1995: 278). The subsequent conception of a viewergraphically differentiated audience on the part of makers, underpinned by reception theorists' emphasis on the construction of various textual pleasures and meanings by microcultures making up the audience, has undermined Potter's sense of drama for a common culture. Any notion of a democratic practice such as Potter's which attempts to make an impact on the cultural landscape of a broad television audience and to challenge doxa across class and education boundaries is now, almost literally, not conceived.

V

In a recent study, Jeremy Tunstall argues that, even in the new post-1990 circumstances, drama producers – and the writers they foster – retain a degree of autonomy, indeed prestige, in quality TV programming (1993: 107–24), although he acknowledges that producers have, 'less security, more responsibility' (1993: 15) than hitherto. But as the publishing rather than production model comes to dominate all the main British television channels, three or four executive producers, as noted, effectively control the commissioning of the whole of TV drama output, and their focus is on ratings.[10] Tunstall notes that, after the reorganization of the British commercial television sector in 1990, ITV

> stressed its dedication to 'quality-popular' drama in continuing series form. Much of this quality-popular material featured detective stories, but reflected an effort to reduce the Hollywoodesque and violence-on-the-streets overtones of earlier police series. Series such as *Inspector Morse* (Central Television), *The Ruth Rendell Mysteries* (TVS), *Taggart* (Scottish) and *Poirot* (LWT) epitomized the popular-quality series notion (1993: 112).

These drama series, though all well-made in terms of accepted production values and thus relatively expensive, largely lack the radical tec(h) of *NYPD* or *BTL*, let alone *TSD*. They would seem to illustrate a trend towards bland, essentially conservative, formulae rather than demonstrating the agency of producers and writers to make innovative or challenging series.

BTL evidences the possibility for an entertaining, popular drama in a fast-cut, glossy form to shake normative perceptual frames. But the forces in the field described in this study may yet overwhelm notions of quality other than those based on ratings. Without a renewed PSB ethos to circulate values to offset commercial interests, there is little to deflect the drives of ratings discourse. Thus the case for valuable programmes within the industry needs to be made in terms of distinctions of worth. Cultural and aesthetic values are thus the topic of the next chapter.

9 For What It's Worth
Problematics of Value and Evaluation

TROILUS: What's aught, but as 'tis valued?
HECTOR: But value dwells not in particular will.
           It holds his estimate and dignity
           As well wherein 'tis precious of itself
           As in the prizer.

(Shakespeare, *Troilus and Cressida*, II. ii. 50–5).

I CONTEXT

Why can we not say quite simply that x is good TV drama? In discussions accompanying the writing of this book, I have been exhorted by some colleagues simply to distinguish the worthwhile from the rubbish. This chapter deals directly – if at times a little abstractly – with why such an approach is untenable; it deals in short with the problematics of value and evaluation.

Simply to proclaim the worthwhile would, in the view of many contemporary commentators, be merely to assert and privilege my own tastes and perhaps that of the class fraction to which – as a university teacher of contemporary arts – I belong. For, in a world without truth or centre, value-judgements always betray an interest and can apparently be neither privileged nor widely shared. According to utter relativists, there are no common values only differences, the multiple taste-formations of fragmented micro-cultures. Willis celebrates the fact that, '[t]here is no longer a sense of a "whole culture" with allocated places and a shared universal value system' (1990: 13). Or, as Prime Minister Thatcher put it, 'there is no such thing as society, only individuals (and their families)'. Taking liberal individualism to an extreme, the notion of value has thus steadily been reduced to personal taste, to individual preference underpinned by the ethic of consumer sovereignty.

I turn shortly to the problem of establishing facts and values, but it is helpful first to place the sense of loss of a 'centre', a standpoint for evaluation, amongst the many dislocations of postmodernity noted in this book. Owing in part to its colonial and imperial history, European culture was able to impose its values throughout much of the world, its alleged aesthetic superiority being imbricated with its martial and political might. European culture (particularly in the nineteenth century) perceived itself as superior to 'other', allegedly more 'primitive' cultures but, briskly to characterize a lengthy historical process, with the diminution (post Second World War) of economic and political influence of some Western countries such as Britain and the emergence to economic and relative political power of Eastern countries such as Japan, Korea, and Malaysia, a former Euro-centric hegemony has dissipated. Critical intervention reclaiming space and identity for formerly marginalized 'other' cultures has assisted what is for Europeans a dislocation of fixed bearings but for others, perhaps, a means of empowerment.

Within British culture in addition, to focus upon a European national example, a parallel challenge to specific standards of value has been mounted on the bases of class, gender and ethnic origin. Initially to oversimplify the class argument in the media quality debate, the traditional valences have been inverted. Where Reith assumed the worth of high culture and the beneficial influence on the populace to be gained through dissemination of it, popular culture is now itself frequently placed beyond question, leading, in Schudson's words, to 'an undiscriminatingly sentimental view of it' (1987: 51). In part, this inversion is a political strategy located in Gramsci's concepts of 'praxis' and 'hegemony' – a practical politics operating through shifts in social power relations. In imposing its preferences as 'good taste', so the argument runs, the dominant social group devalues and marginalizes the tastes of those subordinate to it. The hegemonic dominant assumes that its own tastes and understanding are superior whilst asserting that its ways of seeing are in the best interests of all (as with Reith). Emergent power groups seek in turn to secure consensus by eliciting broad agreement with new axiological frameworks.

Amidst the dislocations of the new circumstances of postmodernity, the economic ascendancy of 'new managerialism' in the newly expanded technological and service sector, noted in Chapter 3, privileges instrumental rational efficiency in a free market economy. Its economic outlook is matched by the assertion of a more popular taste formation – apparently located in individual choice – at a time of loss of assurance worldwide of recognized values. But because of its particular educational background (see Chapter 3), the newly hegemonic group has not entirely rejected established culture; rather it approaches it in its own distinctive manner. Cultural transitions in recent years bear this out.

It is as if both sides of 'the great divide' between 'high art' and 'popular culture' have given ground. Popular culture can no longer be clearly distinguished from high art in the European tradition. In the contemporary products and processes of both domains, the territorial boundaries between discrete high artforms and artefacts of popular culture have become increasingly blurred, particularly since the emergence of pop art in the 1960s. Indeed, a distinctive feature of contemporary aesthetics is precisely the both/and hybrid. TV advertisements draw on the graphic variety of modernist art. MTV pop videos borrow avant-garde art strategies – indeed MTV has an avant-garde art slot. Events formerly associated with particular sectional interests such as soccer matches (proletarian) and opera/classical music concerts (elitist) have become more fluidly patronized. Opera, notably in a highly visualized 'designer' mode of production, has attracted in Britain a socially broader audience in recent years than formerly. Classical music, in edited forms such as Classic FM, has gained popularity. Furthermore, there have been operas about soccer, just as 'Nessun Dorma' became the theme tune of the soccer World Cup, and the 'three tenors' CD became a best-seller.

Thus, in addition to the inversion by populists of cultural valences, there has been in the social reformation of postmodernity, a notable blurring of aesthetic boundaries. As discussed in addition, the application of traditionally academic approaches (historiographies, semiotic analyses, biographies) to artefacts of popular culture (rock, rap, comics) is another boundary-blurring feature of the new times as access to Higher Education has widened. Only partially taking on 'high culture' – indeed using it in new ways to its own ends – the emergent taste formation tends to gesture towards, though at times it rejects outright, the forms and grammars of high aesthetic tradition, in favour of more play, in both the senses of fun and flexibility.

In this transitional phase of fast-changing fashions, there is a marked tendency for value to be ascribed through attitude towards artefacts and processes in the immediate moment rather than justification for the worth of things in terms of universals. Much interpretative theory, as for example that of the Roland Barthes of *Image, Music, Text* (see 1977: 142–8), lends support to this stance by emphasizing the reader and the process of production, of her subjective construction of meaning in reading the text. In marked contrast with former notions of the (passive) reception of an 'objective' meaning inherent in the text and guaranteed by the 'Author-God' (1977: 146), readers are allegedly liberated actively to take their own pleasures and make their own meanings. A parallel between such theory and ethnographers' emphasis on resistant sub-cultural practices is also evident.

Privileging the short-term is another distinctive aspect of contemporary culture. Where the telos of grand narratives is denied in theory, and where life-threatening conditions such as Aids put a practical future in doubt for some, self-denial in the short-term for the benefits of longer-term ideals may seem inappropriate. But 'short-termism', a feature of fast economic turn-round on the one hand, is also a matter of political expediency which has tended to drive out ethical considerations. Politicians, widely regarded as cynical, are thought to manipulate policy to get themselves re-elected in a context where media image in the short-term moment matters most (see Galbraith, 1992).

In the view of some recent commentators, questions of aesthetics – both in the academy and on the streets – have thus been reduced entirely to matters of politics – of gender, sexual preference and ethnicity as well as class. Tester, for example, sums up the implications of what he calls 'the cultural studies project' in terms of a plain power struggle. With particular relevance to cultural and aesthetic value, he concludes that:

> the tendency of cultural studies to be concerned with questions of practical politics means that it tends to adopt a sympathetic – or at least a not entirely critical – attitude towards those cultural practices which it is possible to identify as forms of resistance to the existing relationships of domination and leadership (1994: 18–19).

According to some cultural populists, then, there is no intrinsic aesthetic value in the artefacts of any group but merely a process of worth ascribed by the taste formation of the structure in emergence.

An account of the popular (or populist) challenge to established hierarchies over the past two decades, however, tells only part of the story of changing attitudes to value. At first sight it appears that the displacement of established hierarchies extends a democratic impulse – traceable back to Dada and the Surrealists – to bridge the gap between everyday life and art. Instead of confining the arts to specialist places (galleries, concert halls, theatre buildings), the preserves mainly of a cultural elite, the aesthetic realm should be prised open and art made accessible to all. Insofar as this democratizing principle has been effected in the new circumstances of postmodernity, liberating and empowering formerly repressed groups and their cultural expression, the changes of the past two decades are to be celebrated. But, contrary to the avant-garde project's sense that aesthetic developments accompanied a political transformation of society along egalitarian lines, the Reagan and Thatcher years are characterized by a political swing to the right and the reaffirmation of free-market capitalism. Though late capitalism has seen economic change and empowerment for some, its repressions and inequities remain manifest. As noted in Chapter 3, the bottom third of Western countries are perhaps more seriously disenfranchised than ever, whilst peripheral Fordism has created inhumane conditions of work and life elsewhere.

It appears that the celebrants of diversity and the new revisionism have mistaken limited cultural shifts, particularly in the aestheticization of everyday life and its psychological 'empowerments', for the transformation of society as a whole. In effect, a diverse range of microcultures conveniently corresponds with the postmodern market's need for diversity and flexibility. A parallel may be drawn, furthermore, between the tastes and dispositions of the emergent group in the new social configuration and key concepts in postmodern or poststructuralist thought in the expanded academy. Metaphors of fluidity, diversity, difference, relativism have replaced, as noted, those of fixity, rigidity, homogeneity, consensus. The concept of the public good has accordingly been virtually effaced as a sensibility of dislocation, diversity and choice erodes the common ground necessary for conviction about cultural value.

The very sense of culture as a whole way of life becomes increasingly problematic when it is far from clear what constitutes

a cultural group with discernible shared practices. The formation of nation states in the nineteenth century may have led to
notions of communities more 'imagined' than grounded, as
Benedict Anderson has argued (see 1983: 15–16 ff). In this
regard, to explode myths is to liberate. But local intersubjective
senses of identity are far from set free as national identities
fragment, since a new transnational world-view is urgently promoted by forces seeking to construct a sense of world regional
identity (the new Europe or Pacific Rim, for example). Transnational conglomerates, furthermore, take advantage of fast
communication systems to encourage the notion of a global culture of consumerism. CocaCola and McDonald's hamburgers
insinuate themselves virtually worldwide as the universal signs
of the good life in a way which poses the question as to precisely who has been liberated in the shake-up of traditions (see
Tomlinson, 1991: 103–22). New identities demanded by shifts in
the social fabric within (post-)industrialized nation states, then,
are as much constructions as those they displace. The populist
idea of the authentic, sovereign individual as free agent would
indeed seem to be a fiction.

Contemporary theory in the academy has been much concerned with the problems of individual identity and liberty
in new circumstances. As illustrated in Chapter 7, some commentators have sought to interpret the deconstruction of fixed
or 'essential' identities as unequivocally liberating, implying
that individuals can be anything they want by changing their
metaphors and buying into the range of images on offer in an
extended consumer culture. As in the American Dream that
anybody can make it, even to be president, however, this overlooks the palpable constraints of the socio-economic circumstances of most people. The time of the working-class, black,
lesbian president may yet be to come, but by what means will
radical change be effected if market mechanisms satisfy needs
through the play of images, leaving the entrenched political
hierarchies substantially in place? For sure, the extent to which
politics now operates through mediated culture, as distinct from
a democracy based in citizenship, is at the heart of the debate.

In the new bourgeois cultures of Western countries, life for
the relatively wealthy is increasingly privatized and domestic-
ated as individuals travel from their secure homes by car to
security-protected work-places. The public sphere diminishes

as interpersonal communication by electronic means – cell-phone, fax and the InterNet – increases. Back home, digital technology – television, computers, CDs – provide 'infotainment'. Media culture's importance mounts in direct proportion to its pervasiveness and, as politics and justice (witness the O.J. Simpson trial) is subsumed almost wholly into media culture, the means of change must be addressed in, and through, the media.

With specific reference to the centrality of television as a cultural mediator, Kroker and Cook instance a plausible ideal type, a nightmare vision of a society where the TV audience is the only social community. Its fascinations are worth quoting at some length. In this virtual '*anti-community* . . . electronically composed', a person is reduced to a:

> TV self . . . the electronic individual *par excellence* who gets everything there is to get from the simulacrum of the media: a market-identity as a consumer in the society of the spectacle; a galaxy of hyperfibrillated moods . . . ; traumatized serial being (television blasts away everything which cannot be reduced to the technological limitations of good visuals) (1988: 274).

Kroker and Cook further propose that:

> TV is the real world of postmodern culture which has *entertainment* as its ideology, the *spectacle* as the emblematic sign of the commodity-form, *lifestyle advertising* as its popular psychology, pure, empty *seriality* as the bond which unites the simulacrum of the audience, *electronic images* as its most dynamic, and only, form of social cohesion, *elite media politics* as its ideological formula, the buying and selling of *abstracted attention* as the locus of its marketplace rationale, *cynicism* as its dominant cultural sign, and the diffusion of a *network of relational power* as its real product (1988: 270; Kroker and Cook's emphases).

Whilst this vision is exaggerated, resembling the worlds of William Gibson novels more than those actually inhabited by most people, there may be in it sufficient resonances with the emergent affective order sketched in this book to alarm rational human beings.

In a 'society' so anaesthetized that its members share no more

than a response in isolation to the intensity of a sign scream-
ing out of the sensory information overload, a loss of liberty
is evident at least as great as that encountered in the oppres-
sions of a society administered by instrumental Enlightenment
Reason. If the development of the world envisioned by Kroker
and Cook is to be resisted, however, a value critique of TV culture would seem necessary within any conceivable human psychological norms. But we are thus brought full circle, in what
might be dubbed 'the Nietzschean turn', back to the problem
of value-judgements and the apparent erosion in contemporary
culture of any basis on which to ground evaluation.

Nietzsche's critique of Enlightenment reason, his aestheticism
and its influence on poststructuralist thought are well-docu-
mented,[1] and the kernel of 'the Nietzschean turn' necessary for
debate here is well summarized by Callinicos:

> The plural nature of the self [noted above] is merely one
> instance of the inherently multiple and heterogeneous nature
> of reality itself: running through the whole of nature, includ-
> ing the human world, is what Nietzsche called the 'will to
> power', the disposition of different power-centres to engage
> in a a a perpetual struggle for domination (1989: 64–5).

Since reason itself cannot escape the sway of the will to power,
scientific rationality is neither neutral nor innocent in its claim
to yield objective knowledge of a 'fixed reality'. Not only, then,
are all truth-claims merely interpretations and all assertions of
value no more than wills to power, but any basis for rational
argument in defence of discrimination is also inevitably tainted
by its interests.

There are questions of substance here with regard to evaluation particularly in the new circumstances sketched above:
how can 'the better' or what 'makes for life' be distinguished if
all knowledge is merely a will to power? If no discourse is free
from interests, Habermas asks:

> by what criterion shall critique still be able to propose dis-
> criminations? . . . [I]f thinking can no longer operate in the
> element of truth, or of validity claims in general, contra-
> diction and criticism lose their meaning. To *contradict*, to
> negate, now has only the sense of 'wanting to be different.'
> . . . [Critique] must at least be able to discriminate between

a power that deserves to be esteemed and one that deserves to be devalued (1990: 125).

It is perhaps not surprising in the light of this problematic that commentators have become increasingly reluctant overtly to make value-judgements at all. It is as though, as Connor puts it, 'the operations associated with the transactions of value were always destined to lead to (unjust) hierarchy and (violent) exclusion' (1992: 14).[2]

In universities, for example, a marked refusal of value and evaluation has replaced a former sense of their role as arbiters of taste and ideals (see Schudson, 1987). Instead of espousing values, it has become fashionable to critique established value positions whilst being careful to avoid direct engagement theoretically with questions of esteem. A hesitancy appears to arise from a nervousness – in the light of the multi-perspectival assaults on established discourses of value – that any judgement is liable to be complicit with a white, male, middle-class, heterosexual hegemony with a Euro-centric tendency to imperialism and colonialism.

Insofar as a cultural self-questioning, particularly in the West, has led to awareness of its prejudices and significant social change and meaningful liberations for oppressed or marginalized groups, it is welcomed. But commentators deceive themselves if they take the negative liquefying of established values to be disinterested, since this stance is also to take a position; it is, as they say 'coming from somewhere'. As Connor has observed, 'a period when values are profoundly in question is always equally and correlatively a period of energetic value formation' (1992: 15). Besides the claims to territory of feminisms, gay rights and ethnic movements in a period of change, market discourses have spread exponentially.

The language of market interests has penetrated British universities, for example, which – though never interest-free – traditionally aspired to the best possible standards of disinterestedness through freedom of thought and speech. The now dominant discourse speaks of clients (students), market share (course enrolment), portfolio (curriculum), meeting customer needs (providing a good education), grants (loans), and income-generation (public service and the pursuit of truth). In the poststructuralist wake of Nietzsche, recognition that value positions at the top of the established social hierarchy are not merely objective statements of truth or good taste, but are coloured – if not actually determined – by position in that hierarchy, is welcome. It serves at least to qualify the arrogance and cultural elitism which characterized the early days of the BBC, for example, when Lord Reith famously spoke of, 'giving the public what they need – and not what they want' (1924: 34). At worst, however, the displacement of established hierarchies has dislocated bearings completely, creating a tendency towards an utter relativism such that any value is taken to be equivalent to any other. It should not be overlooked however that the assertion that all values are relative is itself a universal claim.

Foolhardy, perhaps, in the light of 'the Nietzschean turn', I propose in this chapter to re-evaluate the case for distinctions of worth in a common culture. This is not just because I take some TV dramas to be better than others – though, as is evident from my discussion of examples, I do believe some have more to offer – but because people generally make distinctions of worth all the time, about all aspects of life. In this respect, I shall draw on Wittgenstein's sense of language usage more than on Derrida's notion of discourse as an endless process of semiosis.

One of the greatest ironies of the postmodern is its intense preoccupation with subtle distinctions of status in such matters as leisure footwear – not only in the relative worth of Reebok or Nike, but in the merits of fewer or more air bubbles in the sole – at a time when it is apparently not allowable to question the value of such a preoccupation in the first place. It is not necessary to descend to cheap jibes about Skodas versus BMWs to suggest that there is consensus, albeit not universal, that some things are better than others. There remains, in my view, a danger of patronage in suggesting otherwise. For, if we are to talk of interests, it suits the comfortably off – as much as the manipulators of corporate capital – to deny grounds for social critique and to celebrate the diversity of things as they are.[3]

To counter the notion of a TV self electronically constructed as hyperfibrillated consumer, an alternative view of people as citizens is offered in a rational tradition not yet wholly dissolved and worth sustaining on ethical grounds to offset the extremities of privatized sensationalism in postmodern play. The colour of my language here betrays, for sure, an interest – and thus far I might go with Nietzsche – but, with Habermas, I take it that some powers deserve more to be esteemed than others as a matter of practical politics and ethics. The following are proposed as estimable and achievable aims for the media in general and TV drama in particular: to encourage people to think for themselves; to promote feeling for and with people different from themselves and cultural difference; to provide as disinterested information about the world as possible; to offer a range of perspectives affording people a purchase on society as a whole; to encourage self-reflection on value. This proposition demands a case briefly to be made for communicability in language; intersubjective limits on interests; salience – the privileging of one thing over another; and commonality of ethical ends based in terms of our mutual being in the world. Readers impatient to return to direct discussion of the television medium may cut to the summary in Section II (iv).

II   KEY DEBATES

(i)   Language, Rationality and Communicability

Much turns in Western thought of the late twentieth century on language and communicability: on the opposition between Derrida's sense of the ultimate undecidability of utterance or Lyotard's insistence on the incommensurability of language forms (see Connor, 1992: 112) in contrast with Habermas's attempt to sustain the idea of 'communicative rationality'. Post-Lacanian feminism and psychoanalysis, furthermore, has sought to expose, as Aston puts it, that 'the arbitrarily imposed Symbolic (phallic) Order, in which all subjects as members of a communicating social order are required to participate, privileges the male at the expense of the female' (1995: 36). Full consideration of these different approaches to language and meaning is patently beyond the scope of this book, but some core arguments must briefly be made to support its critical stance.

Habermas's conception of an ideal speech situation makes a stronger claim for communicative rationality than is necessary to my case. He argues that a disposition to rationally based agreement is built into the structure of discourse in 'the intersubjective communality of mutual comprehension, shared knowledge, reciprocal trust and accord with one another' (cited in Connor,

1992: 104). Other modern philosophers of a naturalistic conception of language (Wittgenstein, Quine, Davidson) have similarly concerned themselves with tacit assumptions apparently underlying actual language usage. Summarizing the thrust of the theory of such thinkers on a principle of humanity:

> interpretation involves assuming the speaker is rational in a sense that involves setting her in the context of the world which she shares, along with their common human nature, with the hearer (Callinicos, 1989: 108).

Whilst, then, there are numerous documented difficulties with Habermas's project,[4] its key importance, for my purposes, in the basis it proposes for a common ethical sense. Somewhere between Habermas's sense that rationality is constitutive of language and the naturalistic conception of language usage, it is possible to make a case for a sustained disposition to truth-telling.

Far from returning us to the conceptual and discursive binary oppositions of Western metaphysics in which one term is elevated above the other, only by denying its dependence on its contrary (mind privileged over body, male over female, white over black), however, such an ethical disposition can work through both/and thinking. It emerges precisely out of a recognition that subjects of knowledge are embodied and practically engaged with the world, and that the products of their thought inevitably bear traces of their purposes and projects, passions and interests.

Even if Nietzsche is right that human discourse is never free from interests, we may nevertheless be able to distinguish registers of disinterestedness in discursive exchanges, subject to cross-referencing, which save us from collapsing all utterance into rhetoric, a mere will to power. On television, for example, advertising is evidently more commercially interested than *Inspector Morse*, a TV drama sponsored by Beamish Stout – though no doubt the taste for beer of the eponymous hero is gratifying to the sponsor. *Fighting for Gemma*, a documentary drama examining the high incidence of leukaemia amongst children near Sellafield's nuclear reactor, is more sympathetic to the critical case than it might have been had the programme been sponsored by British Nuclear Fuels Ltd. The very title of the programme indicates its interests, though its strategies of presentation are those of documentary 'authenticity'. At the 'objective' end of the scale in development here, the BBC's World Service has an established reputation worldwide for relatively objective news coverage. This does not mean it is neutral, entirely interest-free, but that the basis of its PSB values is known and that it follows recognized strategies for authenticating its evidence.

The need for rational exchange and for truth-telling is made particularly evident by the suasive techniques of media culture. For whatever the intensity of the pleasures of a consumerist democracy and the liberating force of symbolic empowerments in the cultural sphere, they do not fully answer the demands of social ethics and polity. If, in the dislocations of postmodernity, accountability is less secure than ever, and yet the way is open for a more participatory democracy than ever before, citizenship requires a basis in the rational exchange of informed views.

To value the register of rational discourse (thus qualified in recognition of the rhetorical interest in all discourse) and the attempt by human beings to transcend their subjectivities (to take Nagel's broader view) may ultimately be to make a judgement. If so, it is in favour of a more estimable will to power in Habermas's terms. TV drama is not characteristically a medium for rational argument, though documentary drama and certain realist forms, as noted in Chapter 5, do make claims about how the world is. But a rational case is required for what used to be called 'serious drama' in comparison with the *divertissements* of the entertainment industry.

(ii)   Salience . . . 'You Cannot Be Serious!'

In spite of the proliferation of consumer goods, distinguished by fine grades of aestheticization, there has been a marked tendency for a flattening out of hierarchical difference. The consumerist thrust to locate value in the privatized desires of the individual tends to reduce distinctions of worth to Troilus's ascription of value (in the epigraph to this chapter). It 'encourages people to seek private solutions to public problems by purchasing a commodity' (Murdock, 1992: 19). In television, it creates equivalence in value ascribable by each individual (Schroder's 'quality *for the viewers in question*' (1992: 213), my emphasis[5]).

In the flow of television, moreover, horrific images of masses of people dying of starvation in a famine lose their distinction and impact by constant repetition, and by being juxtaposed with items of relative trivia – games shows, for example (see Tester, 1994: 95–8). It is no longer possible to assume that all human beings are inclined to be sensitive to the suffering of others since the bombardment of information in the postmodern world may have had the effect not only of dislocating signs from their referents, but of generally desensitizing people to distinctions of worth. The levelling of hierarchies is linked both to the erosion of the potential for linguistic meaning, and to the emergent affective order of postmodernity generally. In a political context in which the customer rights of individuals constructed as consumers replace the value of intersubjective citizenship and community, a number of forces gravitate towards a selfishness, in the fundamental sense of an erosion of the inclination and ability to sympathize with other people. What matters socially is reduced to what matters to me.

To explore the operation of a scale of values in which the plight of others might take precedence over an individual's direct goals, I instance the development by philosopher Barrie Falk of a scale of differential intensities around the concepts of 'absorption', 'salience' and 'resonance'. Falk takes the literally pedestrian example of a chance encounter in the street in the process of a shopping expedition with 'a man who is old, infirm, obviously wretched' – an example particularly pertinent to the context of postmodernity where shopping for personal goods has become a favoured leisure pursuit.

The question Falk poses concerns the conditions in which pity for the man encountered might be aroused in the shopper whose personal goals are in another direction. He recognizes that the shopper would need to become absorbed by the old man's state of being but that absorption is insufficient for pity. He introduces the refinement of 'resonance' in his absorbed thoughts, 'a certain power which these thoughts may have to modify one's current conative state' (1983: 65). Falk has in mind the precedence that sympathetic involvement in the old man's plight might take over the interest in shopping:

The point is, rather, that even if thoughts about these other matters [shopping] were to occur while I was pityingly absorbed, they would no longer be thoughts about things that concerned me: in the face of a life as bereft of pleasure as this, the decorative state of my room [paint, brushes etc. being the object of the shopping], it would seem to me, no longer matters (1983: 65).

Falk proceeds to claim that, unlike the shopping, an emotion such as pity is not purposive and causal but that its compellingness resides in its 'weakening of one's conative ties with the rest of the world' (1983: 66). Furthermore, Falk believes his account explains variable depths of emotional response in any given circumstance 'by the range and degree of entrenchment within one's life of the concerns it negates' (1983: 66). Taking up the argument above, if the privatized, desensitized consumer is entrenched in her shopping in that sole scale of value privileging the individual as consumer, she may no longer be open to other considerations. Applied more broadly, but put bluntly, the dislocating forces of (post)modernity in destabilizing established communities, have led people to consider others less, in some cases not at all. The levelling tendency of postmodern media culture, moreover, may contribute to this diminution of sympathetic human sensitivity.

In traditional accounts of ethical disposition, an appeal is often made to a moral sense in human nature, but in postmodern thinking it is not possible to take an 'essential' human nature for granted. To a philosopher such as Kant an appeal to exemplariness evidencing common humanity is possible. As Falk puts it:

[i]n the case of finding something beautiful, what replaces the occurrence of rule-guided ordering is the exemplariness of what happens to me: the fact that the feelings I have result not from contingent features of my own personality, but from part of human nature which is common to all (1983: 68).

Falk ultimately wishes to avoid claims about human nature but he finds it possible nevertheless to sustain a case in respect of distinctions of worth for 'transcendence and truth in just the way Kant proposed' (1983: 68).

To this end, Falk further refines his concepts of absorption and resonance with the addition of 'salience'. Salience allows for distinctions of worth relative to an awareness of the hinterground of other, perhaps conflicting or compensatory, situations in the world. It is a matter of what colloquially is termed 'getting things in perspective'. Thus avoiding a simple appeal to a much-disputed human nature, Falk retains a basis on which distinctions of worth might be made with reference to psychological norms which might serve as criteria for rational debate about such matters, without a commitment to nature or absolute values. Falk acknowledges, besides his recognition of the potential shifts in salience and resonance, that differences in what he can only call temperament or a sensitivity which may be repressed (1983: 78) also account for variable responses. For he accepts that '[b]eing in the world is like many things and it is like them simultaneously' (1983: 78). In a note, he acknowledges the advantage of pluralism suggesting that the absorption of apparently disparate views, the one into the other, may make for more complex seeing (1983: 78–9, n7).

That some things can be seen to be more important than others rests, then, not on absolute values or fixed hierarchies, but on people's abilities to recognize the relative unimportance of their short-term ends when faced with matters of more pressing concern. This capacity may need nurturing, but some consensus on matters of relative importance may be an aspect of our being in the world.

(iii) 'Forms of Life' (Wittgenstein): Our Being in the World

Appeals to human nature are problematic both in everyday speech (where all too often today they are used to claim the inevitability of self-assertive aggression in competition) and by philosophers such as Kant (where the opposite assumption of a common humanity prevails). To counter a culture characterized by individualism to the point that how the world is has become a matter of how it seems to me, it is helpful briefly to recall modern accounts, as for example in the later Wittgenstein, of '[w]hat has to be accepted, the given . . . *forms of life*' (1953, reprinted 1994: 226e). Wittgenstein famously argues that consensus about such matters as colour are matters of judgement based upon knowledge of being in the world:

> Can one learn this knowledge? Yes; some can. Not, however,
> by taking a course in it, but through '*experience*' . . . What one
> acquires here is not a technique; one learns correct judg-
> ments (1994: 227e).

There are accordingly limits in the practice of any given circumstances on the extent to which value can simply be ascribed by
individuals. Appeals on the basis of intersubjective agreement
within a speech community are tenable,[6] and subjective ascription may be grounded in shared standpoints beyond personal
whim. As David Wiggins has neatly put it, ' "x is good, because
I like x" and "I like x because it is good" both hold, though the
force of the because is different in each case' (1987: 106).

I suggest, following Wiggins's reading of Wittgenstein, that
practical judgements consist of a customarily unacknowledged
amalgam of ascription and description. Estimations of quality
always come from somewhere: they are grounded in people's
lived experience and people inhabit different places. Thus,
there is always a significant proportion of ascription in people's
aesthetic judgements, informed by their ethical and socio-
political positions. I look to avoid, however, that reification
and reduction of taste merely to those class allegiances noted
of Bourdieu in Chapter 7. Furthermore, judgements are not
reducible to personal whim because they draw on intersubjective agreements within speech communities, and thus may be
defended on a rational basis in discursive exchanges from the
intellectual debate in the academy to the discussion in the
laundrette of last night's episode of a soap.

I suggested above (following Fekete, 1988, and Connor, 1992)
that the idea that evaluation could be avoided is an illusion.
Spurning distinctions of worth in favour of a fashionable undecidability or negative liquifying of established value is in itself
to take a stance. Values are asserted and contested in the praxis
of everyday life. In Chapter 3, I noted a current tendency, in
a period of axiological uncertainty, for an almost whimsical
ascription of value – the disposition towards kitsch, for example.
These aesthetic judgements, however apparently fleeting and
fluid, are, like all estimations, inevitably imbricated with ethics
and politics, that is with questions of how we should live and
how we should organize our societies to promote our ethical
ends. In this light the re-evaluation of popular culture and the

emergent confidence of a broader range of people in their taste-formations might be seen as an extension of democracy. But, in its inference in the process that value is merely a personal matter, the democratic thrust appears to have become unhappily caught up with a populist individualism and hedonism shot through with the interests of late capitalism and dis-articulated from ethics and progressive politics.

Acknowledging the colouring of interests in judgement-making, however, Wiggins challenges

> the long-standing philosophical tendency to strive for descriptions of the human condition by which will and intellect-cum-perception are kept separate and innocent of all insider trading (1987: 97).

In emphasizing that all rational judgments are open to the influence of wilful interests, he acknowledges that human discursive practices are ultimately grounded in practical judgements about life's having a point at all, that is in matters of ethics.

The cultural studies project, in Tester's account above, recognizes political interests in cultural estimation but itself suppresses the intersubjectively affirmed (intrinsic) aesthetic qualities of cultural artefacts. Furthermore, it excludes ethical considerations. This strategy affords more emphasis on individual or group ascription of value, by way of empowering emergent fractions yet to develop distinctive taste formations. Where traditional high art aesthetics may rest on an unsustainable categorial isolation of an aesthetic realm, the cultural studies project collapses aesthetics and ethics into politics. Philosophical postmodernism's challenge to categorial distinctions in attempting to breach the gap between everyday life and art seems not to have extended to the inextricable imbrication of politics, aesthetics and ethics in everyday practices.

At this point I must reflexively acknowledge, as best I can, my interests in making my practical judgements as manifest in this book. It may be that, unconsciously, I am simply trying to justify and sustain a position in which I feel comfortable but which is currently under challenge – that of the modernist intellectual. The force of the argument – and its critics – will no doubt tell. I consciously believe I am seeking to sustain a means of rational critique to afford distinctions between those ideas and practices which claim to empower people – but which

may do so only to a limited, and at worst diversionary, extent –
from others with greater potential to offer formerly disenfranch-
ized people greater power over their own destinies.

In making my estimations, I draw upon another notion of
Wittgenstein's coupled with his conceptual 'family resemblances', softening categorial distinctions. This is his sense of
value intrinsic to artworks in terms of their ability to offer experience not to be had through engagement with other texts. The
two notions, taken together, allow for intrinsic (intersubjectively
affirmed) aesthetic qualities of cultural artefacts to be described.
But no clear dividing line needs to be drawn between 'high art'
and 'popular culture' in this regard since an overlap in terms
of family resemblances affords a both/and approach.

Importantly, this position does not entail a falling back on a
set of essentialist art values *sui generis* and therefore categorially
distinct from ethics and politics, as in aesthetic high modernism.
Whilst worth is not merely defined by class (or other interest
group) ascription, it is acknowledged that such interests are
in play in evaluation. Thus, a more flexible approach is advocated in which aesthetic matters are seen to be engaged with
matters of politics and ethics to illuminate the meaning of life.
The view does rest, then, on assumptions about the end of life
which, as Tilghman summarizes Wittgenstein:

> is not merely to propagate the species, but is to live life in
> a certain way. One feature of living is reflection, reflection
> on human life and its values in general and upon our own
> lives in particular (1991: 175).

Even if, as Rorty tells us, it is a mistake to seek any basis for
solidarity in the core self of human beings, solidarity may be
made not found. In an attempt to embrace diversity without
abandoning entirely the possibility of solidarity, Rorty invites
us 'to see more and more traditional differences (of tribe, religion, race, customs, and the like) as unimportant compared
with respect to pain and humiliation' (1989: 192) and 'to think
of people wildly different from ourselves as included in the
range of "us"' (Rorty, 1989: 192). Art, broadly conceived as in
Wittgenstein's understanding of its role,[7] might serve as a basis
of appeal to embodied subjectivities offering foundations on
which to build such solidarity.

(iv)   Summary

The combined arguments above establish the case for five important aspects of a basis for evaluation:

(1)   that to acknowledge that the conception of a transcendental Reason of the Enlightenment has been found wanting does not (as alleged in Carroll, 1993: 1–8 ff) necessarily leave human value creation wholly without foundation or consensus. There are places on which to take a stand though perhaps less firmly founded than was formerly presumed of the bedrock of Kantian transcendental Reason or, prior to that, religious faith.

(2)   that, providing an anthropocentric perceptual apparatus is accepted, a sense of common meaningfulness is possible. Without reference to 'human nature' a commonality of our being in the world obtains which, though variable in practice, may be located and defended by rational appeal to social and psychological norms. Ascription, or invention, of value operates along with elements of value-focus and discovery to which an appeal may be made in terms of human 'objectivity'.

(3)   that the elements of commonality noted above significantly arrest the slide into utter relativism. There is, for sure, room for diversity, for a variability avoiding the repressive fixity of a conception of human nature which, in its essentialism, resists change by refusing to acknowledge the nuances of human experience in the concreteness of history, on the one hand, and what, on the other, Eagleton calls 'habits of pluralistic thought and feeling, persuading them [the masses] to acknowledge that more than one viewpoint existed than theirs – namely that of their masters (1983: 25).

(4)   that different evaluations by individuals are inevitable in the face of given circumstances at a particular time, and that different values will be privileged at different historical moments. In consequence, as Connor puts it:

> The question of value will always exert an imperative force which disturbs us from our safe inhabitation of ourselves, impelling us to question beliefs, certainties and values with a view not only to their potential betterment, but to the revaluation of the very notions of better or worse (1992: 32).

The paradox of value is that values which seem like fixtures remain perpetually open to reappraisal, and thus a need for reflexion, but not utter relativism, results.

(5)   that communicability of thoughts and feelings is possible though not foolproof, and that the roles of symbolic formations in bridging the gap between subjectivities is likely to be a significant one, on the contested ground of what it means to be human.

Whilst this may not be sufficient to persuade the determined sceptic who would muster support for more nihilistic claims, it is held here to provide a critical basis for distinguishing between the better and the worse on rational grounds whilst acknowledging the sway of the passions and the will.

III APPLICATIONS

Whilst the discussion above might seem distant from the everyday practices of watching drama on television, the more familiar arguments and assertions about what is worth watching, or whether indeed television is worth watching at all, are ultimately rooted – consciously or otherwise – in the debates sketched above.

There would appear to be a measure of intersubjective agreement that television is a force of major importance for good or ill in the modern world. Even the editors of a recent study avowedly contributing to 'the new revisionism' acknowledge that, besides its power in advertising and 'consumer awareness', television is:

> the single most powerful forum of public communication, as well as the primary site of the social negotiation of ideas, values and lifestyles (Skovmand and Schroder, 1992: 12–13).

Precisely because the medium is so important, it must on occasion be taken seriously. In reviewing the new affective order, I have sought to offset the pleasures, liberations and empowerments of a postmodern culture against its downside, using some of the useful tools afforded by poststructuralist thinking.

When linked uncritically with poststructuralist thought, however, the noted tendency of 'new revisionists' to applaud what is on offer in the media and the ways in which it is used, over-emphasizes the meanings and pleasures generated through popular texts by individuals (see Ang, 1991: x, ff). To allow that ethnographers have demonstrated a varied range of responses to television does not mean that other quality judgements are redundant or that they reduce a text to a singular meaning. Nor does engagement in critique of texts entail a return to a crude marxist over-emphasis on the production side of textual encoding.

In the light of the arguments above, it is a matter of distinguishing between forms which raise a topic in a drama such that it might stimulate viewers to chat about it with their families and friends, and an even more valuable symbolic experience which disturbs habitual mind-sets. The implicit value assumptions underlying much media ethnography is that popularly generated meanings and pleasures are inherently worthwhile. The examples of TV drama on which I place most value in this book, in contrast, set criteria of critical reflection on human life and its values in general. Nor is such reflection a merely cerebral matter akin to the traditional (Kantian) disinterested, aesthetic disposition, for it embraces additionally the profound engagement of emotion. In short it asks that viewers think more reflectively and feel more profoundly about human life and value. Even with regard to postmodern compositional principles which might, in their refusal of closure, encourage the viewers in creative play, distinctions of worth may be made between the greater and lesser potential, as we shall see in Chapter 10.

Whilst the flexi-narrative mode currently dominant in the schedules is not precluded from stimulating either play or reflection (as illustrated in Chapter 8), the tendency of the force field sketched in this book would seem to be away from, rather than towards, dramas inviting such responses. Dramatic forms which rapidly inter-cut hotspots of narratives as illustrated tend to engage viewers by pseudo-emotional contrivance. Because they move so quickly from one moment of narrative intensity to the next, they merely raise social issues rather than exploring them contextually to demand from viewers a profounder engagement with those issues. A critical realist TV drama, in contrast, provides resources through additional perspectives with the potential to broaden horizons and loosen viewers' conative ties with the world, opening up new ways of seeing.

In accordance with the principle of diversity, however, the

argument is not against soaps and formulaic popular series but for the inclusion of a range of TV drama which contemporary circumstances threaten to diminish. The strategy of pace and melodramatic narrative energy to catch and hold people's attention in the face of domestic distractions is necessary only if a particular conception of the audience is fixed. But, since viewers and the viewing context vary, not all TV drama needs to follow the flexi-narrative format.

Confirming the capacity for diversity of output, David Morley has pointed out that, 'television is not uniform in this respect – modes of address vary across different genres of programming as do modes of representation' (1992: 206). It is a question of register. A core argument in this book has been that a commercial drive to maximize audiences by way of flexi-narrative and flexiad models may, without attention being paid to the different possible modes of reading, representation and pleasure, extend the current drift to an exclusion of diversity in a range of registers. It is important to stress that my claim is not that the soaps, and *a fortiori* the viewers who regularly watch them, are mindless in respect of the new affective order, but that they might be – and indeed at their best they have been – more mindful. There is a significant element of media mythology in the very idea of a three-minute culture: the attention span is not universally thus reduced and viewers may be willingly re-educated to extend the range of concentration if the rewards were sufficient.

Thus the strategy of leaving everything to find its worth in the market-place (itself value-laden, of course) can be seen to be inadequate. Whilst it appears in its deregulating tendency to be freeing things up and liberally proliferating values, it is questionable in terms of its tendency ultimately to reduce the range of standards of value. As Murdock argues:

> The consumer marketplace offers an array of competing goods, but it doesn't confer the right to participate in deciding the rules that govern either market transactions or the distribution of wealth and income that allows people to enter the market in the first place. It provides choice at a price but without empowerment (1992: 19).

A public service ethos is necessary to sustain diversity in TV drama. Wholly commercial strategies tend, as demonstrated, either to formulaic realism or to a dehistoricized postmodern

bricolage dispersing critical potential. Notwithstanding the fact
that some viewers will re-work the materials in a process of
symbolic play, such provision sells people short.

Accordingly, I support Murdock's advocacy of Britain's Channel 4 as a model on which to base developments of PSB provision for the future. As he remarks:

> Channel 4 continues public broadcasting's core commit-
> ment to accommodate diversity within a mixed programming
> schedule, available to everyone without extra payment. This
> is essential, since a positive response to diversity depends on
> a collective exploration of difference, not the perpetuation
> of separate spheres. This requires a communicative system
> that sets 'local languages of identity alongside a public lan-
> guage of collective aspiration' (Sacks, 1991: 9) (1992: 39).

Such a model embraces diversity without sacrificing a sense
of community. Ideally it would encourage both sympathy with
and respect for others, and contribute to the restoration of a
mutuality based in our common being in the world. It would
sustain a constant reflexivity in evaluation of the public sphere
as mediated and constructed in the influential symbolic formations of TV drama. Commercial interests, whilst by no means
all bad, must be offset by other ethical and political interests,
if reflection on value is to be sustained. In short, more than
one perspective or way of seeing is necessary.

The health of a community, wherever its bounds are drawn,
involves the demands of seriousness as well as of play, of rational
justification as well as abandonment to pleasure and desire,
in the imbrication of ethics and politics with aesthetics outlined. Falk's (1983) account of possible distinctions of weight
or relative seriousness is important to my case for distinguishing between more and less 'serious' TV drama. The comfortable pleasures engendered by much formulaic television drama
might, in certain circumstances, be expected to give way to
engagement with matters of more weight. This is the ethical
case – in consonance with the principle of diversity – for more
challenging TV drama intermixed in the schedules with the
consolatory formulaic series. Just as there is nothing objection-
able in seeking to buy decorating materials, there may be no
principled objection to escapism in TV drama. But in a medium
as omnipresent and culturally significant as television, advocacy

of a schedule of pure escapism (or arguments that seek uncritically to justify what is on offer) work to diminish the broader frame of reference by which sensitive appeals to psychological norms might be fostered.

In the context of market research, described in Chapter 4, it may well be that respondents would not choose a programme of ethical seriousness over a comforting escapist formulaic realism, it should be noted, since the salience and resonance Falk describes would not obtain without context. Indeed, Falk's argument might account for variable responses at different times, and in different contexts, in a way which does not wholly denigrate 'lesser' concerns in the manner of an Arnoldian or Adornoesque contempt for an allegedly trivial popular culture. Just as where frustration at the failure to find the desired decorating materials would be misplaced in the broader context of a food crisis, so a critique of the pleasures of escapism has force only where a wider perspective presents more pressing concerns.

Enjoyment of a popular TV drama such as *Heartbeat*, to return to that example, is as understandable and unobjectionable as the pursuit of decorating materials in the given circumstances. Nevertheless, it is possible to make a case in Falk's framework for more 'serious' drama, *Boys from the Blackstuff* for example, on the grounds that, in specific at the historical moment of its transmission (1982), the pressing concerns of contemporary unemployment and, more generally, 'our bond with the world' (Merleau-Ponty, 1974: 143), demanded a certain precedence over the diversionary simulations of *Heartbeat*. The 'condition of postmodernity' may warrant the redressing of an imbalance between hedonism and rationality. Tester's complaint that students are preoccupied with 'Mills & Boon romances or Levi Jeans commercials – and meanwhile rape goes on in Bosnia (1994: 3) is directed against a culture apparently anaesthetized to the point where its ability to loosen conative ties to make distinctions of relative seriousness appears to be in doubt.

Falk modestly proposes:

only that we *think* of ourselves as being such that, sometimes, how the world seems to us manifests not just how, because of some interest or mood, it seems to us but isn't; but how it seems, in the sense of what it is indeed like, for all of us (1983: 76–7).

It may be, however, that in the culture of postmodernity we have stopped thinking of ourselves in terms of an awareness of what it is like for all of us to be in the world. And if we have, taking a cue from Rorty, we should perhaps – under the sign of the pursuit of good lives for all – (re)construct our sense of citizenship. Rorty sees symbolic formations and television in particular as important factors in this construction process (see 1989: xvi). The proposal may indeed seem too utopian for TV drama were it not that examples exist of products of popular culture in that medium which are equally artworks in Wittgenstein's sense of symbolic formations which show what cannot be said: the value and meaning of life in its diversity and in the family resemblance at the core of its human cultural practices.

10 Coda – Critical Postmodernism: Critical Realism

Twin Peaks and *Our Friends in the North*

> It is thus not truth that varies with social, psychological and cultural contexts but the symbols we construct in our un-equally effective attempts to grasp it (Geertz, 1993: 212).

I

It is an irony – though not of that postmodern kind which places everything in inverted commas like raised eyebrows – that, at the time of completion of this book, the BBC made and transmitted a social realist serial, *Our Friends in the North* (BBC2), written by Peter Flannery. That a single dramatist was given – or more precisely fought for – a major space for a political drama is rare at a time when writing teams predominate. TV drama production practice increasingly equals the challenge to authorship posed by poststructuralist theory. Being one dramatist's interpretation of the political history of Britain in the period of postmodernity, furthermore, *Our Friends* defies fragmented, flexiad drama by tracing the lives of four central characters through thirty years in nine episodes running over three months (January–March, 1996). It demands a sustained viewing, premissed on the realist aesthetic assuming a correspondence (though not a transparency) between fictional construct and historical events. It is a factitive fiction in the critical realist tradition. It took a considerable risk by BBC2 to make such a serial in the early 1990s, the more particularly since *Our Friends* commanded the highest budget of any UK drama series ever produced by the BBC.

Twin Peaks, running for thirty episodes, transmitted in US in the 1988–90 and 1990–91 seasons, followed shortly in Britain.

Hailed in critical discourse as the ultimate postmodern text, *Twin Peaks*, so its advocates allege, has almost single-handedly effected a paradigm shift in TV drama, changing its (sur) face for ever.[1] In the light of postmodernism's dismissal of authorship to emphasize textual multivalency and the fluidity of process, the habitual connection of *Twin Peaks* with David Lynch as *auteur* is also ironic, since a range of writers and directors were co-authors of the serial.[2] Despite considerable differences between episodes, however, the serial's look and feel are indeed marked with Lynch's distinctive *auteur* signature, as established in his films. Thus *Twin Peaks* serves as an example of the kind of both/ and text noted at the outset where a (postmodernist) non-authored sense of writing or textuality is not incompatible with a (modernist) distinctive authorial signature.

Given the fragmentation of audiences in the US multi-channel context, the commissioning of *Twin Peaks* might in part be explained by a move away from network, catch-all, 'lowest common denominator' programming to niche marketing of specific products to attract different segments of the audience at different times of the day. Following the 'quality demograpics' approach established in *Hill Street Blues* a decade since, *Twin Peaks*, along with *Moonlighting* and *Thirtysomething*, aims to appeal to the young professionals (in the jargon 'baby boomers' or 'yuppies') whose relatively high disposable income is attractive to advertisers.

Detailed discussion of either *Twin Peaks* or *Our Friends* is not possible in the remaining space here. As *Twin Peaks* has already received wide critical attention beyond my brief discussion of the series in Chapter 2, I shall treat the more recent *Our Friends* at a little more length. But the purpose of this coda – in the light of the need established constantly to reflect on the evaluation of value – is to set in juxtaposition the progressive potential in TV drama, as we approach the twenty-first century, of a critical postmodernism and an ever-adapting critical realism.

To take *Twin Peaks* first, there is a considerable difference between its assemblage of disparate discourses and that of *Heartbeat*, though there are superficial similarities. *Twin Peaks*, whilst it appears to be set in a 1990s 'present' sustains a sense of the 1950s just as *Heartbeat* blurs a temporal distinction between the 1990s and the 1960s. The compilation in *Heartbeat* of different strands of catchment established in viewergraphics to maximize

an audience primarily for commercial interests amounts, however, neither to Potter's attempt to construct a common culture
by bridging the popular culture/high art divide, nor to a deconstructive strategy inviting play. *Twin Peaks'* critical potential lies
in its refusal ultimately to centre itself, to make discursive or
narrative sense of its allusive, multi-layered construct. But its critical effectivity is realized only if it promotes through its multiple
coding a recognition in viewers of the constitutive nature of all
discourse.

In opposition to formulaic realism's tendency to make sense
of everything and thus to naturalize the status quo, postmodernist bricolage, in not resolving the contradictions between
its discourses, may in theory de-centre the subjectivity of viewers.
It may in praxis, so the poststructuralist argument goes, allow
individuals to sense that they are not constrained by an essentialist self, but are constituted by the cultural discourses of the
society they inhabit. Recognition that individual identities are
thus not fixed but capable of change opens up the possibility
of all kinds of liberations. Since, as argued in Chapter 7, this
amounts to no tangible change in the first instance, there can
be no assurance that a resistant critical strategy beyond psychological empowerment will result.

In the context of postmodernity where fun is encouraged,
perhaps at the expense of social critique, *Twin Peaks* offers a
range of pleasures to its audience. The combination of various
television fiction modes (the soap opera, the detective series, the
horror film, the commercial, the sit-com, the western), underscored by specific intertextual references, affords something for
everyone. Seen in this way, *Twin Peaks* could offer, like *Heartbeat,*
discrete pleasures for the semi-attentive viewer selecting appealing morsels from an extensive menu. As I have acknowledged,
the rethinking of the pleasures of fantasy has formed a significant part of feminist and psychoanalytic projects. They have
shown, at least, that fantasy must be recognized as a dimension of people's actual experience and not cast as illusion, the
binary opposite of 'reality'. Nevertheless, from a critical point of
view, the politics of pleasure remain problematic. Moreover,
if 'the pleasure of fantasy lies in its offering the subject an
opportunity to take up positions which she could not assume
in real life' (Ang, 1996: 93), a level of credibility in the constructed world would appear to be needed quite contrary to

that awareness of textual process as discursive practice posited
by poststructuralists.

But *Twin Peaks*, as Brent assesses it:

> gives you a lot of traditional pleasures – the narrative, the
> whodunit mystery, the various romantic intrigues. But while
> it gives you these pleasures with one hand, it takes them away
> with the other (cited in Lavery, 1995: 178).

In this view, accessibility to a broad audience is facilitated by
the availability of a range of traditional TV drama pleasures, but
the effectivity of the text precludes simple pleasures or even the
pleasure of mere play in the spaces between discourses. Precisely because the different strands are not woven into a harmonious whole, viewers are not merely afforded the opportunity
but are actually required to shift – at times violently and uncomfortably – from one discourse to another, and in and out of
emotional states. Providing, then, that some allowance is given
to the positioning tendency of particular textual constructs
(rather than shifting the site of construction of meanings and
pleasures entirely to the reader), *Twin Peaks* is an interrogative
text. Through its radical disjunctions of different channels of
discourse in juxtaposition, it draws viewers in emotionally along
some channels whilst, almost simultaneously, distancing them
with irony in others.

As many commentators seeking to retain some sense of
potential for change for the better have come to acknowledge,
however, the dislocations of postmodernity, whilst they free
things up, do not guarantee change, let alone progress (Laclau
and Mouffe, 1985; Caughie, 1990). Laclau and Mouffe point
out the need for articulation, for 'establishing a relation among
elements such that their identity is modified as a result of the
articulatory practice' (1985: 105). For any kind of change in
subjectivity to occur, that is to say, identities, once dislocated,
must be articulated anew. The proliferation of positions and
identifications on offer in play with postmodern texts may well
result in recursion precisely because articulations are inevitably
contextual. The discourses affirming patriarchy in social praxis,
for example, may still exert more influence than those speaking gender and sexual pluralism. Similarly, in a context where
the dominant disposition of the target audience may be playful

and gestural, inclined more to the style of striking an attitude than with re-articulation, the odds might appear to be stacked against cognitive or affective reorientation.

In these circumstances, postmodern texts constructed such that they provoke, 'a careful and purposeful consideration of representational alternatives' (Collins, 1989: 138), rather than the mere pastiche of past styles thrown together with no other thought than to maximize audience, have greater critical potential. As Foster puts it, 'a resistant postmodernism is concerned with a critical deconstruction of tradition, not an instrumental pastiche of pop- or pseudo-historical forms' (1985: xii). *Twin Peaks* may be regarded as an example of critical postmodernism in these terms. That it is not 'easy watching', however, contributes to its cult status, the downside of which is that a large number of viewers find the serial difficult to follow and switch off. The viewing figures declined significantly once the key enigma – who killed Laura Palmer? – reached a point of closure.

It may well be that the de-centring tendencies of *Twin Peaks*, its refusal to accommodate the desire for followability or to allow comfortable viewing positions are precisely those features which a regular audience rejects. Culture is in continual process, as this book has stressed. But the new affective order, disposed to bricolage by way of the aggregation of short-term gratifications, retains nevertheless a residual desire for sense-making frames – the audience's need for answers. That is why critical realism may yet be the most productive strategy for changing hearts and minds, particularly where the context of production and distribution enables it to be sensitive to local resonances.

Turning then to *Our Friends in the North*, a weft of narrative threads traces the fortunes of four friends brought up together in Newcastle-upon-Tyne: Nicky, Mary, Tosker and Geordie. As *Our Friends* is likely to be unfamiliar to some readers, it is helpful briefly to sketch the serial's scope and concerns. Newcastle and the North East region of England have a strong working-class heritage connected with iron and steel production and ship-building, heavy industries which have been largely depleted with attendant mass redundancies in the post-Fordist period of the serial's concern. Newcastle, or more specifically Jarrow, resonates in Britain with working-class resistance to an economic structure whose periodic crises result in dislocation and mass unemployment. The famous Jarrow march to London represents

– both politically at the time, and metonymically in visual and oral history – the plight of those most detrimentally affected by the 1930s Depression.

The historical context of *Our Friends*, then, has national and regional resonances making its stories widely 'usable', but in a smaller audience frame than that required for transnational products such as *Dallas* or even *Middlemarch*. Hence the irony of its production by the BBC in the mid-1990s when the serial had for fifteen years been under consideration and had 'passed through the hands of four producers, five directors and four controllers of BBC2'.[3] Indeed without the commitment of executive producer Michael Wearing, who had long since championed the project, *Our Friends* would almost certainly have been displaced from the budget in the corporate shift to period costume drama at the expense of the contemporary and political.

In addition to its lack of potential in the transnational market, *Our Friends* has the disadvantage of all serials from the scheduler's perspective since viewers are known to disregard a serial if they miss episodes, suspecting that they will not be able to follow the story. Unlike flexi-narrative hybrids such as *Casualty*, there is in *Our Friends* no fresh self-contained narratives each week or indeed complete narrative strands introduced halfway through. Whilst it is possible to pick up the threads, and in some instances to enjoy an episode in its own right as if it were a single play, *Our Friends* basically demands a regular following. The value for those viewers who do remain hooked is a developed and complex narrative structure, sustained over a significant period of time which sees the characters change and develop in response to their experience. Agency is situated in structure.

Unlike the melodrama of soaps in which the high temperature of the action with contrived mini-climaxes complicates the characters' lives at the level of narrative but often with all too little consequence in terms of character development, *Our Friends* affords understanding of how people change in response to the context of their environment (in the widest sense). Furthermore, since it traces a period of significant social and cultural change from the 1960s through to the 1990s, *Our Friends* offers a view of changing cultures. At the outset, for example, Mary and Nicky do not, in the phrase of the time, 'go all the way' in their sexual relationship since working-class Catholic social codes and fear of pregnancy constrain them. Mary's later seduction by Tosker, for whom she evidently cares less, to some extent reflects the liberalising sexual mores of the 1960s but, because of a resultant pregnancy, the couple are nevertheless forced to marry. By the 1970s, the time of the final breakdown of the marriage which has only been sustained for the sake of the children, however, Mary can initiate a sexual relationship with Nicky, unfettered by social stigma.

TV drama's noted general tendency to deny consequence is exacerbated in postmodern texts which recycle the styles of history but, privileging the synchronic over the diachronic, emphasize a dehistoricized, perpetual present. More formally traditional realist series and serials such as *Our Friends*, in contrast, besides dealing with the consequences of actions, approximate to what Geertz (1993) calls 'thick description' in an anthropological approach which tries to unmask the complexity of experience lived through time.

Peter Flannery's project is ambitious. He interweaves the personal histories of his four protagonists with broader political issues such as police corruption implicating politicians at the highest level of government. *Our Friends* also explores the housing problems of Newcastle's badly-built, modernist high-rise and the Rachmanite scandals of the rented housing sector. The serial is undoubtedly coloured by that perspectivism acknowledged by modern anthropologists to be inevitable (Clifford, 1986). Flannery, and the production team, construct the world they present since, all descriptions being constitutive, realist TV drama cannot, as noted, neutrally describe.

Furthermore, the conventions of realist drama, repressing as they do the means of production, encourage self-reflexion by different means from those postmodern texts which draw attention to their compositional devices. The many intertextual references in *Twin Peaks*, for example, amount to an acknowledgement that the text is re-working pre-existing languages, reiterating – and at best re-articulating – familiar tropes. *Our Friends*, in contrast, purports to be giving a true (albeit fictional) account of cultural and political change in UK over thirty years.

The series carries conviction since some aspects of it – Newcastle's high-rise scams and the Metropolitan Police corruption – have a demonstrable basis in historical fact. Social realism, particularly when its discursive position stands outside

the Establishment as does that of *Our Friends*, has the capacity
to reinterpret history and politics to viewers. It invites critical
reflection precisely because it invites its audience to look at
things from a particular perspective (arguably centred in male
working-class experience in this case) rather than offering absolute truth. It might imply – counter to the official view of an
ordered society led by honest and conscientious politicians for
the good of all and supported in their aims by an inviolable
police force – that, when viewed from another angle, the self-
interest of individuals at the expense of the many (or their interest in perpetuating a power structure which serves some people
better than others) may seem paramount.

Our Friends' discursive position is neither singular nor simplistic. Flannery has acknowledged that his own political views
have modified from 1980, when the first stage version of *Our
Friends* was written for the RSC, to 1993, when he delivered his
third screenplay version. A shift from enthusiastic radicalism to
political uncertainty is manifest in the central character, Nicky,
as the TV serial offers a retrospective on key moments in British
political history. Nicky's youthful political idealism is already
dented by his discovery of corruption and nepotism in the
housing policy of Newcastle's Labour Council at the time of
Wilson's Labour government in 1965. Whilst he remains opposed
to the subsequent emergence of Margaret Thatcher and new
Toryism, however, Nicky is inadvertently drawn into careerism.
After a spell as researcher for a new Labour MP from the North
East, Nicky becomes disillusioned with the parliamentary process as means to change. Eschewing parliamentary democracy,
he joins a militant undergound political faction committed to
direct action at the time of the conservative government under
Edward Heath. But, illustrating the gap between intentions and
effects, his chosen 'cover' role as radical photographer leads
ultimately to mainstream success through the publication of a
well-received book.

The strength of *Our Friends* as critical realist drama is the
avoidance of agit-prop or programmatic political mouthpieces
by intermingling the personal and political. Flannery discovered
to his surprise when the series was finished that he had written a piece about parenting.[4] The story of Nicky, the political
activist, is intricately intervowen, with Nicky's family and love-
life. He is banned from the family home by his father when a

'revolutionary's' automatic weapon is found under his bed by his mother. Later in the serial, as noted, he becomes sexually involved with Mary who, echoing 1970s feminism, has herself become actively involved in local politics, rising to lead the County Council just when Nicky is side-lined. Their subsequent marriage breaks up partly because Nicky finds it hard to handle his wife's centrality in local (and potentially national) politics whilst he feels so ineffectual.

This last quality is particularly emphasized through Nicky's renewed relationship with his father, a former Jarrow marcher who carries a deep bitterness towards politicians which the serial never fully explains. Father and son have shared neither a close relationship nor political outlook. To Nicky, his father seems cold, hard, distant and disapproving. He is also incommunicative such that his political cynicism is difficult to fathom. In the final two episodes by which time Mr Hutchinson is in a residential home having developed Alzheimer's disease, Nicky makes a sustained effort to communicate with his father and perhaps a final attempt to seek his approval. But a chance opportunity to revisit a key moment on the Jarrow march and to unlock Mr Hutchinson's psyche fails miserably. Driving his father home, however, Nicky finally decides that his father simply is a 'bastard' and thus sees through the romantic illusion he has cherished of a sympathetic alliance with him. In one reading, Nicky's radicalism is an attempt to succeed to change things where the Jarrow march failed; psychologically, Nicky has spent his life attempting to fulfil the law of the father when he thought he was changing the world.

The final sequence of the serial sees Nicky literally chasing his estranged wife's car as she departs from his mother's wake. Having run through ginnels down the hill to the river Tyne, he catches up with Mary. They walk towards each other and in a brief verbal exchange agree to have lunch that day rather than the next, suggesting perhaps a realisation that personal relationships, and possibly family life, have a priority over more public politics. In this reading, *Our Friends'* final note would seem to advocate the uncertainty of the political contemporary. Tosker, the working-class Tory is successful, indeed happy with his second wife with whom he has developed a new business. Mary remains involved with the Labour Party, though, with diminished conviction as roots are severed with the emergence of

'new Labour'. In civic, radical and sexual politics, Nicky seems
to have lost direction.

It is difficult to convey in little space a serial of more than
eleven hours' duration. Adding to a sense of the serial's trajectory conveyed in Nicky's journey, a brief look at the beginning
of Episode 4 gives a further sense of the interweaving of the
regional and national political contexts with each other and
with the personal lives of the characters. The episode, set in
early 1970s, begins with Geordie Peacock who – having fled
from an impending forced marriage in Newcastle – has worked
for a decade in the gangland underworld of London's Soho
peddling sex and pornography (affording the series a number
of sex scenes). He seeks out his long-lost pal, Nicky, in his supposedly secret London hideaway. Following a drink together in
a strip-club where it emerges that Geordie and Nicky no longer
share the same values, they visit a group of tramps under the
railway arches. Nicky has led Geordie there by way of explaining why he still wants 'to change things' whilst in Geordie's view,
'things are as they are; it's inevitable'. Nicky sees people where
Geordie sees tramps, arguing that 'nobody has to sleep under
a bridge'. It is ironic in the light of this remark that, later in
the serial, Nicky finds Geordie sleeping rough on London's
Embankment.

The episode then turns to one of the key concerns of the
early part of the serial: corruption in the Metropolitan Police
Force. An informant leads *The Times* newspaper to print an
exposé of corruption, naming names. Evidential tapes mention
Geordie's name as somebody who can vouch for the trustworthi-
ness of a particular detective. To edit a convoluted story, in the
ensuing investigation an incorruptible inspector is brought from
Newcastle to head the inquiry team, whilst a member of the Met.
CID, pursuing another inquiry into corruption in local government, goes north to Newcastle to interview Austin Donohue,
the Labour Council leader to whom Nicky Hutchinson was assist-
ant in his early years. It emerges in the course of the episode
that the two lines of inquiry are in fact linked and go to the
heart of national government. At the local level in Newcastle,
Austin Donohue feels protected because his dubious associate
in the building of high-rise flats, one Mr Edwards, employed the
MP Claude Seabrook (recently promoted to Home Secretary
in the Conservative government) to lend a respectable face to

the board for reasons of international sales. In the Metropolitan Police inquiry which is stalled at every turn by 'widespread and systemic corruption', Inspector Fox sends direct to Seabrook his advisory report that the Metropolitan Police should be fundamentally overhauled. The Home Secretary, however, is on first name terms with the Metropolitan Commissioner who happens to mention how awkward it might be for Seabrook if the findings of the Newcastle investigations ever came to light. The Metropolitan report is returned without comment.

By means of cross-plotting and interweaving the various strands of his narrative, Peter Flannery conveys a sense of a corruptly self-sustaining Establishment. The implication, as in *Between the Lines*, is of the self-interest of Establishment 'truth', brought out graphically at the end of the episode when Claude Seabrook takes the moral highground in giving an after-dinner speech about the need to restore standards in the face of moral decline. The issues, however, do not sit uncomfortably in the drama since *Our Friends'* success overall is to ground the political questions in the everyday lives of its four central characters. Indeed the more personal aspects of the drama are amongst the most powerful scenes and perhaps ultimately marginalize more public politics.

The comparison with *Between the Lines* highlights a possible limitation of *Our Friends'* kind of historical realism for (post)modern viewers. The production style is reminiscent more of the early Garnett/Loach 'authenticity' particularly in the lighting and the design of costumes and locations, than of the high-gloss of *Twin Peaks* or even *Between the Lines* itself. Nor does *Our Friends* have the black humour and disjunctive devices of *Boys from the Blackstuff* with which it has inevitably been compared, since between 1982 and 1996 it is difficult to recall another social realist TV drama series. *Our Friends* is unashamedly social realist. Performances of considerable conviction, particularly from Mr and Mrs Hutchinson in the living-room of their back-to-back terrace, restored to TV drama the compulsion of viewing private lives set against public events. Eschewing the flexiad approach, *Our Friends* inevitably lacked instant or short-term gratifications. The viewing figures testify, however, to the willingness of large numbers of people to sustain attention as well as viewing commitment.

The serial was a success from BBC2's point of view both in

terms of ratings, which exceeded 5 million (high for a 'minority' channel), and a critical success. *Our Friends* achieved something of the status of 'an event', distantly echoing those moments when *The Wednesday Play* provoked discussion in pubs up and down Britain (see Chapter 1). It is gratifying to Flannery, moreover, that his large postbag revealed interest across a wide range of ages and social positions. The serial was not only enjoyed, either nostalgically or in critical reflection, by people over forty who had lived through the 1960s–1990s period. Indeed, younger correspondents notably revealed an interest in the series precisely in terms of a dramatized history such as postmodern television effaces. Besides lending support to the argument that audiences may enjoy, if it were on offer in the TV drama schedules, something 'with more to it', this interest leaves in question what the size of the audience might have been had *Our Friends* been aired on BBC1.

II

Postmodern texts might be summarily characterized by a formal openness, a strategic refusal to close down meaning. They create space for play between discourses allegedly empowering the reader to negotiate or construct her own meanings. In the post-structuralist view of the indeterminacy of meaning in an endless process of semiosis, readers are freed from the hegemonic imposition of a dominant ideology (inoculation even, in the old hypodermic communication model) into a democratizing trajectory of multiple meanings-making. From the marxist perspective on which (following Jameson and Harvey) I have drawn in this book, however, the discursive position of this view is complicit with capitalist postmodernity's espousal of difference and variety in the market. From this standpoint, radical indeterminacy is, at worst, indistinguishable from complicit obfuscation.

Attempting to bridge the two positions, Ang has recently argued that postmodernity's defining characteristic is an admixture of complicity and resistance. She reacts to the 'new revisionist' charge, however, by asserting the need

> to embrace fully the primacy of the indeterminacy of meaning which . . . is essential for understanding how and why capitalist postmodernity is a 'true realm of uncertainty' (1996: 171).

Ang is right, I believe, to note that 'critical theory has changed because the structure of the capitalist order has changed' (1996: 171) and, indeed, I have drawn attention throughout this book to homologies of metaphor between shifting theories and a developing market-place. But it is difficult to see the distinction between capitulation and resistance when Ang herself acknowledges earlier in her book that:

> the agents of commercialism' . . . now have virtually complete power in defining our televisual pleasures for us: hedonism is now the official ideology of the television institution, intimately linked to the desire-producing logic of consumer capitalism (1996: 33–4).

The argument seems to rest on a premise that, post-cold-war and after the fall of the Berlin wall, capitalism has won its historical battle with socialism. Even if it is the case that no viable alternative to capitalism is currently on offer, it remains possible to be critical of a contradictory and inequitable system.

A both/and strategy seeks to sustain critique whilst acknowledging the inevitability of implication. In distinguishing a critical from a popular postmodernism above, I look to sustain the possibility of a space in which to think and feel the possibility that things might be otherwise and, in the case of postmodern texts, a space for re-articulation. Fully to embrace indeterminacy would be to abandon, as I have argued, the attempt to conduct urgently needed debate at a global level on matters of ethics and politics to redress inequities and injustices which cannot be reduced to the play of semiosis and for which market forces have no answer.

To acknowledge the authority of a voice sending a message in a language we speak does not, as Ang suggests (1996: 164–5), set us on a recursive trajectory back through dominant ideology in colonialism and imperialism to the law of the father. The important contribution of audience ethnography has been to show that situated people do not passively consume all they are offered. Indeed, it may be easier to resist attempted imposition if the message is closed and unambiguous rather than open and polysemic.

A realist TV drama like *Our Friends* might purport to say 'this is how it is', but viewers may well not consent; it might propose 'see it this way', and viewers may or may not be persuaded. Such an interaction is dialogical precisely if we accept what ethnographers tell us, that positioned truths are negotiated by situated readers in a context in which meanings are 'inexorably contextual'. In its accessibility, critical realism may yet be more productive of a dialogic exchange with potential for cognitive reorientation than critical postmodern discourses whose disjunctions and refusal of the audience's need for answers may still lead television viewers literally to switch off.

Whether new mind-sets come eventually to dominate and, if they do, whether indeterminacy is an ultimately liberalizing democratic strategy must remain to be seen. But if agency is not completely outmoded, it may be possible to intervene in the debate to change things for the better, rather than to submit helplessly to indeterminacy and undecidability. The importance of the television medium, and the significance of TV dramas in its schedules, places them at the centre of a debate to which this book is a contribution. *Our Friends* takes the British audience to the threshold of 'new Labour'. Amidst the various transitions, it is important that debate continues.

Appendix

Casualty, 'No Place to Hide', 16 October 1993: segment breakdown

(1)	(2)	(3)	(4)	(5)	(6)	(7)
TITLES CUs – accidents action	admission on stretcher trolley	MS Charlie in office	CU Charlie → MS	MS Norma in reception	M3S by bed of 'Mr Miller' → interrupted by wife (who isn't)	Charlie meets Chief Exec + Mark Calder
'mozaic' – ambulance rescue	MS/CU documentary feel	– interrupt CU of Norma	Shot/Reverse shot Norma		[ENIGMA Ia]	[ENIGMA (?) 2] [overstaffed?]
50 secs.	68 secs.	24 secs.	20 secs.	12 secs.	21 secs.	11 secs.

(8)	(9)	(10)	(11)	(12)	(13)	(14)
police with 'Mr Miller' and wife	Charlie with Chief Exec	coin swallowed – parents + child	Mrs Miller returns home to find husband Peter wounded	Ken and Duffy → Charlie	Peter and wife → police	Norma and Mr Calder Chief Exec
identity?					[ENIGMA 1A CLOSURE] [ENIGMA 1B OPENS]	
42 secs.	40 secs.	68 secs.	24 secs.	20 secs.	43 secs.	22 secs.

(15)	(16)	(17)	(18)	(19)	(20)	(21)
Calder and Jane at reception	police at the Millers ↓ drugs discovery	Charlie's office Duffy (Ken's partner)	Peter Miller arrested	Ken and partner in canteen	Peter and wife at hospital 'drugs morality'	as (19) Charlie enters
22 secs.	65 secs.	73 secs.	13 secs.	54 secs.	30 secs.	26 secs.

(22)	(23)	(24)	(25)	(26)	(27)	(28)
NEW STORY clothes w/shop Chris Weston Sonia Kate → Anne Weston visits	Mrs Miller + listening nurse 'emotional moral discussion'	Kate/Chris 'ultimatum' [ENIGMA 3]	Mr Miller treated 'disparage wife'	NEW STORY Mr Phipps admitted	Mr/Mrs Miller – self-pity – argument – slap (climax)	Hugh Phipps treated by Ken [ENIGMA 4]
2 mins. 58 secs.	1 min. 43 secs.	53 secs.	41 secs.	40 secs.	78 secs.	1 min

(29)	(30)	(31)	(32)	(33)	(34)	(35)
Mrs Miller + listening nurse as (23)	Mr Phipps to X-ray 'Burma fit'	W/shop over-time	Hugh to Ken confidential 'p.o.w in Burma' 'racism justified'(?)	Kate with kids in lift 'accident'	W/shop	Lift
41 secs.	57 secs.	72 secs.	1 min. 18 secs.	35 secs.	11 secs.	10 secs.

(36)	(37)	(38)	(39)	(40)	(41)	(42)
W/shop	Lift Kate seeks help	W/shop	Lift Kate in trouble	Exterior W/shop	Lift	Exterior W/shop Anne at lift
				Anne arrives		
12 secs.	53 secs.	7 secs.	16 secs.	8 secs.	3 secs.	7 secs.

(43)	(44)	(45)	(46)	(47)	(48)	(49)
Kate under threat	Ken talks to Hugh	Mr Miller charged by police	fire-brigade	Mr Dwyer	rescue Sarah & Kate	rescue Danny
Fall/Screams	'no future'	Deb stands by him	'the cavalry arrives'	'concern for the Major'		
		[CLOSURE 1B?]				
36 secs.	37 secs.	40 secs.	2 mins. 24 secs.	56 secs.	50 secs.	25 secs.

(50)	(51)	(52)	(53)	(54)	(55)	(56)
Hugh Phipps & Mr Dwyer reminisce ↓ reception party	Norma Charlie as (3) ↓ Mark Calder 'Norma tells it how it is'	Kate/Chris at hospital	Reception Norma/Charlie Calder 'Norma blows it'	Kate treated Danny treated	Sarah + Anne + Chris + Sonia 'tensions'	Chris + Kate
1 min. 09 secs.	77 secs.	44 secs.	24 secs.	47 secs.	1 min. 14 secs.	1 min. 12 secs.

(57)	(58)	(59)	(60)	(61)	(62)	(63)
Danny treated	Sarah Anne/Chris 'truth time'	Charlie/Ken (Duffy + a.n. other) 'did you see that?' [TO BE CONTINUED]	Anne/Chris 'showdown'	Phipps leaves Ken 'thanked' [CLOSURE 4] [ENIGMA 4]	Chris rejected by both women in tears marginalized [CLOSURE?] [ENIGMA 3]	TITLES
27 secs.	1 min.	19 secs.	1 min. 40 secs.	43 secs.	26 secs.	1 min.20 secs.

Notes

Introduction

1. I am indebted in my account to Brunsdon's avowedly schematic review of television criticism.
2. 'Populism' is used here in the sense of structures which neutralize the opposition between people and power structures in society.
3. A number of recent films (e.g. *Schindler's List* and *Heat*) and TV dramas (*Inspector Morse*) have exceptionally long running times against the drift of the new affective order.
4. Throughout the book, I use 'articulated' as does Hall, following Laclau, to refer to 'the complex set of historical practices by which we struggle to produce identity or structural unity out of, on top of, complexity, difference, contradiction' (Grossberg, 1986: 63).
5. Giddens proposes that, '[s]ocial activity is always constituted in three intersecting moments of difference: temporally, paradigmatically (invoking structure which is present only in its instantiation) and spatially. All social activities are *situated* activities in each of these senses' (1979: 54). In what follows, I shall use 'situated practices' and 'agency in structure' to evoke Giddens's formulation.
6. The phrase alludes to the title of Galbraith (1992).
7. McGuigan has similarly concluded that 'the reinsertion of aesthetic and ethical judgement into the debate is a vital rejoinder to the uncritical drift of cultural populism and its failure to dispute laissez-faire conceptions of consumer sovereignty' (1992: 159).
8. See, for example, Bannett (1993: 88–112).
9. The framework of 'family resemblances' affords the acknowledgement of differences between members of the family, quite marked between some, whilst sustaining a conceptual continuum of overlapping shared features. Kosko (1993) develops similarly the notion of 'fuzzy logic'.
10. See Leavis (1972) for an account of his great tradition of the English novel.
11. The phrase is borrowed from the title of Huyssen (1986).

1 From Electronic Theatre to . . . Cyberspaces? Technology and Televisual Form

1. For an account of *Blackstuff*'s impact, see Millington and Nelson (1986: 152–73).
2. A pioneering aspect of the production of *Blackstuff* was its mix of video and film mediums and hybrid shooting methods. For an account, see Millington and Nelson (1986: 91–108).
3. For details and an analysis of the significance of these hommages and that of film noir style in *Twin Peaks*, see Chion (1995: 113–14).
4. For a discussion of a range of quotations and allusions for the sheer

fun of it, since they have no thematic or plot significance, see Lavery (1995: 176–7).

5. That US viewers left the series at this point may suggest that narrative drive remains a key hook, though other factors complicate the issue (see Chion, 1995: 101).

6. Parataxis – literally 'the placing together of sentences, clauses or phrases without a conjunctive word' (Random House Dictionary, New York, 1966) – is used here applied to a structuring principle in the arts whereby traditional sense-making grammars give way to looser assemblages juxtaposing images without causal connection.

7. Fiske summarizes this tendency not only in the production and reading of texts but also in the making sense of social experience (1987: 15). Eagleton is critical of the reduction of social experience into language, rhetorically asking the poststructuralists, 'Was language really all there was? What about labour, sexuality, political power?' (1983: 111).

8. For a discussion of C.S. Peirce's classification of signs as they relate to cinema, see Wollen (1972: 123–4).

9. Bourdieu's research findings suggest a correlation between class and reading practices, the working class reading literally by the basic code alone, whilst the educated classes with cultural capital take note of the aesthetic (see 1992: 32–9).

10. For a succinct account of television and film production methods, see Rose, D. and Bevan, T. in BFI *Film and Television Handbook 1990* (1989: 25 and 27).

11. For an endorsement of this view by a filmmaker, see John Schlesinger in BFI *Film and Television Handbook 1990* (1989: 29).

12. For an account of the conditions of performance of European Naturalist theatre, see Styan (1983: 1–81).

13. Stephen Neale, in discussing Metz, makes the point that, 'Like theatre and opera, cinema engages a large number of perceptual registers. But, unlike them, the various perceptual mechanisms centre around objects which are not in themselves physically present' (1980: 32). My point is that in television, a sense of immediate presence is partially retained in spite of the fact that, as in cinema, the objects themselves are not physically present.

14. Raymond Williams first introduced the concept of 'flow' in television (see 1974: 96).

15. In the schedules of early television, breaks were built in. The acts in plays were punctuated with 'interludes' featuring music over images perhaps of the props and set from the play.

16. I am indebted to Ellis (1982, revised 1992) for establishing a number of features of the film and television mediums I develop in this book.

17. In an obituary TV tribute to Dennis Potter on BBC1, 8 June 1994, Gareth Davies, a TV drama director, recalls how he could walk the length of his commuter train and everybody would be talking about the play shown on the previous night. Actor Jack Shepherd made a similar observation in a discussion of TV drama organized by the BFI at MOMI on 2 May 1995.

18. Some advertisements in the 1990s have turned into mini-soaps. See, for example, the 1994 campaign for Nescafé Blend 37 coffee featuring the relationship between a young man and a young woman in a post-modern designer setting suggesting fluid personal identity. See also, Flitterman (1983).

19. In the discussion of televisual and film aesthetics in relation to politics in this study, I am indebted to initial insights in Maltby (1983).

20. I am grateful to Bob Millington for pointing out that D.W. Griffith used cross-cutting to gain pace in *Birth of a Nation*, for example, whilst Metz's parallel montage offers a creative – and potentially critical – use of the device.

21. Potter cited in *The Guardian*, 2, 6 April 1994: 3.

22. Populism is used here in the sense of structures which neutralize the opposition between people and the power block.

23. Imagery constructed of digital bits, a pattern of alternative options registered in a computer's memory, has no original in the sense that a photographic image has a negative. Furthermore, any additional imagery created from digital samples similarly has no original against which 'authenticity' might be tested. The implications of such technology for referentiality are considerable.

2 Flexi-Narrative from Hill Street to Holby City: Upping the Tempo; Raising the Temperature

1. I am indebted in the following account of MTM and *Hill Street Blues* to various contributors in Feuer *et al.* (1984).

2. See *Radio Times*, 18–24 September 1993: 28.

3. Contemporary academics and market strategists alike challenge the concept of a consensual, mass audience. Indeed rather than an agglomeration of individuals, the audience is reconceived in terms of segments, variously broken down by factors such as age, class, gender ethnicity. Most recently – as illustrated in Chapter 2 – groups are targeted in terms of purchasing power relative to 'VAL's . . . "values and lifestyles"' (Kroker and Cook, 1988: 278).

4. Ratings based on British Audience Research Board figures as published in *Radio Times*, 16–22 October 1993: 22.

5. Special Effects Generators, SEGs, are standard features of electronic vision mixers and editing suites. Their capacity to manipulate visual imagery electronically varies in sophistication from the inexpensive domestic to the computer-driven, professional apparatus and is greatly extended with digital technology.

6. It has become a convention of television news and documentary programmes to use the SEG mosaic to mask the face of a person whose identity is to be protected.

7. *Casualty* is shot on Betacam SP in Bristol. Accident sequences are shot on location, but the 'hospital' scenes shot on a purpose built set.

8. Information given in an unpublished interview at his home with Robin Nelson on 14 June 1994.

9. For a discussion of a range of structural relations between plots in Renaissance drama, for example, see Levin (1971).
10. See, for example, Caryl Churchill's play, *Serious Money* (1990).
11. For a discussion of Charlie's ambiguous sexuality and its significance for his narrative centrality, see *Radio Times* 17–23 September 1994: 37–8.
12. A parallel might be drawn between TV drama in this respect and children's play in which adult experience is rehearsed or educational drama which explores learning through vicarious experience in an imaginary situation but where the line between actuality and the imaginary is merely blurred (see Heathcote, 1990).
13. Williams makes this point in relation to the development of drama in the twentieth century (see 1973: 386).
14. Series and soaps with rural settings have proved particularly popular. Viewers frequently give the location as their reason for watching. The implications of the preference for cultural reassurance in rural locations in an industrial (or postindustrial) age is discussed in Ch. 4.
15. For a discussion of the developing inter-relationship between the private and public spheres see Sennett (1977).
16. See *Radio Times*, 18–24 September 1993: 28.
17. See *Radio Times*, 18–24 September 1993: 28.
18. See *Radio Times*, 9–15 October 1993: 123; and 30 October – 5 November 1993: 129.

3 Dislocations of Postmodernity: Transition in the Political Economy of Culture

1. (1982: 30). The screenplay is published by Granada, the series, first shown on BBC1, 1982.
2. In 'George's Last Ride', emphasis is placed particularly by Mrs Malone on the efforts of the workers to resist the worst aspects of exploitation (see Bleasdale, 1982: 206). Harvey, however, supplies a broader socio-economic context for the 'boys' predicament (see 1989: 125–40).
3. See, for example, Lyotard (1984: 6–9), and Jameson (1993: 95–6).
4. Callinicos points out that changes in manufacturing are less pronounced than some commentators claim and demand a more subtle analysis than theorists of 'postindustrial society' characteristically offer (see 1989: 122–3).
5. Though a technical standard of production has been established through custom and practice in the deployment of different techniques and technologies as noted in Chapter 1, the success – technically, aesthetically and commercially – of a number of low-budget productions calls in question the direct relationship between high budgets and quality.
6. See, for example, Inglis (1990: 88) and Kumar (1977: 234).
7. See, for example, Ang (1991: 5–6), and Dowmunt (1993: 1–15).
8. See Ang (1996: 26–34) for an account of changes in Dutch television and culture.
9. The number of households in Britain with satellite TV dishes rose from

2.5 million in 1991 to 3 million in 1993 and to almost 3.5 million by 1995 (figures *Marketing*, 7 March 1996). Cable penetration has almost doubled between 1986 and 1993 from 12.2% to 21.1% of TV homes (figures from *BFI Film and Television Handbook 1995*).

10. The Government White Paper of Summer 1994 confirmed renewal of its charter for the next decade.

11. The dramatic increase in the last decade and particularly the past five years was confirmed by contributors from C4, BBC Research Dept., and ITV Network Audience Planning at 'Doing Television Research', University of Manchester Broadcasting Symposium, Channel 4, London, 3 Decenber 1993.

12. See report in *The Guardian*, 22 April 1995: 1.

13. For a discussion of *Dallas* as an imperialist text, see Tomlinson (1991: 45–50). Other commentators, notably Katz and Liebes (1985) and Cubitt (1988) have noted diverse readings of *Dallas* in various speech communities but, I would suggest, against the preferred meaning on offer.

14. Murdoch in the McTaggart Memorial Lecture, Edinburgh, 1988.

15. Whereas in the past C4 was financed from advertising revenue generated by ITV, it will in the future find its own funding through a direct relation with advertisers.

16. See Sean Cubitt (1988: 46–8) for a refinement of Robins and Webster's tendency to overemphasize the power of advertising.

17. Cited in *The Guardian*, 22 April 1995: 2.

18. *The Guardian*, 22 April 1995: 1.

19. For a discussion, see Robin Murray, 'Benetton Britain: The New Economic Order' (in Hall and Jacques, 1990).

20. Cited in *The Guardian*, 27 May 1994: 1. Writers and directors of 'authored' single drama retain high status in the television industry and, more particularly, beyond it with those influential in political decision-making. 'Accordingly, every single applicant for a major Channel 3 franchise promised, in its application, to increase the output of single plays and films. Little has been heard of these promises since the new franchisees started work on January 1, 1993 (*BFI Film and Television Handbook 1995*: 60).

21. See, for example, Bourdieu (1992), Featherstone (1989), Lasch (1978).

22. Callinicos suggests that undecidability in political terms arises from the disillusion, post 1968, with the idea of social transformation through marxist revolution and that the generation of 68 have accordingly adopted an aesthetic pose, having no real faith in capitalist democracy, but enjoying its benefits with a certain ironic detachment (see 1989: 162–71).

23. Jim Collins (1992: 337) locates the initial usage with reference to the making of meanings from disparate fragments in anthropological accounts of tribal cosmologies.

24. Many contemporary advertisements draw on surrealism in the construction of their images. The Guinness campaign featuring Rutger Hauer in 1993–4, for example, and the shampoo advertisement isolating

individual models emerging as if propelled from the desert sand, their long hair defying gravity. Other advertisements have consciously imitated impressionist paintings, whilst others have used computer graphics to disorientate spatio-temporal norms.

4 Signs of the Times? *Heartbeat* and *Baywatch*

1. Figures taken from *Radio Times*, 23–29 October 1993.
2. See *Radio Times*, 20–25 November 1993: 22.
3. *Heartbeat* emerged to be the highest rated original TV drama production of 1993 (see *BFI Film and Television Handbook 1995* (1994). Following three series, its popularity has led to repeats in 1996.
4. For the marketing information in what follows, I am indebted to David Brennan, Controller of Audience Planning ITV Network Centre, in a contribution to 'Doing Television Research', University of Manchester Broadcasting Symposium, Channel 4, London, 3 December 1993. For additional production information, I am indebted to Stuart Doughty, producer of the first series (and a personal friend), in a number of informal discussions.
5. Nick Berry also had a number 1 chart success with 'Every Loser Wins', a song used in *EastEnders*. He thus carries associations of a pop star along with his other credits.
6. '[W]hat the French neatly call *la mode retro*, retrospective styling' (Jameson, 1985: 116) refers to the tendency in postmodernism (contra modernism) to reclaim the history of the arts and culture more generally but, denying history itself, simply to recirculate its signs in a perpetual present.
7. In the episode of 17 September 1995 – just prior to the submission of this thesis – Kate Rowan died of leukaemia having given birth to a baby girl, to be called Kate. This might be seen as a melodramatic but palatable solution to the problem of losing an actor from the series.
8. *BFI Film and TV Handbook, 1994* (1993: 49).
9. Award winning series and serials include *GBH* (C4, 1991), *Anglo-Saxon Attitudes* (BBC, 1992), *Prime Suspect* (Granada, 1991) and *Prime Suspect 2 and 3* (Granada/WGBH, 1992/93), *Band of Gold* (ITV, 1995), *Cracker* (ITV, 1995).
10. Hal Foster distinguishes similarly between a 'postmodernism of resistance' and 'the "false normativity" of a reactionary postmodernism' (1985: xii).
11. Williams records that in the 1960s there were, 'very large audiences for disturbing and controversial plays . . . in many ways embarrassing to the broadcasting authorities and orthodox public opinion' (1974: 58).
12. Post-feminists have, of course, reviewed attitudes of women to their representations as glamorous sex-objects, finding them less unacceptable than their 1970s feminist predecessors.
13. Since my analysis, the titles of *Baywatch* have been slightly revised but my points still hold.

5 TV Drama Forms: Tradition and Innovation: Gradual (Un)realizations

1. A concise account is offered in Williams (1981: 216–19 and 257–62).
2. For an account of Realism in the visual arts, see Nochlin (1971: 13–57).
3. Williams points out that the artistic method of imitating everyday, ordinary life is timeless; the difference between earlier episodes of realism in drama and what subsequently is termed bourgeois realist drama is concerned with 'a whole form' in a specific historical moment (1977, 61–4).
4. In formulating these characteristics, I am indebted to my colleague Derek Akers and his unpublished MA thesis, 'Aspects of naturalism in relation to opera', University of Keele, 1981.
5. For a discussion of structuralism and semiotics, see Hawkes (1977).
6. See 'Ideology and the State Apparatus' (Althusser, 1977: 121–73) and Barthes (1973: 117–74).
7. To paraphrase Williams (1977: 68).
8. For a discussion of the development of the subject and subjectivity, see Smith (1988).
9. See particularly the work of the Glasgow Media Group (1976, 1980, 1982).
10. In *Philosophical Investigations*, the 'later' Wittgenstein revises and develops his earlier philosophy, coming to think that the structures of language shape human thinking about the world and that words mean, to put it very simply, what they are used to mean. See Wittgenstein (1994).
11. Undertaking an elementary ethnographic study in the preliminary stages of this study at a sheltered housing development in Alsager, Cheshire, I asked residents in the form of a simple questionnaire to list which TV dramas they most watched and liked. Findings inadvertently revealed that a number of respondents did not distinguish clearly between factual and fictional programmes. Michael Palin's very popular travelogue was listed by many as a drama, in the sense of a narrative with attractive settings, much as they might view *Heartbeat.*
12. For a discussion of *Cathy Come Home*, see Brandt (1981: 194–216).
13. See, for example, the accounts of the reception of Bleasdale's *The Monocled Mutineer* and Plater's *A Very British Coup* in Brandt (1993: 11–12).
14. See Gottlieb (1993: 47–8).
15. See Gottlieb (1993: 52).
16. In rare cases of TV dramas, such as *Lovejoy* (BBC1) and *House of Cards* (BBC1), the main character talks directly to camera or, as it were, directly to viewers. This device serves not so much to 'break the frame', however, as to extend complicity between viewers and character. As noted, unusual angles of vision, or breaches of established codes and conventions, can be accommodated given the very familiarity of the format.
17. See Lukács (1969). Lukács favours the Realist novel for its ability to reveal the underlying dynamics of society. See Brecht (1964: 179–

209). Brecht advocates the exposure of the means of theatrical production to reveal the processes of construction.

18. For a discussion of the presumptions and limitations of scientific knowledge, see Rorty (1980).

6 Framing 'the Real': *Oranges, Middlemarch, X-Files*

1. In the past three years, lesbian relationships have been represented
    in the mainstream British soaps, *Brookside, EastEnders* and *Emmerdale.*
    Otherwise overt treatment of particularly physical lesbian relationships
    in TV drama is rare, but see, for example, *Portrait of a Marriage* (BBC2,
    1990), a biography of Vita Sackville West. See also the discussion of
    Between the Lines in Chapter 8.

2. For the views attributed to Andrew Davies and insights into the adapta-
    tion process, I am indebted to a lecture he gave about making *Middle-
    march* in the Department of Arts Education, University of Warwick, 9
    March 1994.

3. Brecht sought a theatrical strategy to invite 'complex seeing'. He
    famously disputed with Lukacs the best means by which this might be
    achieved. As Nichols summarizes, 'Lukács located the beginnings of
    this process in experiential qualities of narration, which offer both pleas-
    ure and recognition, involvement and awareness simultaneously. Brecht
    held out for reason joined to passion, Lukács for insight embedded in
    classic narrative structure. In either case, ideological struggle and polit-
    ical change follow from the changes of habit that art . . . can provoke'
    (1991: 194).

4. For a more lengthy critical discussion of MacCabe's position, see
    Christopher Williams (1994: 275–92).

5. Weill indeed appears to have anticipated Brecht's use of the terms
    '*Gestus*' and '*gestich*' to denote action which took an attitude to what
    it depicted. See Willett (1964: 42n).

6. Winterson, Bennett and Wood all feature in their comedy the faded
    seaside town of Morecambe, itself made something of a British national
    joke in the patter of comedians Morecambe and Wise.

7. *Oranges Are Not the Only Fruit* (1990) won Winterson the Whitbread
    prize for first novel.

8. See Barthes (1973: 117–74).

9. As Auerbach observes, in Flaubert's novels '[h]is opinion of his char-
    acters and events remains unspoken; and when the characters express
    themselves it is never in such a manner that the writer identifies him-
    self with their opinion or seeks to make the reader identify himself
    with it (1953: 486). George Eliot is a much more intrusive author not
    sharing so fully with Flaubert the belief that 'the truth of the phenom-
    enal world is also revealed in linguistic expression' (cited in Auerbach,
    1953: 486).

10. See 'The Work of Art in an Age of Mechanical Reproduction' (Ben-
    jamin, 1992: 211–44).

7 The Public Stock of Harmless Pleasure: Pleasures, Meanings, Responsibilities

1. John Corner has recently noted the influence of the postmodern debate on documentary style (Corner, 1995: 96–7).
2. Ellis points out that in television, '[s]ound holds attention more consistently than image, and provides a continuity that holds across momentary lapses of attention' (1992: 128).
3. In Shakepeare's *Twelfth Night* Act III. Sc. iv. the self-entranced Puritan Malvolio is gulled into dressing unfashionably and ridiculously in cross-gartered yellow stockings.
4. Jameson observes that, 'the posing of the category of 'mode of production' as the fundamental one of Marxian social analysis and the endorsement of a 'problematic' that asks such systemic questions about contemporary society would seem essential for political people who are still committed to radical social change and transformation' (1984: xv).
5. Enzenberger argues that, 'the new media are egalitarian in structure'. He recognizes, however, that '[o]nly a free socialist society will be able to make them fully productive' (1974; 107) since prevailing market mechanisms constrain and neutralize.
6. Adorno's critique (with Horkheimer) of the culture industry (1979) and its denial of freedom through the commodification of leisure may well be overstated and – with regard to jazz, for example – smack of conspiracy theory. It should not be forgotten, however, that Adorno was writing at the height of the most nihilistic deployment of the aestheticization of mass media and the manipulation of signs in contemporary history. His critique, though perhaps overstated, still carries some force.
7. In *Times Higher Education Supplement*, 18 Nov. 1994: iii.
8. Barthes distinguishes between a *scriptible* (writerly/writable) and a *lisible* (readerly/readable) text in the introduction to *S/Z* (1970). Although he proceeds to demonstrate in his discussion of Balzac's *Sarrasine* that a readerly text may be read against the grain, his distinction would seem to suggest that some texts are more conducive to the acceptance or transgression of codes and conventions than others.

8 Diverse Innovations: Radical 'Tec(h)s': *NYPD Blue*, *Between the Lines*, *The Singing Detective*

1. Cited in *Radio Times*, 15–21 October 1994: 30.
2. *Cop Rock* might be described as Bochco's attempt to be Potter. A police series with all Bochco's high-gloss hallmarks, it differed by its characters breaking into song and dance numbers mid-narrative. The realist context resumed without acknowledging any disjunction.
3. It should be acknowledged that complaints were to some extent orchestrated by the self-appointed Viewers for Quality Television Group which has established standards for the programmes it supports (see Brower, 1992: 170–7).

4. I am indebted for this insight to *EoD* producer, Michael Wearing, in a research interview for Millington and Nelson (1986).
5. Cited in *Radio Times*, 15–22 October 1994: 30.
6. *Radio Times*, 2–8 October 1993: 30.
7. This episode was written by Nicholas Martin, directed by Peter Smith and produced by Peter Norris.
8. For a discussion of this point, see Saynor (1993: 12).
9. This episode was written by Rob Heyland, directed by Roy Battersby and produced by Peter Norris. *BTL* is made by Garnett's company Island World, in association with the BBC.
10. Currently (1995), in the BBC, Alan Yentob (BBC1) and Michael Jackson (BBC2) are the key schedulers including for drama, whilst for ITV Network, Vernon Lawrence is responsible for commissioning decisions about drama output.

9 For What It's Worth: Problematics of Value and Evaluation

1. For a clear exposition, summary and critique, see Callinicos (1989: 62–91).
2. Throughout the following discussion I am particularly indebted to Connor (1992).
3. Callinicos makes an interesting case about the '68 generation's abandonment of radical politics along these lines (see 1989: 162–74).
4. For a critical discussion, see Connor (1992: 102–13).
5. Schroder argues that quality is entirely relative to the viewer of television, though he acknowledges ethical, aesthetic and ecstatic dimensions. Thus the housewife, in his example, whose 'ecstatic' engagement with *Dynasty* is evident in her building her life around it, finds quality for her in the programme, and there is little more to be said (see 1992: 212–13).
6. Even between speech communities, according to Wittgenstein, understanding is possible: 'The common behaviour of mankind is the system of reference by means of which we interpret an unknown language' (1994: 82e).
7. Since Wittgenstein's writings are famously oblique, his conception of art referred and cited here is that summarized by Tilghman (1991), to whose detailed study of Wittgensteinian aesthetics I am indebted.

10 Coda – Critical Postmodernism: Critical Realism: *Twin Peaks* and *Our Friends in the North*

1. Whilst postmodernism might be seen more as a disposition of viewers than a feature of textual construction, where postmodern TV drama texts are concerned, there are few besides *Twin Peaks*. *Wild Palms* was widely regarded as imitative of *TP*, often referred to as *Wild Peaks* or *Twin Palms*. Otherwise antecedents might include *Moonlighting, Thirtysomething, The Wonder Years* and even *Cop Rock*. In the face of the preponderance of TV drama remaining within realist aesthetics – albeit

in developed forms – the assertion of a paradigm shift in TV drama culture, allegedly heralded by *TP*, appears to be premature.

2. For an account of the range of writers, directors and their contributions see Lavery (1995: 5 and 208–58).

3. *The Guardian*, 1 Jan. 1996: 2. The two-page spread on *OFN* recounts the production history.

4. I am indebted to Peter Flannery for a number of insights shared in an interview with Robin Nelson and Janine Moss at the writer's flat on 1 May 1996.

References

ADORNO, Theodor (1992) 'Letters to Walter Benjamin' in Taylor, R. (ed.) (1992) *Aesthetics and Politics* (Verso, London).

ADORNO, Theodor and HORKHEIMER, Max (1979) *Dialectic of the Enlightenment* (trans. Herder from 1944 *Dialektik der Aufklarung*) (Verso, London).

ALLEN, Robert C. (ed.) (1992) *Channels of Discourse, Reassembled* (2nd edition, Routledge, London).

ALTHUSSER, Louis (1977) *Lenin, Philosophy and Other Essays* (trans. Brewster, B.) (New Left Books, London).

ANDERSON, Benedict (1983) *Imagined Communities* (Verso, London).

ANG, Ien (1990) 'Culture and Communication. Towards an Ethnographic Critique of Media Consumption in the Transnational Media System', *European Journal of Communication*, no. 5: 239–60.

ANG, Ien (1991) *Desperately Seeking the Audience* (Routledge, London).

ANG, Ien (1996) *Living Room Wars* (Routledge, London).

ANSCOMBE, G.E.M. (trans.) (1994) *Philosophical Investigations* (Blackwell, Oxford).

ARENDT, Hannah (ed.) (1992) *Walter Benjamin: Illuminations* (trans. from 1955 *Schriften*, Suhrkamp Verlag, Frankfurt am Main) (Fontana Press, London).

ARMES, Roy (1994) *Action and Image* (Manchester University Press, Manchester).

ASTON, Elaine (1995) *An Introduction to Feminism and Theatre* (Routledge, London).

AUERBACH, Erich (1953) *Mimesis: The Representation of Reality in Western Literature* (trans. Trask, W.R., from 1947, Francke, Berne) (Princeton University Press, New Jersey).

BANNET, Eve Tavor (1993) *Postcultural Theory* (Macmillan, Basingstoke and London).

BARTHES, Roland (1970) *S/Z* (trans. Miller, R.) (Jonathan Cape, London).

BARTHES, Roland (1973) *Mythologies* (trans. Lavers, A.) (Paladin, London).

BARTHES, Roland (1976) *The Pleasure of the Text* (trans. Miller, R.) (Jonathan Cape, London).

BARTHES, Roland (1977) *Image, Music, Text* (trans. Heath, S.) (Fontana Press, London).

BAUDRILLARD, Jean (1988) 'Simulacra and Simulations' in Poster, Mark (ed.) (1988) *Jean Baudrillard: Selected Writings* (Polity Press, Cambridge).

BBC Education (1994) *Middlemarch: A Viewer's Guide* (BBC Education, London).

BELSEY, Catherine (1980) *Critical Practice* (Methuen, London).

BENJAMIN, Walter (1992) 'The Storyteller', 'On Some Motifs in Baudelaire', 'The Work of Art in an Age of Mechanical Reproduction', 'Theses on the Philosophy of History', in Arendt, H. (ed.) (1992) *Illuminations* (Fontana Press, London).

BENNETT, Tony (ed.) (1983) *Formations of Pleasure* (Routledge & Kegan Paul, London).

BENNETT, Tony *et al.* (eds) (1981) *Popular Television and Film* (British Film Institute/Open University, London).

BERMAN, Marshall (1993) *All That Is Solid Melts Into Air* (Verso, London, 1983 rep. 1993).

BHABA, Homi (1993) *The Location of Culture* (Routledge, London).

BILLEN, Andrew (1994) 'Beach Bums', *The Observer*, 2 January, pp. 16–25.

BLEASDALE, Alan (1982) *Boys from the Blackstuff* (Granada Publishing, St Albans and London).

BONDEBJERG, Ib (1992) 'Intertextuality and Metafiction: Genre and Narration in the Television Fiction of Dennis Potter' in Skovmand, M. and Schroder, K.C. (eds) (1992) *Media Cultures* (Routledge, London).

BOOTH, Wayne C. (1988) *The Company We Keep: An Ethics of Fiction* (University of California Press, LA and London).

BOURDIEU, Pierre (1992) *Distinction* (1979, rep. 1992, trans. Nice, R.) (Routledge, London).

BRANDT, George (ed.) (1981) *British Television Drama* (Cambridge University Press, Cambridge).

BRANDT, George (ed.) (1993) *British Television Drama in the 1980s* (Cambridge University Press, Cambridge).

BRECHT, Bertolt (1964) 'The Modern Theatre is the Epic Theatre' in Willett, John (ed.) (1964) *Brecht on Theatre: The Development of an Aesthetic* (Methuen, London).

BRECHT, Bertolt (1992) 'Against Georg Lukács' (trans. from 1967 *Schriften zur Kunst und Theater*, Frankfurt, in Taylor, R. (ed.) (1992).

BRIGGS, Asa (1985) *The BBC, the First Fifty years* (Oxford University Press, Oxford).

British Film Institute (1989) (1990) (1993) (1994) *BFI Film and Television Handbook 1989, 1990, 1993, 1994, 1995* (British Film Institute, London).

BROWER Sue (1992) 'Fans as Tastemakers: Viewers for Quality Television' in Lewis, Lisa (ed.) (1992: 163–84).

BRUNSDON, Charlotte (1990a) 'Aesthetics and Audiences' in Mellencamp, P. (ed.) (1990).

BRUNSDON, Charlotte (1990b) 'Problems with Quality', *Screen* (Spring) vol. 31, no. 1: 67–90.

BURGER, Peter (1986) *Theory of the Avant-Garde* (Manchester University Press, Manchester).

BURGIN, Victor (1986) *The End of Art Theory* (Macmillan, Basingstoke).

BUXTON, David (1990) *From The Avengers to Miami Vice* (Manchester University Press, Manchester).

BYATT, A.S. (1994) *Middlemarch: A Viewer's Guide* (BBC Education, London).

CALLINICOS, Alex (1989) *Against Postmodernism* (Polity Press, Oxford).

CARROLL, John (1993) *Humanism* (Fontana, London).

CAUGHIE, John (1990) 'Playing at Being American: Games and Tactics' in Mellencamp, P. (ed.) (1990).

CHION, Michel (1995) *David Lynch* (trans. Julian, R.) (British Film Institute Publishing, London).

CHURCHILL, Caryl (1990) *Serious Money* in *Two Plays: Caryl Churchill* (Methuen, London).

CLIFFORD, Andrew (1991) 'Small Pleasures', *Sight & Sound* (November) vol. 1, Issue 7: 18–20.

CLIFFORD, James (1986) *Writing Culture* (University of California Press, Berkeley and London).

COLLINS, Jim (1989) *Uncommon Cultures* (Routledge, London).

COLLINS, Jim (1992) 'Postmodernism and Television' in Allen, R.C. (ed.) (1992).

COLLINS, Richard, *et al.* (eds) (1986) *Media, Culture & Society: A Critical Reader* (Sage, London).

CONNOR, Stephen (1989) *Postmodernist Culture* (Blackwell, Oxford).

CONNOR, Stephen (1992) *Theory and Cultural Value* (Blackwell, Oxford).

COOK, John R. (1995) *Dennis Potter: A Life on Screen* (Manchester University Press, Manchester).

CORNER, John (1992) 'Presumption as Theory: "Realism" in Television Studies', *Screen* (Spring) vol. 33, no. 1: 97–102.

CORNER, John (1994) 'Debating Culture: Quality and Inequality', *Media, Culture & Society*, vol. 16: 141–8.

CORNER, John (1995) *Television Form and Public Address* (Edward Arnold, London).

CUBITT, Sean (1988) 'Reply to Robins and Webster', *Screen* (May–August) vol. 27, no. 3–4: 46–8.

CUBITT, Sean (1990) in Tomlinson, A. (ed.) (1990) *Consumption, Identity, Style* (Routledge, London).

CURRAN, James (1990) 'The New Revisionism in Mass Communications Research. A Reappraisal', *European Journal of Communications*, no. 5: 135–64.

CURRAN, James *et al.* (eds) (1977) *Mass Communications and Society* (Edward Arnold/Open University, London).

DEBORD, Guy (1992) *Society of the Spectacle and Other Films* (trans. Parry, R., from 1978 *Oeuvres Cinematographiques Completes*) (Rebel Press, London).

DERRIDA, Jacques (1978) *Writing and Difference* (trans. Bass, A.) (Routledge & Kegan Paul, London).

DONALD, J. and MERCER, C. (1981) 'Reading and Realism' in *Form and Meaning*, Course U203, Popular Culture (Open University, Milton Keynes).

DOWMUNT, Tony (1993) *Channels of Resistance* (British Film Institute, London).

DRUMMOND, P. and PATERSON, R. (eds) (1985) *Television in Transition* (British Film Institute, London).

EAGLETON, Terry (1983) *Literary Theory: An Introduction* (Blackwell, Oxford).

ECO, Umberto (1979) *The Role of the Reader* (Indiana University Press, Bloomington and London).

ELLIS, John (1992) *Visible Fictions* (2nd edition, Routledge, London).

ENZENBERGER, Hans Magnus (1974) *The Consciousness Industry* (Roloff, M. ed.) (The Seabury Press Inc., New York).

FALK, Barrie (1983) 'The Communication of Feeling' in Schaper, E. (ed.) (1983).

FEATHERSTONE, Mike (1989) 'Postmodernism, Cultural Change and Social Practice' in Kellner, D. (1989).

FEKETE, John (ed.) (1988) *Life After Postmodernism: Essays on Value and Culture* (Macmillan, Basingstoke and London).

FEUER, Jane (1986) 'Narrative Form in American Network Television' in MacCabe, Colin (ed.) (1986).

FEUER, Jane *et al.* (eds) (1984) *MTM: 'Quality Television'* (British Film Institute, London).

FISKE, John (1987) *Television Culture* (Methuen, London).

FISKE, John (1992) 'The Cultural Economy of Fandom' in Lewis, Lisa (ed.) (1992: 30–49).

FLITTERMAN, Sandy (1983) 'The *Real* Soap Opera: TV commercials' in Kaplan, E. Ann (ed.) (1983).

FOSTER, Hal (ed.) (1985) *Postmodern Culture* (Pluto Press, London).

FOUCAULT, Michel (1978) *The History of Sexuality* (Penguin, Harmondsworth).

FOUCAULT, Michel (1984) 'Panopticism' in Rabinow, Paul (ed.) (1984).

FRITH, Simon (1983) 'The Pleasures of the Hearth: The Making of BBC Light Entertainment' in Bennett, T. (ed.) (1983).

GALBRAITH, J.K. (1992) *The Culture of Contentment* (Sinclair-Stevenson, London).

GEERTZ, Clifford (1993) *The Interpretation of Cultures* (Fontana, London).

GIDDENS, Anthony (1979) *Central Problems in Social Theory: Action, Structure and Contradiction* (Macmillan, London).

GLASGOW MEDIA GROUP (1976) *Bad News* (Routledge & Kegan Paul, London).

GLASGOW MEDIA GROUP (1980) *More Bad News* (Routledge & Kegan Paul, London).

GLASGOW MEDIA GROUP (1982) *Really Bad News* (Writers & Readers Publishing Co-operative Society, London).

GOTTLIEB, Vera (1993) '*Brookside*: "Damon's YTS Comes to an End" (Barry Woodward): Paradoxes and Contradictions' in Brandt, George (ed.) (1993).

GRAMSCI, Antonio (1971) *Selections from the Prison Notebooks* (trans. and ed. Hoare, Q. and Nowell Smith, G.) (Lawrence & Wishart, London).

GROSSBERG, Lawrence (1986) 'History, Politics and Postmodernism: Stuart Hall and Cultural Studies', *Journal of Communication Inquiry*, vol. 10, pt 2: 61–7.

GROSSBERG, Lawrence (1987) 'The In-Difference of Television', *Screen* (Spring) vol. 28, no. 2: 28–45.

GUREVITCH, M. *et al.* (eds) (1982) *Culture, Society and Media* (Methuen, London).

HABERMAS, Jürgen (1976) *Legitimation Crisis* (trans. McCarthy T. from 1973, Suhrkamp Verlag, Frankfurt am Main) (Heinemann Educational, London).

HABERMAS, Jürgen (1990) *Philosophical Discourse of Modernity* (trans. Lawrence, F. from 1985, Suhrkamp Verlag, Frankfurt am Main) (Polity Press, Cambridge).

HALL, Stuart (1984) 'The State – Socialism's Old Caretaker', *Marxism Today* (November) vol. 28, no. 11: 24–9.

HALL, Stuart (1986) 'On Postmodernism Articulation', *Journal of Communication Inquiry*, vol. 10, part 2: 45–60.

HALL, Stuart (1987) 'Minimal Selves', *ICA Documents 6: Identity* (Institute of Contemporary Arts, London).

HALL, Stuart *et al.* (eds) (1980) *Culture, Media, Language* (Hutchinson, London).

HALL, S. and JACQUES, M. (eds) (1990) *New Times* (Lawrence & Wishart, London, 2nd edition).

HAMER, D. and BRIDGE, B. (eds) (1994) *The Good, the Bad and the Gorgeous* (Pandora, London).

HARVEY, David (1989) *The Condition of Postmodernity* (Blackwell, Oxford).

HAWKES, TERENCE (1977) *Structuralism and Semiotics* (Methuen, London).

HEATHCOTE, Dorothy (1990) *Collected Writings on Education and Drama* (Johnson, L. and O'Neill, C. (eds) Stanley Thorne, Cheltenham).

HINDS, Hilary (1992) '*Oranges Are Not the Only Fruit*' in Munt, Sally (1992).

HMSO (1994) *The Future of the BBC: Serving the Nation, Competing Worldwide* (HMSO, London).

HOARE, Q. and NOWELL SMITH, G. (ed. & trans.) (1971) *Antonio Gramsci: Selections from the Prison Notebooks* (Lawrence & Wishart, London).

HOBSON, Dorothy (1982) *Crossroads: The Drama of a Soap Opera* (Methuen, London).

HUNNINGHER, Joost (1993) 'The Singing Detective (Dennis Potter): Who Done It?' in Brandt, George (ed.) (1993).

HUTCHEON, Linda (1989) *The Politics of Postmodernism* (Routledge, London).

HUYSSEN, Andreas (1986) *After the Great Divide: Modernism, Mass Culture, Postmodernism* (Macmillan, Basingstoke and London).

INGLIS, Fred (1988) *Popular Culture and Political Power* (Harvester Wheatsheaf, Hemel Hempstead).

INGLIS, Fred (1990) *Media Theory: An Introduction* (Blackwell, Oxford).

INGLIS, Fred (1993) *Cultural Studies* (Blackwell, Oxford).

JAMESON, Fredric (1984) Introduction to Lyotard, J.-F., *The Postmodern Condition: A Report on Knowledge* (trans. Bennington, G. and Massumi, B.) (University of Minnesota/Manchester University Press, Manchester).

JAMESON, Fredric (1985) 'Postmodernism and Consumer Society' in Foster, H. (ed.) *Postmodern Culture* (Pluto Press, London).

JAMESON, Fredric (1993) *Postmodernism or The Cultural Logic of Late Capitalism* (Verso, London).

JENCKS, Charles (1989) *What is Postmodernism?* (1986 rev. 1989) (Academy Editions, London).

KAPLAN, E. Ann (ed.) (1983) *Regarding Television: Critical Approaches – An Anthology* (America Film Institute, Los Angeles).

KAPLAN, E. Ann (1987) *Rocking Around the Clock* (Methuen, London).

KATZ, E. and LIEBES, T. (1985) 'Mutual Aid in the Decoding of *Dallas*: Preliminary Notes from a Cross-Cultural Study' in Drummond, P. and Paterson, R. (eds) (1985).

KEATS, John (1953) 'Ode on Melancholy' in Quiller-Couch, Sir A. (ed.) (1953) *The Oxford Book of Modern Verse* (Clarendon Press, Oxford).

KELLNER, D. (ed.) (1989) *Postmodernism/Jameson/Critiques* (Harvard University Press, Cambridge, Mass. and London).

KERR, Paul (1984) 'Drama at *MTM*: *Lou Grant* and *Hill St Blues*' in Feuer, J. *et al.* (ed.) (1984).

KOSKO, Bart (1993) *Fuzzy Thinking: The New Science of Fuzzy Logic* (Flamingo, London).

KROKER, A. and COOK, D. (1988) *The Postmodern Scene: Excremental Culture and Hyper-Aesthetics* (Macmillan, Basingstoke and London).

KUMAR, Krishn (1977) 'Holding the Middle Ground: The BBC, the Public and the Professional Broadcaster' in Curran, James *et al.* (eds) (1977).

LACLAU, E. and MOUFFE, C. (1985) *Hegemony and Socialist Strategy* (Verso, London).

LASCH, C. (1978) *The Culture of Narcissism* (Norton, New York and London).

LAURETIS, T. de and HEATH, S. (1980) *The Cinematic Apparatus* (Macmillan, Basingstoke and London).

LAVERY, David (ed.) (1995) *Full of Secrets* (Wayne State University Press, Detroit).

LEAVIS, F.R. (1972) *The Great Tradition* (Pelican, London).

LEE, Martyn (1993) *Consumer Culture Reborn* (Routledge, London).

LEVIN, Richard (1971) *The Multiple Plot in English Renaissance Drama* (Chicago University Press, Chicago).

LEWIS, Lisa (ed.) (1992) *The Adoring Audience* (Routledge, London).

LOVELL, Terry (1980) *Pictures of Reality: Aesthetics, Politics, Pleasure* (British Film Institute, London).

LOWRY, Brian (1995) *The Official Guide to The X Files* (HarperCollins Publishers, London).

LUKACS, Georg (1969) *The Historical Novel* (Harmondsworth, Peregrine).

LYOTARD, Jean-Francois (1984) *The Postmodern Condition: A Report on Knowledge* (trans. Bennington, G. and Massumi, B.) (University of Minnesota/Manchester University Press, Manchester).

LYOTARD, Jean-Francois (1993) *Libidinal Economy* (trans. Hamilton Grant, I., from 1974 Les Editions de Minuit) (The Athlone Press, London).

MacCABE, Colin (1974) 'Realism in the Cinema: Notes on Brechtian Theses', *Screen* (Summer) vol. 15, no. 2: 7–27.

MacCABE, Colin (1976) *Days of Hope* – a Response to Colin McArthur', *Screen* (Spring) vol. 17, no. 1: 98–101.

MacCABE, Colin (ed.) (1986) *High Theory/Low Culture* (Manchester University Press, Manchester).

MALTBY, Richard (1983) *Harmless Entertainment* (The Scarecrow Press, Metuchen, New Jersey).

MARSHMENT, M. and HALLAM, J. (1994) 'From String of Knots to Orange Box: Lesbianism on Prime Time' in Hamer, D. and Bridge, B. (eds) (1994).

MARTIN, Troy Kennedy (1964) 'Nats Go Home: First Statement of a New Drama for Television', *Encore* (March/April) no. 48.

MASUDA, Yoneji (1990) *Managing in the Information Society* (Blackwell, Oxford).

McGRATH, John (1977) 'TV Drama: The Case Against Naturalism', *Sight and Sound* (Spring) vol. 62, no. 2: 100–5.

McGUIGAN, Jim (1992) *Cultural Populism* (Routledge, London).

MELLENCAMP, Patricia (ed.) (1990) *Logics of Television: Essays in Cultural Criticism* (Indiana University Press, Bloomington).

MEPHAM, JOHN (1990) 'The Ethics of Quality in Television' in Mulgan, G. (ed.) (1990).

MERCER, Colin (1983) 'A Poverty of Desire' in Bennett, T. (ed.) (1983).

MERLEAU-PONTY, Maurice (1974) *The Prose of the World* (trans. from 1969, Editions Gallimard) (Heinemann, London).

METZ, Christian (1985) *Psychoanalysis and Cinema: The Imaginary Signifier* (trans. Britton, C. *et al.* from 1977 Union Generale d'Editions) (Macmillan, Basingstoke and London).

MILLER, Daniel (1987) *Material Culture and Mass Consumption* (Blackwell, Oxford).

MILLINGTON, B. and NELSON, R. (1986) *'Boys from the Blackstuff': The Making of TV Drama* (Comedia, London).

MORLEY, David (1980) *The Nationwide Audience* (British Film Institute, London).

MORLEY, David (1986) *Family Television: Cultural Power and Domestic Leisure* (Comedia, London).

MORLEY, David (1992) *Television Audiences and Cultural Studies* (Routledge, London).

MOUFFE, Chantal (1988) 'Radical Democracy: Modern or Postmodern' in Ross, A. (1988).

MULGAN, Geoff (ed.) (1990) *The Question of Quality* (British Film Institute, London).

MULVEY, Laura (1975) 'Visual Pleasure and Narrative Cinema', *Screen* (Autumn) vol. 15, no. 3: 6–18.

MUNT, Sally (ed.) (1992) *New Lesbian Criticism* (Harvester Wheatsheaf, Hemel Hempstead).

MURDOCK, Graham (1992) 'Citizens, Consumers and Public Culture' in Skovmand, M. and Schroder, K.C. (eds) (1992).

MURRAY, Robin (1990) 'The Benetton Economy' in Hall, S. and Jacques, M. (eds) (1990).

NAGEL, Thomas (1986) *The View from Nowhere* (Oxford University Press, Oxford).

NASH, Christopher (1987) *World Games: The Tradition of Anti-Realist Revolt* (Methuen, London).

NEALE, Stephen (1980) *Genre* (British Film Institute, London).

NEUMAN, W. Russell (1991) *The Future of the Mass Audience* (Cambridge University Press, Cambridge).

NICHOLS, Bill (1991) *Representing Reality* (Indiana University Press, Bloomington and Indianapolis).

NOCHLIN, Linda (1971) *Realism* (Penguin, Harmondsworth).

POOLE, M. and WYVER, J. (1984) *Powerplays: Trevor Griffiths in Television* (British Film Institute, London).

POSTER, Mark (ed.) (1988) *Jean Baudrillard: Selected Writings* (Polity Press, Cambridge).

POSTMAN, Neil (1987) *Amusing Ourselves to Death* (Methuen, London).

PROPP, Vladimir (1968) *The Morphology of the Folk Tale* (University of Texas Press, Austin).

RABINOW, Paul (ed.) (1984) *The Foucault Reader* (Penguin, London).

RANDOM HOUSE (1966) *The Random House Dictionary of the English Language* (Random House Inc, New York).

REDMOND, James (1979) *Drama and Society* (Cambridge University Press, Cambridge).

REITH, John (1924) *Broadcast Over Britain* (Hodder & Stoughton, London).

ROBINS, K. and WEBSTER, F. (1988) 'Broadcasting Politics: Communications and Consumption', *Screen* (May–August) vol. 27, no. 3–4: 30–45.

RORTY, Richard (1980) *Philosophy and the Mirror of Nature* (Princeton University Press, New Jersey).

RORTY, Richard (1989) *Contingency, Irony, Solidarity* (Cambridge University Press, Cambridge).

ROSE, D. and BEVAN, T. (1989) 'British Film – Where New?' in *BFI Film and Television Handbook 1990* (British Film Institute, London).

ROSS, Andrew (1988) *Universal Abandon* (University of Minnesota Press, Minneapolis).

SAMUEL, Raphael (1982) 'The SDP and the New Political Class', *New Society*, 22 (April): 124–7.

SARUP, Madan (1993) *An Introductory Guide to Poststructuralism and Postmodernism* (Harvester Wheatsheaf, Hemel Hempstead).

SAYNOR, James (1993) 'Imagined Communities', *Sight & Sound*, vol. 3, no. 12: 11–13.

SCHAPER, E. (ed.) (1983) *Pleasure, Preference and Value* (Cambridge University Press, Cambridge).

SCHLESINGER, John (1989) 'British Film – Where Now?' in *BFI Film and Television Handbook 1990* (British Film Institute, London).

SCHRODER, K.C. (1992) 'Cultural Quality: Search for a Phantom?' in Skovmand, M. and Schroder, K.C. (eds) (1992).

SCHUDSON, Michael (1987) 'The New Validation of Popular Culture. Sense and Sentimentality in Academia', *Critical Studies in Mass Communications*, vol. 4, no. 1: 51–68.

SEITER, Ellen *et al.* (eds) (1989) *Remote Control* (Routledge, London).

SENNETT, Richard (1977) *The Fall of Public Man* (Cambridge University Press, Cambridge).

SKOVMAND, M. and SCHRODER, K.C. (eds) (1992) *Media Cultures* (Routledge, London).

SMITH, Paul (1988) *Discerning the Subject* (University of Minnesota Press, Minneapolis).

SPARKS, Richard (1992) *Television and the Drama of Crime* (Open University Press, Buckingham).

STERN, J.P. (1973) *On Realism* (Routledge & Kegan Paul, London).

STOPPARD, Tom (1968) *Rosencrantz and Guildenstern are Dead* (Faber & Faber, London).

STOREY, John (1993) *An Introductory Guide to Cultural Theory and Popular Culture* (Harvester Wheatsheaf, Hemel Hempstead).

STYAN, J.L. (1983) *Modern Drama in Theory and Practice 1: Realism and Naturalism* (Cambridge University Press, Cambridge).

TAYLOR, Ronald (ed.) (1992) *Aesthetics and Politics* (Verso, London).

TESTER, Keith (1994) *Media, Culture and Morality* (Routledge, London).

TILGHMAN, B.R. (1991) *Wittgenstein, Ethics and Aesthetics* (Macmillan, Basingstoke and London).

TOMLINSON, Alan (ed.) (1990) *Consumption, Identity, Style* (Routledge, London).

TOMLINSON, John (1991) *Cultural Imperialism* (Pinter Publishers, London).

TRILLING, Lionel (1980) *Beyond Pleasure: Essays on Literature and Learning* (Oxford University Press, Oxford).

TULLOCH, John (1990) *TV Drama: Agency, Audience and Myth* (Routledge, London).

TUNSTALL, Jeremy (1993) *Television Producers* (Routledge, London).

VINCENDEAU, Jeanette (1995) 'Unsettling Memories', *Sight & Sound*, vol. 5, no. 7: 30–2.

WIGGINS, David (1987) *Needs, Values, Truth* (Blackwell, Oxford).

WILLETT, John (ed.) (1964) *Brecht on Theatre: The Development of an Aesthetic* (Methuen, London).

WILLIAMS, Christopher (1994) 'After the Classic, the Classical and Ideology: The Differences of Realism', *Screen* (Autumn) vol. 35, no. 3: 275–92.

WILLIAMS, Raymond (1973) *Drama from Ibsen to Brecht* (Pelican, Harmondsworth).

WILLIAMS, Raymond (1974) *Television: Technology and Cultural Form* (Fontana, London).

WILLIAMS, Raymond (1975) *Writing in Society* (Cambridge University Press, Cambridge).

WILLIAMS, Raymond (1977) 'A Lecture on Realism', *Screen* (Spring) vol. 18, no. 1: 61–74.

WILLIAMS, Raymond (1980) *Problems in Materialism and Culture* (Verso and New Left Books, London).

WILLIAMS, Raymond (1981) *Keywords* (Flamingo, London).

WILLIS, Paul (1990) *Common Culture* (Open University Press, Buckingham).

WINTERSON, Jeanette (1990) *Oranges Are Not the Only Fruit* (Bloomsbury, London).

WINTERSON, Jeanette (1994) *Great Moments in Aviation and Oranges Are Not the Only Fruit* (Vintage Books, London).

WITTGENSTEIN, Ludwig (1961) *Tractatus Logico-Philosophicus* (trans. Pears, D. and McGuiness, B.F.) (Routledge & Kegan Paul, London).

WITTGENSTEIN, Ludwig (1994) *Philosophical Investigations* (trans. Anscombe G.E.M.) (Blackwell, Oxford).

WOLLEN, Peter (1972) *Signs and Meanings in the Cinema* (Indiana University Press, Bloomington).

WOLLEN, Peter (1980) 'Discussion' in de Lauretis, T. and Heath, S. (1980) *The Cinematic Apparatus* (Macmillan, Basingstoke and London).

ZOLA, Emile (1964) *The Experimental Novel and Other Essays* (trans. Sherman, B.) (Haskell House, New York).

Index